100 Days with Jesus

*A Guide to Transformation by Knowing
God and Living in His Presence*

Edward N. Gross

Parson's Porch Books

www.parsonsporchbooks.com

100 Days with Jesus: A Guide to Transformation by Knowing God and Living in His Presence
ISBN: Softcover 978-1-949888-26-3
Copyright © 2018 by Edward N. Gross

All rights reserved. No part of this book may be reproduced or transmitted in any form or by any means, electronic or mechanical, including photocopying, recording, or by any information storage and retrieval system, without permission in writing from the publisher.

All Scripture quotations from the preface up to day 40, unless otherwise indicated, are taken from the English Standard Version Bible copyright 2001 by Crossway, a publishing ministry of Good News Publishers

All Scripture quotations following day 40, unless otherwise indicated, are taken from the New International Version (NIV). Copyright 1973, 1974, 1984, 2011 by Biblica Inc.

Table of Contents

Preface 17
10-Day Period 1 23
    Discipleship and Our Repenting
Day One 24
    The Name of God
Day Two 28
    God – The Holy One
Day Three 32
    God - the Light
Day Four 36
    God - the Easily Entreated One
Day Five 40
    God - The Forgiving One
Day Six 44
    God – The Transformer
Day Seven 48
    God - The Judge
Day Eight 52
    God - The Destroyer
Day Nine 56
    God - The Fire
Day Ten 60
    God - The Renewer
10-Day Period 2 64
    Discipleship and our Believing

Day Eleven 65
    God – The I AM
Day Twelve 69
    God – The Personal One
Day Thirteen 73
    God – The Knowable One
Day Fourteen 77
    God – The Promising One
Day Fifteen 81
    God – The Believable One
Day Sixteen 85
    God – The True One
Day Seventeen 89
    God – The Faithful One
Day Eighteen 93
    God – The Living One
Day Nineteen 97
    God – The Real One
Day Twenty 101
    God – The Good One

10-Day Period 3 105
    Discipleship and our Following Jesus
Day Twenty-one 106
    God - the All-Seeing One
Day Twenty-two 110
    God - the Caller
Day Twenty-three 114
    God - the Ever Present One

Day Twenty-four 118
   God – the Example
Day Twenty-five 122
   God – the Inviting One
Day Twenty-six 126
   God – the Leader
Day Twenty-seven 129
   God – the Marvelous One
Day Twenty-eight 133
   God – the Shepherd
Day Twenty-nine 137
   God – the Friend
Day Thirty 140
   God – the Indwelling One
10-Day Period 4 144
   Discipleship and our Obeying Jesus
Day Thirty-one 145
   God – The King
Day Thirty-two 149
   God – The Father
Day Thirty-three 153
   God – The Commander
Day Thirty-four 157
   God – The Covenant Maker
Day Thirty-five 161
   God – The Just One
Day Thirty-six 165
   God – The Gracious One
Day Thirty-seven 168
   God – The Lawgiver

Day Thirty-eight 172
    God – The Lord of Hosts
Day Thirty-nine 175
    God – The Worker
Day Forty 179
    God – The Rewarder
10-Day Period 5 182
    Discipleship and our Mastering the Words of Jesus
Day Forty-one 183
    God – The Creator
Day Forty-two 187
    God – The Rock
Day Forty-three 190
    God – The Near One
Day Forty-four 194
    God – The First One
Day Forty-five 198
    God – The Teacher
Day Forty-six 202
    God – The Wise One
Day Forty-Seven 205
    God – The Word
Day Forty-eight 209
    God – The Life
Day Forty-nine 213
    God – The Enjoyed One
Day Fifty 217
    God – The Liberator
10-Day Period 6 220
    Discipleship and our Understanding the Teaching of Jesus

Day Fifty-one 221
   The Glory of God
Day Fifty-two 224
   God – The Triune One
Day Fifty-three 227
   God – The Unchanging One
Day Fifty-four 231
   God – The Eternal One
Day Fifty-five 235
   God – The Sovereign One
Day Fifty-six 239
   God is Love
Day Fifty-seven 243
   God – The Jealous One
Day Fifty-eight 247
   God – The Pure One
Day Fifty-nine 251
   God – The Righteous One
Day Sixty 255
   God – The Worshipped One
10-Day Period 7 259
   Discipleship and our Imitating the Life of Jesus
Day Sixty-one 260
   God – The Great One
Day Sixty-two 263
   God – The Choosing One
Day Sixty-three 267
   God – The True One
Day Sixty-four 270
   God – The Anointing One

Day Sixty-five 274
   God – The Giver
Day Sixty-six 278
   God – The Tester
Day Sixty-seven 282
   God – The Hated One
Day Sixty-eight 286
   God – The Orderly One
Day Sixty-nine 290
   God – The Servant
Day Seventy 294
   God – The Savior
10-Day Period 8 297
   Discipleship and our Duplicating in the Kingdom of Jesus
Day Seventy-one 298
   God – The Owner of All
Day Seventy-two 302
   God – The Worthy One
Day Seventy-three 306
   God – The Pattern
Day Seventy-four 310
   God – The Witness
Day Seventy-five 314
   God – The Pleader
Day Seventy-six 318
   God – The Patient One
Day Seventy-seven 322
   God – The Redeemer
Day Seventy-eight 326
   God – The Joyful One

Day Seventy-nine 330
   God – The Delighting One
Day Eighty 333
   God – The Victorious One
10-Day Period 9 336
   Discipleship and our Praying in Jesus' name
Day Eighty-one 337
   God – The Powerful One
Day Eighty-two 341
   God – The Hearer of Prayer
Day Eighty-three 345
   God – The Uniter
Day Eighty-four 349
   God – The Listener
Day Eighty-five 353
   God – The Helper
Day Eighty-six 356
   God – The Mother-like
Day Eighty-seven 360
   God – The Healing One
Day Eighty-eight 364
   God – The Happy One
Day Eighty-nine 367
   God – The Uplifting One
Day Ninety 371
   God – The Destroyer of Satan
10-Day Period 10 375
   Discipleship and our Going to Make Disciples of Jesus
Day Ninety-one 376
   God – The Strong One

Day Ninety-two 380
    God – The Compassionate One
Day Ninety-three 384
    God – The Peaceful One
Day Ninety-four 387
    God – The Opposed One
Day Ninety-five 391
    God – The Provider
Day Ninety-six 395
    God – The Overcomer
Day Ninety-seven 399
    God – The Preserver
Day Ninety-eight 403
    God – The Coming One
Day Ninety-nine 407
    The Wrath of God
Day One Hundred 411
    God – The Triumphant One
Appendix One 417
    Are YOU a Christian or a Disciple?
Appendix Two 418
    A Faith that does not Save
Appendix Three 422
    Is Total Submission Too Radical for YOU?
Appendix Four 425
    Jesus and Obedience
Appendix Five 429
    Following Jesus by a Memorized Mastery of His Word
Appendix Six 433
    Following Jesus' Teaching concerning the Old Testament Law

Appendix Seven 438
    Following Jesus' Way of Life

Appendix Eight 443
    Truly Witnessing like NT Disciples

Appendix Nine 450
    Why Most Christians Prayers are NOT Answered

Appendix Ten 452
    Truly Fulfilling Jesus' Great Commission

Dedication

I lovingly dedicate this book to the memory of
3 pastors who greatly influenced my walk with Christ:

Nathan Rakestraw (C&MA)
Gordon Hay (GARBC)
Arthur Froehlich (BPC)

And to 12 brilliant and brave disciples, some in Glory and others still bearing their crosses here below, whose examples and writings have most helped me to understand, embrace and promote a
Renewal of Biblical Discipleship which helps Christians become true disciples of Jesus committed to making disciples globally:

Brother Lawrence
Charles Hodge
Charles Spurgeon
Andrew Murray
Dietrich Bonhoeffer
Martyn Lloyd-Jones
Dallas Willard
Juan Carlos Ortiz
Jerry Trousdale
Brother Yun
Gene Edwards
Bill Hull

Preface

Yes, I know it is an unusual request. To expect a 100-day commitment in our quick-read, deliver now-or-never age. But I have a good reason for it. The deep and thorough change we need simply cannot be quickly and easily achieved. I wish it could. Both Scripture and church history show that walking with God in power usually takes some time to experience.

I have designed this book to help Christians who are *ready* to walk with Jesus. And especially for those who have had some basic training in the elements of NT Discipleship. As you start, if you are extremely blessed, you may become a disciple in 100 days. It took the Apostles over 1000 days in the direct, miraculous, personal presence of God, Himself! That is why 100 days might not be nearly enough time. But, *with the Holy Spirit's help*, it could be more than enough. And you could even find yourself so blessed that God uses you to start a Disciple Making Movement (DMM), which reaches your entire area for Christ! This has happened before and is happening today.[1] Why not in and through you? God's great love is for you and your region, too!

But you will have to have the grace to bid "Easy Christianity" farewell. Forever. What Jesus demanded of others, He demands of you--**No turning back**. Today's low-cost, Western options for "following Jesus," are not working. They can barely save our souls, much less disciple the nations, which is what Christ commanded in His Great Commission, "make disciples of all nations" (Matt 28:19).

So, if you want a fast-moving and entertaining devotional, this will disappoint you. Not only am I asking for an unusually long commitment of 100 days, I am also using an unusual approach. I am insisting that you will have to become somewhat of a theologian if you try to follow Jesus today. Theological training has never been popular, a thing for "the common Christian." But this must change if you are to walk in the presence of Jesus.

I will have you thinking about God more than you probably are used to. Every morning and throughout the day. For 100 days! But it is this very thing that will begin to challenge and transform your life. You see, you must know a good amount about God if you intend to follow Him and devote your life to Him. You cannot be expected to submit yourself entirely to one whom you hardly know. I want you to experience for yourself the awesome, unparalleled love and power of Jesus. You will never do that if you do not

---

[1] See Jerry Trousdale's *Miraculous Movements* and my *The Amazing Love of Paul's Model Church*. Trousdale will introduce you to the Discovery Bible Study (DBS) method of disciple making— a proven, simple, reproducible way to make disciples of "people of peace" with whom God connects you as you are following Jesus daily.

know Him well. And you can do this only with the living Word of God in your hand, mind and heart.

Today's cheap brands of Christianity cost little and produce little. Jesus did not leave us with an easy and safe way to live. But rather with a demanding, sacrificial life of selfless love. A life that is always perilous and, so, always in need of divine protection. The moment you get serious about surrendering to Jesus, the real Jesus[2], you enter the battle. A war that Christ intends for you to win. This book is a guide to help make you an overcomer, by His grace. For there are no other types of "Christians" who apparently make it to heaven, according to John and Jesus![3]

He called us to follow Him, that is, to be His disciples. And He commanded us, while we live day-by-day, to make disciples. So, let me ask you: **How many disciples have you made?** How successfully are you fulfilling Christ's command? You can't make another what you are not yourself. Christians who are not disciples can worship, give and go—but they cannot make disciples! And that is His will for us all. I pray this guide will help you make disciples.

Theologian, James I. Packer, wrote a classic entitled, *Knowing God*. He drew from Daniel's prophecy: **"...but the people who know their God shall be strong and shall do exploits"** (KJV). The behavior of all people follows their beliefs. If we know little about God (beliefs), we will attempt little for God (behavior). But if our minds are consumed with who God really is, we will much more likely follow Him and live bravely in a world that wants both to remove His image and overthrow His rule.

We are addressing a huge problem in Christians today. Many of us know much *about* God and yet do not feel as though we know Him. There is a huge difference between "knowing about God" and "knowing God!" Disciples truly know Jesus and follow Him, while many Christians today only know the biblical facts *about* Jesus.

Not only will this guide greatly increase your knowledge of God, it will also bring you into a living, transforming contact with Him. We all need to experience Him daily. To be taught by God. That will happen more while you lovingly obey Jesus than when you are sitting comfortably at home merely thinking about Him. We need a working knowledge of God—one that is alive, acting and leading us down the path of discipleship. Only this will answer the prayer of Jesus uttered on the night He was betrayed. "Father, the hour has come; glorify your Son that he might glorify you, since you have given him authority over all flesh, to give eternal life to all whom you have

---

[2] 30+ years after Jesus was on earth, the devil was already successfully foisting "another Jesus" upon the Church! See 2 Cor. 11:1-4!
[3] See 1 John 5:4; Rev. 2:1, 7, 11, 17, 26; 3:1, 5, 12, 21.

given him. And this is eternal life, **that they know you, the only true God, and Jesus Christ whom you have sent**" (John 17:1-3).

Jesus believed that eternal life proceeds from the knowledge of God! Without this knowledge of God and His Christ, there can be no salvation. I know that you want God to touch your life daily with the unparalleled glory of His actual presence.

So, I have made the major part of this book to be a daily, brief-but-thorough study of 100 attributes of God. During the 100 days of your walk with Jesus, you will be learning about 100 aspects of His amazing being. As you really get to know Him, your love and trust in Him will grow. You will soon be transformed, becoming "theologians of love," fulfilling Jesus' prayer—"I have made you known to them, and will continue to make you known in order that the love you have for me may be in them and that I myself may be in them" (John 17:26-NIV). God's deepest love flows from those who know and walk with Him!

Western Christianity is undeniably and seriously declining.[4] But, at the same time, the Holy Spirit is raising up millions of simple disciples all over the world who are following Jesus with a staggering fruitfulness that parallels the productivity of the Church in Acts![5] Don't let anything or anyone prevent you from joining them! Ask yourself: "Do I want to die and stand before God empty-handed? Having made no disciples?" If you believe the Bible, it clearly warns us all that it is neither wise nor safe to do so.[6]

So, if you are ready, I truly welcome you into a daily fellowship with God and one another, my friends! Here are 6 ground rules to help guide you into what could be both a very surprising and a very fruitful trip:

1) Don't start and QUIT – Jesus warned disciples about doing that.[7]
2) Don't start and modify the program—see it through to the end- all 100 days[8]
3) Determine that you are not joining merely to LEARN but to LOVE and OBEY
4) Do get a sincere Christian friend to join you – Jesus commanded His disciples to go "two by two"[9]
*5) Do seek the **daily** help of the Holy Spirit, without Whom this way of life is impossible*

---

[4] See John Dickerson's *The Great Evangelical Recession*, the Barna Group's recent books, etc.
[5] See Trousdale, Pat Robertson's, *Father Glorified*; David Watson's, *Contagious Disciple Making*; and David Garrison's, *A Wind in the House of Islam*
[6] See my *"Fruitful or Unfruitful? Why it really matters"* for the shocking reality!
[7] "Jesus said to him, 'No one who puts his hand to the plow and looks back is fit for the kingdom of God" (Luke 9:62)
[8] You are not mainly being **taught** you are being **trained**—and this takes time
[9] See Matt 10:1-5; Mark 6:7; Luke 10:1 (also Mark 11:1; 14:13; 16:12)

*6) Do **PRAY**, always acknowledging Jesus' real presence to help you with every step?*

I have written mainly for those who know they need to change but have found it difficult. For those ready to step out in obedience to His call, "Follow Me." Jesus taught that His new wine needs to be poured into new wineskins; but, we have not appreciated just how hindering the old skins may be. Many of our existing Christian institutions and much of our Christian education, programs, outreach, devotions and even worship should be reworked or replaced by the renewing paths and practices of New Testament Discipleship. Our churches need to truly follow Jesus.

We are seeing today, where believers are willing to "deny themselves and take up their crosses and follow (Christ)" (Lk 9:23), that the Holy Spirit is filling and flowing through them, helping them to glorify God and fruitfully fulfill the Great Commission. That could be you, too.

Jesus asked Peter, "So, could you not watch with me **one hour**? Watch and pray that you may not enter temptation. The spirit indeed is willing, but the flesh is weak" (Matt 26:40-41). You will be greatly rewarded by spending the morning hour with Jesus! It will transform your day and, eventually, your life – along with many others.

Here are some Helpful Hints-- Begin the daily discipline of walking with God early each morning, if possible. You will need 30-60 minutes. As it was with all NT era disciples, Bible memorization is indispensable and will help remind you at 9, noon and 3 to continue walking by faith rather than merely by sight.[10] Recognize that this discipleship manual follows the outline of the Lord's Prayer, focusing first on God and then on us, with 7 essential elements for our daily walk with Jesus:

1) God's Nature (Adoration-Hallowed be thy name)
2) God's Kingdom (Strategy-Thy kingdom come) and
3) God's Will (Obedience-Thy will be done on earth as it is in heaven)
4) Our Needs (Petitions-Give us this day our daily bread),
5) Our Sins (Confession- Forgive our trespasses as we forgive ...),
6) Our Temptations (Walk- Lead us not into temptation) and
7) Our Deliverance (Victory-Deliver us from evil)

True disciples learn to "pray without ceasing" (1 Thess 5:17) and to "keep in step with the Spirit" (Gal. 5:25), implying constant guidance by and obedience to the Spirit's promptings. All of us will obey the Word

---

[10] Breaking for prayer was the practice of biblical believers: Psalm 55:17; Acts 3:1. Every NT era disciple memorized verbatim the teaching of his rabbi. Jesus commanded and expected the same of all who followed Him (John 8:31-32; 14:23, 26; 2 Cor 10:5; etc.)

imperfectly. Your growth process will take time and may often look like a child crawling and stumbling rather than walking and running. Here are some great resources available to help us walk with God.[11] But the Spirit and Word will be our greatest Helpers.

The Holy Spirit can accelerate the process of true discipleship very rapidly, as He did in NT times. The keys to your progress are your belief in: (1) the presence of Christ, (2) the love of the Father, (3) the truth of His Word, (4) the power of the Spirit and (5) the certainty of both Christ's and our victory, in Him! In discipling others, you will benefit greatly from mastering the simple DBS method which is being used so powerfully throughout the world.[12]

Take note that the 100 aspects of God are put in 10 periods, each covering 10 days. Please prepare for what's coming in each 10-day period by reading the brief introductions to biblical discipleship on the first day of each new period. They are in the 10 appendices at the close of the book.

I have given you some space to write down immediate responses. Do NOT proceed without writing something down. Your partners should hold you accountable, so share them daily—as they will with you. You will probably want to journal daily in another place as your walk begins to astound you by its fruitfulness!

Our chief goal is to help you develop a disciple-based way of life over time. Your Rabbi or Teacher is Jesus, alone as He emphatically told the Apostles (Matt 23:8-12). By living in His presence, with the Spirit's help, you will soon begin to reflect the 5 spiritual disciplines that every true disciple of Jesus vowed:

> 1) Total Submission/Obedience (to what the rabbi commanded)[13]
> 2) Total Mastery/Memorization (of what the rabbi taught)
> 3) Total Understanding (of the unique beliefs held by the rabbi)
> 4) Total Imitation (of the rabbi's lifestyle)
> 5) Total Duplication (once the way of the master had been learned and applied)

---

[11] Here are a few – My favorite – Brother Lawrence's *The Practice of the Presence of God*. Plus, Dallas Willard's *Hearing God*, Juan Ortiz's *God is Closer than you Think*, and Gene Edwards' *Living Close to God*.

[12] Contact me at ed.gross@comcast.net for more info on DBS training through Renewals of Biblical Discipleship (RBDs) and beyond. See also Trousdale's Miraculous Movements chapter 13 and Jim Lily's Great Commission Disciple making chapters 3-5.

[13] By "Total" I **never** mean "**perfect**", but full or complete. See Are You a Christian or a Disciple for how these 5 commitments were evident in Jesus' disciples and defined just what He meant when He used the word "disciple"

Each of the 100 days aims at inspiring and activating your faith. I want Jesus and His powerful presence to become real to you. So, I have chosen a combination of sources to touch your minds and hearts in new and transforming ways—the Bible, old and new spiritual songs and quotes from Christian writers—woven together in daily steps of obedience and accountability. There is even a daily section where you can be taught by the Spirit, producing a personal "I will statement" that will bring you into actual contact with the convicting Spirit of God!

My goal is not to advance one way of discipling, though I strongly recommend and use one myself, the Discovery Bible Study (DBS) method. The reason for this is basic. It does not matter which method you master if you, yourself, do not absolutely and obviously love Jesus "with all your heart, soul, strength and mind." You cannot effectively lead others where you have not gone. So, let's go into the world and make disciples of Jesus because we have become devoted disciples, ourselves, by His enabling grace.

I welcome you to follow our global ministry on Facebook where we often give reports.

-Ed Gross
April 2018

10-Day Period 1

Discipleship and Our Repenting

**Begin by reading Appendix One – Are YOU a Christian or a Disciple?

This is all about you and Jesus. If you want a living, moment-by-moment, powerful and fulfilling life with Him in heaven, you better start it on earth! By His grace, you can walk with Him, as did His disciples of old. And, like them, filled with the Spirit and His Truth, you can be used to advance His Kingdom and make many disciples who do the same. But this will not happen without significant, biblical changes occurring in your life. I would love to help you move forward with Jesus.

For the next 10 days you and your chosen partner will be focusing on following Jesus through *repentance*. Why start there, you might wonder? Because Jesus did! His way shows us that there is no life here without death. No resurrection without a crucifixion. No crown without a cross. We need to learn the absolute necessity of dying daily. "Unless a grain of wheat falls into the earth and dies, it remains alone, but if it dies, it bears much fruit. Whoever loves his life must lose it…." (John 12:24-25). Each morning we awake to die and be filled with the Spirit and the resurrection power of Jesus.

John the Baptist preached "repent!" He then baptized those who did. And to all who repented, Jesus first said, "The time is fulfilled, and the kingdom of God is at hand, *repent* and believe in the gospel" (Mark 1:15). How strange! Jesus demanded repentance of those who had just repented! Why? We often need to repent of our repentance! It is often incomplete, outward, insincere, and temporary. These next days, as you hear the call of Christ "follow Me." you will be able to do so only if you are willing to repent. Repentance has a sound (confession of sin) *and* a sight (walking with God). There is no true repentance without inward and outward change. Let us, for 10 days, humbly confess and willingly turn from those sins shown to us by the Spirit's conviction. During this time, out of love for Jesus who goes with and before us, and wanting to be used by Him, let us truly and deeply REPENT, as you focus on Him, learning of His nature, you cannot talk too often with Jesus during these next 10 days. Holy Spirit help us!

Day One

The Name of God

ADORATION

We are known by our names. They are our primary identifiers. When you call out a name, only the one to whom it belongs comes. When a person signs his name to something, that name stands for the entire person, himself. So serious is one's name, that it is a criminal act for a person to forge the name of another person. Our names are sacred things because we are special creatures made in the image of our holy God. His name uniquely represents Him, too. As David prayed, "May the Lord answer you in the day of trouble! May the name of the God of Jacob protect you." (Ps 20:1). The Lord and His name are one and the same.

An early expression of true worship followed the birth of Seth, when "people began to call on the name of the Lord" (Gen 4:26). Conversely, the apostasy of those at Babel was characterized by a desire to "make a name for ourselves" (Gen 11:4). But Abram "built an altar to the Lord and called upon the name of the Lord" (Gen 12:8). The Lord's name, which stood for the personal presence and power of the Lord, was a most sacred thing. So, as a part of His Law, God commanded, "You shall not take the name of the Lord your God in vain, for the Lord will not hold him guiltless who takes his name in vain" (Ex 20:7). Care had to be taken when speaking the name of God, for whenever it was spoken, God, Himself was being invoked. David affirmed, "I bow down toward your holy temple and give thanks to your name...for you have exalted above all things your name and your word" (Ps 138:2). Only fools questioned God's word and misused His name. So, today, speak His names with love and fear.

In the New Testament (NT), power is repeatedly linked with the name of Jesus. In Acts chapters 3-5, the name of Jesus is at issue, referred to 11 times in 3 chapters (3:6,16; 4:7,10,12,17-18, 30; 5:28,40-41)! The opponents asked Peter & John, "By what power or by what name did you do this?" (4:7). The presence of Jesus was revealed whenever something was done in His name. So great was Jesus' name, that even unbelievers could sometimes use it to do miracles (Matt 7:22; Acts 19:13). God has given Jesus a name above every name-a place of matchless majesty and peerless power (Phil 2:9; Heb 1:3-4). Since Jesus lives and we are commanded "And whatever you do, in word or in deed, do everything in the name of the Lord Jesus"

(Col 3:17)-let us realize that when we pray, speak or act in His name, we are trusting in His presence and power! We are living like His true disciples. So, today, be ready to repent when you do not consciously in all your ways acknowledge Him, seeing Him powerfully make your paths straight (Prov. 3:6).

Response

I thank you God for showing me _____

STRATEGY

Follow Jesus today, whose name means "Jehovah saves," and think about His words in **Luke 13:1-5** (Read now)

As I follow Jesus today I will remember _____

OBEDIENCE (I will statement)

The Spirit is convicting or leading me today to do or stop doing:

_____

_____

PETITIONS (Following your reciting of The Lord's Prayer)

I pray for these scheduled meetings today:

I pray also for these pressing needs of myself, my family, my church, my disciples,[14] my world:

CONFESSION and REPENTANCE

I confess these, my sins with every intention to never repeat them, but rather to live as Jesus would live, by Your enabling grace and Spirit ...

---

[14] Those whom you are discipling may be considered "your" disciples in the same way Paul meant when he told the Corinthians, "Be imitators of me as I am of Christ" (1 Cor 11:1)

*Never confess without a faith that looks to the cross of Christ, where the guilt and penalty of all our sins was paid!

WALK (Think about the following hymn)

Take the Name of Jesus with You

1) Take the name of Jesus with you,
Child of sorrow and of woe;
It will joy, and comfort give you,
Take it then where'er you go.

Precious name, oh how sweet!
Hope of earth and joy of heav'n,
Precious name, oh how sweet!
Hope of earth and joy of heav'n.

2) Take the name of Jesus ever,
As a shield from ev'ry snare;
When temptations round you gather
Breathe that holy name in prayer.

3) Oh, the precious name of Jesus!
How it thrills our souls with joy!
When His loving arms receive us
And His songs our tongues employ.

4) At the name of Jesus bowing,
Falling prostrate at His feet,
King of kings in heav'n we'll crown Him
When our journey is complete.[15]
(Lydia Baxter, 1800-1874)

Response

Help me Jesus, to _____

_____.

---

[15] Most hymns quoted from free online sites like: www.hymnary.org; www.hymnsite.com; www.hymnlyrics.org; www.cyberhymnal.com, etc.

VICTORY

Memorize *Acts 4:12* by reading it 5 times, reciting (without looking) 5 times and repeating it throughout the day 5 times (at least at 9AM, 12 noon and 3PM when you STOP the day to worship and talk to God).

**IF YOU STRUGGLE MEMORIZING OR QUESTIONING W*HY* IT IS CRUCIAL, PLEASE READ <u>APPENDIX 5</u> NOW

"Freely you have received, freely give" (NIV-Matt 10:8) – Remind yourself to speak peace (Luke 10:5) wherever you go and to whomever you speak, and always be ready to share something of the Word if the person is receptive and has time to listen. Be prepared to ask, "the person of peace question" (PoP) to anyone who seems ready and willing to be discipled.[16]

Be prepared for opposition (spiritual warfare) and expect victory in Jesus' name.

Write down the name (s) of those with whom you shared today and pray for them.

_____

_____

_____ Check when the day is completed with praise and glory to God, alone!

---

[16] PoP question: "Would you like to discover for yourself what God is like and how God wants you to live?"

Day Two

God – The Holy One

ADORATION

The biblical concept of holiness is two-sided: including both moral purity and total consecration or devotion to God. "There is none holy like the Lord" (1 Sam 2:2a).

God's "eyes are too pure to look on evil" (with approval - Hab 1:13- NIV). He is absolutely holy.

Immorality and sin are the opposites of holiness, so God's holiness sets Him against sin. He cannot be apathetic to sin. He must stand against it because His nature demands it. He calls us to moral purity when He says, "be holy, because I am holy" (Lev. 11:45; 1 Pet 1:15-16).

Holiness also involves set apart-ness or consecration. Aaron's garments, the anointing oil, the tabernacle and all its furnishings were declared to be holy-that is, to be totally devoted to the service of God (Ex. 28:2; 30:22-31; 40:9).

In fact, all of Israel was declared to belong to the Lord, to be devoted to Him (Lev 20:26; Ex 19:5-6). Peter called Jewish and Gentile disciples (so, us), "a holy nation, a people for his own possession" (1 Pet 2:9a).

Of all the many attributes of God, it is significant that His holiness is particularly attributed to the Spirit of God. In fact, 89 of the 177 times the word "holy" is used in the NT, it is a reference to the *Holy* Spirit. As we depend on the Spirit for all that we do, we must never take our sin lightly. God's holiness is so inflexible that it demanded no less a solution for our sin problem than the death of the sinless Son of God, Himself. Those who think little of sin must, therefore, think little of the cross and of the Christ who died thereon. But those who truly repent of sin, reveal that the Holy Spirit is significantly working in them.

Believers are chosen in Christ "before the foundation of the world that we should be holy and blameless before him" (Eph 1:4). We are urged by Paul "to offer (our) bodies as living sacrifices, holy and pleasing to God" (Rom 12:1). So, true holiness includes both a separation from sin and a devotion to God. The one cannot exist without the other. Justification without sanctification is as useless as a counterfeit coin that is engraved on only one side (2 Tim 2:20-21). So, when people either act morally, apart from the fear of the Lord (Prov 15:8) or worship without a loving, pure heart (1 Cor 13: 1-3), they are not exhibiting true holiness.

Since God is unchangeably holy, sin will always offend Him and must be dealt with. So, throughout the day, guard your heart-where sin begins its deceptive work within us (Jer 17:10; James1:15-17). Jesus warned us all, "Remember Lot's wife!" (Lk 17:32). Guard your emotions and look often to Christ, our righteousness, as the One who keeps us from God's just punishment (Rom. 8: 1). Since God loves holiness, devotion delights Him, especially the devotion of a heart filled with love (Rev. 2:4-5; 3:15-16). Follow Christ closely today and be devoted to Him, cutting your compromising alliances with sin and the world (I John 2:15). "Do not follow the crowd in doing wrong" (Ex 23:2-NIV). "Choose this day whom you will serve" (Josh 24:15). But always remember since Adam's first sin, "I am the Lord who makes you holy" (Ex 31:3). His love and wisdom made a way, through Christ, for our sin to be replaced by His gift of holiness! Christ has become our holiness (1 Cor 1:30). Praise and serve Him forever!

Response

I thank you God for showing me _____

_____.

STRATEGY

Follow Jesus today, humbled by His holiness, like Peter was as seen in **Luke 5:1-11.** (Read now)

As I follow Jesus today I will remember _____

_____.

OBEDIENCE (I will statement)

The Spirit is convicting or leading me today to do or stop doing:

_____

_____.

PETITIONS (Following your reciting of The Lord's Prayer)

I pray for these scheduled meetings today:

I pray also for these pressing needs of myself, my family, my church, my disciples,[17] my world:

CONFESSION and REPENTANCE

I confess these, my sins with every intention to never repeat them, but rather to live as Jesus would live, by Your enabling grace and Spirit …

*Never confess without a faith that looks to the cross of Christ, where the guilt and penalty of all our sins was paid!

WALK (Think about the following hymn)

Fountain of Purity

Fountain of purity opened for sin
Here may the penitent wash and be clean;
Jesus, Thou blessed Redeemer from woe,
Wash me and I shall be whiter than snow.

Whiter than snow, whiter than snow,
Wash me, Redeemer,
And I shall be whiter than snow.

Though I have labored again and again,
All my self-cleansing is utterly vain;
Jesus, Redeemer from sorrow and woe,
Wash me and I shall be whiter than snow.

Cleanse Thou the thoughts of my heart, I implore,
Help me Thy light to reflect more and more;
Daily in loving obedience to grow,
Wash me and I shall be whiter than snow.

---

[17] Those whom you are discipling may be considered "your" disciples in the same way Paul meant when he told the Corinthians, "Be imitators of me as I am of Christ" (1 Cor 11:1)

> Whiter than snow! nothing further I need,
> Christ is the Fountain; this only I plead;
> Jesus, my Savior, to Thee will I go,
> Wash me and I shall be whiter than snow.
> (C Newman Hall, 1816-1902)

Response

Help me Jesus, to _____

_____.

VICTORY

Memorize *1 Peter 1:15*

Be prepared for opposition (spiritual warfare) and expect victory in Jesus' name.

Write down the name (s) of those with whom you shared today and pray for them.

_____

_____.

_____Check when the day is completed with praise and glory to God, alone!

Day Three

God - the Light

ADORATION

"God is light; and in him is no darkness at all" (1 John 1:5b). The chief characteristic of light is its radiance. Light shines. Darkness conceals but light reveals. In the world there are different degrees of light: a flickering candle, a car's headlights, the brilliance of the sun. Even the sun's light is limited, with countless other universes unreached by its rays. But the light of God is boundless, "unapproachable light" (1 Tim 6:16)-greater than a million suns, for, unlike our sun, the light of God cannot be extinguished. He will never stop radiating all that is good and holy. "He wraps himself in light as with a garment" (Ps 104:2-NIV).

God is light both in Himself and in His relationship with us (1 John 1:6-7). In His presence we experience the ultimate that life has to offer, as the Psalmist declared, "in your light we do see [experience, enjoy] light [life's fullness]" (Ps 36:9). We should remember that the first recorded words spoken by God at creation were, "Let there be light" (Gen 1:2). This was not because God needed light to see (Ps 139:12); but, rather because we need light to see. These first words well represent the great purpose of God in creating the world: to gloriously display to rational creatures His awesome nature! God created us so that we could love and adore him through his works (Ps 19: 1) His Word (Ps 119:105), and especially His Son, Jesus who most clearly displays His peerless radiance (Heb 1:1-3). The light of His glory is seen "in the face of Jesus Christ" (2 Cor 4:6).

The greatest darkness, then, is not located in the deepest cave, in the lowest depths of the ocean or even in the eyes of the blind. It exists with those who have eyes to see with, but who never truly see (Is 6:9-10; Matt 13:13-16; Rev 3:17-18). The most devastating darkness exists wherever God's creatures refuse to see and glorify their Creator. This is an inexcusable blindness gripping many of God's image-bearers (Job 24:13; Rom 1:18-25), dooming them to a life of woe (Is 5:20). It is for them, the blinded and perishing, that Christ, "the light of the world" (John 8:12) came offering "recovering of sight to the blind" (Lk 4:18). And it is for them that Christ made all His disciples to be "the light of the world" (Matt 5:14-16), to shine in word and deed so that they might see and be saved.

Since the light of God's smile comes to us only through Christ, let us ever live "in Christ" and "for Christ" (Num 6:22-27; John 1:4). Let us never be ashamed of Jesus, for "Blessed are those who have learned to acclaim you, who walk in the light of your presence, O Lord" (Ps 89:15-NIV).

Response

I thank you God for showing me _____

_____.

STRATEGY

Follow Jesus today, as He spoke to His opponents in **John 8:12-20.** (Read now)

As I follow Jesus today I will remember _____

_____.

OBEDIENCE (I will statement)

The Spirit is convicting or leading me today to do or stop doing:

_____

_____.

PETITIONS (Following your reciting of The Lord's Prayer)

I pray for these scheduled meetings today:

I pray also for these pressing needs of myself, my family, my church, my disciples,[18] my world:

CONFESSION and REPENTANCE

I confess these, my sins with every intention to never repeat them, but rather to live as Jesus would live, by Your enabling grace and Spirit …

*Never confess without a faith that looks to the cross of Christ, where the guilt and penalty of all our sins was paid!

---

[18] Those whom you are discipling may be considered "your" disciples in the same way Paul meant when he told the Corinthians, "Be imitators of me as I am of Christ" (1 Cor 11:1)

WALK (Think about the following hymn)

Stepping in the Light

Trying to walk in the steps of the Savior,
Trying to follow our Savior and King;
Shaping our lives by His blessed example,
Happy, how happy, the songs that we bring.

How beautiful to walk in the steps of the Savior,
Stepping in the light, stepping in the light,
How beautiful to walk in the steps of the Savior,
Led in paths of light.

Pressing more closely to Him Who is leading,
When we are tempted to turn from the way;
Trusting the arm that is strong to defend us,
Happy, how happy, our praises each day.

Walking in footsteps of gentle forbearance,
Footsteps of faithfulness, mercy, and love,
Looking to Him for the grace freely promised,
Happy, how happy, our journey above.

Trying to walk in the steps of the Savior,
Upward, still upward, we follow our Guide;
When we shall see Him, "the King in His beauty,"
Happy, how happy, our place at His side.
. (Eliza E Hewitt, 1851-1920)

Response

Help me Jesus, to _____

_____.

VICTORY

Memorize *John 8:12* by reading it 5 times, reciting (without looking) 5 times and repeating it throughout the day 5 times (at least at 9AM, 12 noon and 3PM when you STOP the day to worship and talk to God).

"Freely you have received, freely give" (NIV-Matt 10:8) – Remind yourself to speak peace (Luke 10:5) wherever you go and to whomever you speak, and always be ready to share something of the Word if the person is receptive and has time to listen. Be prepared to ask, "the person of peace question" (PoP) to anyone who seems ready and willing to be discipled.[19]

Be prepared for opposition (spiritual warfare) and expect victory in Jesus' name.

Write down the name (s) of those with whom you shared today and pray for them. _____

_____.

____ Check when the day is completed with praise and glory to God, alone!

---

[19] PoP question: "Would you like to discover for yourself what God is like and how God wants you to live?"

Day Four

God - the Easily Entreated One

ADORATION

We all know what is meant when someone is described as, "a tough nut to crack." We all have been obstinate. Rigid. Unwilling to yield. Demanding our "pound of flesh" from our offenders. God is just the opposite! It is He whom Jesus portrayed as the prodigal son's father, who "saw him and felt compassion; and ran and embraced him and kissed him ...saying, "Bring quickly the best robe and put it on him...Bring the fattened calf and kill it and let us eat and celebrate. For this my son was dead and is alive again; he was lost and is found" (Luke 15:20ff).

If we only knew just how ready God is to forgive, to restore, to advance us. Listen to Isaiah's description of God to stubborn, sinful Israel: "Therefore the Lord longs to be gracious to you; he rises to show you compassion...O people of Zion...you will weep no more. How gracious he will be when you cry for help! As soon as he hears, he will answer you" (Isa 30:18-19-NIV). It is He who says, "Come now, let us reason together, says the Lord." (Isa 1:18a).

When you pray, believe! Do not question the willingness of God to forgive and help you. He says, "If you, then, who are evil, know how to give good gifts...how much more will your Father who is in heaven give good things to those who ask him!" (Matt 7:11). He is more ready than the most willing parent. Only one thing will block God's desire of mercy from being poured out on us-it is SIN (See Jonah 2:8; Isa. 59:1-2). "If I had cherished iniquity in my heart, the Lord would not have listened; but truly God has listened. He has attended to the voice of my prayer. Blessed be God, because he has not rejected my prayer or removed his steadfast love from me!" (Ps 69:18-20). Repentance precedes blessing. Always remember, "The wisdom that comes from heaven is... easily entreated" (James3:17-KJV).

Look at Manasseh, the most abominable of all of Judah's kings. He had "done things more evil than all that the Amorites did, who were before him" (2 Kgs 21:10b; see 21:2-9 for his list of shocking sins). Yet, at the end of his life, following decades of sorcery, murder and idolatry, Manasseh humbled himself and prayed. And what happened? "God was moved by his entreaty and heard his plea; and brought him again to Jerusalem into his kingdom. Then Manasseh knew that the Lord was God" (2 Chron 33:13).

It does not matter how evil a person is, God "is patient with you, not wishing that any should perish, but that all should reach repentance" (2

Pet 3:9). Is wicked Egypt, the great enemy of ancient Israel, hopelessly lost and written off by God? "And the Lord will strike Egypt; striking and healing, and they will return to the Lord, and he will listen to their pleas for mercy and heal them" (Isa 19:22).

So, today, don't make reconciliation with God a hard thing, for He "is actually not far from each one of us" (Acts 17:27b). God can easily be won over to your side-if you are willing to forsake your sin and follow Christ. "Do not say in your heart, who will ascend into heaven? or, who will descend into the abyss? The word is near you; in your mouth and in your heart; that is the word of faith that we proclaim. (Rom 10:6-8). Satan says, "You're a lost cause." But the Spirit and the bride disagree and say, "Come!" (Rev 22:17).

Response

I thank you God for showing me _____

_____.

STRATEGY

Follow Jesus today, amazed at the access to God that His death has given us as seen in what happened to the veil of the temple in **Mark 15:33-39.** (Read now)

As I follow Jesus today I will remember _____

_____.

OBEDIENCE (I will statement)

The Spirit is convicting or leading me today to do or stop doing:

_____

_____.

PETITIONS (Following your reciting of The Lord's Prayer)

I pray for these scheduled meetings today:

I pray also for these pressing needs of myself, my family, my church, my disciples,[20] my world:

CONFESSION and REPENTANCE

I confess these, my sins with every intention to never repeat them, but rather to live as Jesus would live, by Your enabling grace and Spirit ...

*Never confess without a faith that looks to the cross of Christ, where the guilt and penalty of all our sins was paid!

WALK (Think about the following hymn)

Come, Ye Sinners

1) Come, ye sinners, poor and needy
Weak and wounded, sick and sore
Jesus ready, stands to save you
Full of pity, love and power
He is able, He is able, He is able,
He is willing, doubt no more!

2) Let not conscience let you linger,
Nor of fitness fondly dream;
All the fitness he requireth
Is to feel your need of him.
This he gives you, This he gives you, This he gives you:
'Tis the Spirit's glimmering beam.

3) Come ye weary, heavy laden,
Bruised and mangled by the fall;
If you tarry till you're better,
You will never come at all.
Not the righteous, Not the righteous, Not the righteous;
Sinners Jesus came to call.

4) Agonizing in the garden,
Lo! your Maker prostrate lies!
On the bloody tree behold Him:

---

[20] Those whom you are discipling may be considered "your" disciples in the same way Paul meant when he told the Corinthians, "Be imitators of me as I am of Christ" (1 Cor 11:1)

> Hear Him cry, before He dies:
> "It is finished!" "It is finished!" "It is finished!"
> Sinner, will this not suffice?
>
> 5) Lo! The incarnate God ascending,
> Pleads the merit of His blood;
> Venture on Him, venture freely;
> Let no other trust intrude.
> None but Jesus, None but Jesus, None but Jesus
> Can do helpless sinners good
> (Joseph Hart, 1712-1768)

Response

Help me Jesus, to _____

_____.

VICTORY

Memorize Hebrews *4:15*

Be prepared for opposition (spiritual warfare) and expect victory in Jesus' name.

Write down the name (s) of those with whom you shared today and pray for them. _____

_____.

____ Check when the day is completed, never beating yourself up if you did not finish; but, just asking Jesus to help you next day!

Day Five

God - The Forgiving One

ADORATION

    We want to be at peace with others. But at times something serious comes between us, a deep wrong occurs-and peace is broken. And unless the issue is dealt with, the wrong is admitted and forgiveness sought, there can be no deep and true reconciliation. Time does NOT heal ALL wounds. Sometimes the breach is between husband and wife, between friends or colleagues. Between father and child. Those wounds may never heal-and horror may be the result unless forgiveness occurs.

    God revealed Himself to Moses as One "keeping steadfast love for thousands, forgiving iniquity and transgressions and sin, but who by no means will clear the guilty...." (Ex 34:7). The psalmist says, "For you, O Lord, are good and forgiving, abounding in steadfast love to all who call upon you" (Ps 86:5) "If you, O Lord, should mark iniquities, O Lord, who could stand? But with you there is forgiveness; that you may be feared" (Ps 130:3-4).

    We know that God does not forgive everyone. Since He is a God of pure justice, every wrong between Him and us must be rightly dealt with. He said, "It may be that the house of Judah will hear all the disaster that I intend to do to them, so that everyone may turn from his evil way; and that I may forgive their iniquity and their sin" (Jer 36:3). But they didn't turn from sin to His way. So, He sent them into Babylonian captivity and exile for 70 long years. And there some of them learned about their God and His heart of pure justice and forgiving love!

    Since we do not have the moral ability to despise sins, we cannot repent of them without His help. He must give us the gift of repentance! He must kindly lead us to repentance or else we will rush ahead in rebellion! (See Rom 2:4) God does this all by His grace.

    He sent Christ to live righteously and then pay for our sins' penalty. Then He and the Son poured out the Spirit to change our hearts, so we can confess and forsake our sins. Otherwise, forgiveness from God and reconciliation between us and God could never have occurred. "In him we have redemption through his blood, the forgiveness of trespasses, according to the riches of his grace" (Eph 1:7). At the Last Supper Jesus said, "for this is my blood of the covenant, which is poured out for many for the forgiveness of sins" (Matt 26:28). And the covenant He referred to is the New Covenant promised long before He came, "For I will forgive their iniquity and will remember their sin no more" (Jer 31:34). Forgiveness is God's gift to you through Christ!

Cherish that gift. You may be justified before God, and heaven be your destination, but do not deal lightly with your daily sins. You're free from God as a condemning Judge, but you still must relate to Him as a Father. He will not walk closely and powerfully with you unless you admit your sins and seek His fatherly forgiveness. "If we confess our sins, he is faithful and just to forgive us our sins" (1 John 1:9). We are to pray to our Father, "and forgive us our debts, as we also have forgiven our debtors...For if you forgive others their trespasses, your heavenly Father will also forgive you" (Matt 6:12-14). Let peace and healing come and forgiveness occur by humbly and honestly confessing your sin to God and one another (James 5:16).

Response

I thank you God for showing me _____

_____.

STRATEGY

Follow Jesus today, remembering His propensity to forgive sin as seen in **Mark 2:1-12**(Read now)

As I follow Jesus today I will remember _____

_____.

OBEDIENCE (I will statement)

The Spirit is convicting or leading me today to do or stop doing:

_____

_____.

PETITIONS (Following your reciting of The Lord's Prayer)

I pray for these scheduled meetings today:

I pray also for these pressing needs of myself, my family, my church, my disciples,[21] my world:

CONFESSION and REPENTANCE

I confess these, my sins with every intention to never repeat them, but rather to live as Jesus would live, by Your enabling grace and Spirit ...

*Never confess without a faith that looks to the cross of Christ, where the guilt and penalty of all our sins was paid!

WALK (Think about the following hymn)

Forgive our Sins as we Forgive

1) 'Forgive our sins as we forgive,'
you taught us, Lord, to pray,
but you alone can grant us grace
to live the words, we say.

2) How can your pardon reach and bless
the unforgiving heart,
that broods on wrongs and will not let
old bitterness depart?

3) In blazing light your cross reveals
the truth we dimly knew:
what trivial debts are owed to us,
how great our debt to you!

4) Lord, cleanse the depths within our souls,
and bid resentment cease;
then, bound to all in bonds of love,
our lives will spread your peace.
(Rosamond Herklots, 1906-1987)

Response

---

[21] Those whom you are discipling may be considered "your" disciples in the same way Paul meant when he told the Corinthians, "Be imitators of me as I am of Christ" (1 Cor 11:1)

Help me Jesus, to _____

_____.

VICTORY

Memorize Hebrews *4:16*

Be prepared for opposition (spiritual warfare) and expect victory in Jesus' name Write down the name (s) of those with whom you shared today

_____

_____.

____ Check when the day is completed, never beating yourself up if you did not finish; but, just asking Jesus to help you next day!

Day Six

God – The Transformer

ADORATION

  In a presidential election year in America, amazing amounts of money and time are spent to bring about change. We should remember Daniel, who, prayed "He changes times and seasons: he removes kings and he sets up kings" (Dan 2:21). Yes, we might and ought to work hard for something; but, it will always serve us well to yield our expectations to, "Your will, not mine, be done." The psalmist sang, "No one from the east or west can exalt a man. But it is God who judges: He brings one down, he exalts another" (Ps 75:5-6-NIV). God is the great Changer or Transformer.

  He told Abram, "And I will make you into a great nation and I will bless you and make your name great, so that you will be a blessing" (Gen 12:2). When God says He will do something, even the impossible, He does it. "In the beginning, you laid the foundations of the earth, and the heavens are the work of your hands. They will perish, but you remain; they will all wear out like a garment. Like clothing you will change them, and they will be discarded" (Ps 102:25-26 -NIV). Nothing is impossible with our God.

  Are the winds blowing with destructive force upon your soul? God can change the wind, scattering the locusts. "And the Lord changed the wind to a very strong west wind" (Ex 10:19a- NIV). Is your mind so troubled by doubts, fear and uncertainties that you cannot sleep? Hear the words of a distressed victim of drought and famine, "You have put more joy in my heart than they have when their grain and wine abound. In peace I will both lie down and sleep, for you alone, O Lord, make me dwell in safety" (Ps 4:7-8). Are you "small potatoes," forgotten and overlooked? Not if you trust God, like little shepherd David did, to whom God said, "And I will make for you a great name, like the name of the great ones of the earth" (2 Sam 7:9b). And when he went to war, facing great enemies, the prayer was sung, "May he grant you your heart's desire and fulfill all your plans!" (Ps 20:4). Just believe because God changes things!

  Even Jesus had to wait for the Father to change things. "The Lord says to my Lord: Sit at my right hand until I make your enemies your footstool" (Ps 110:1). Change often comes slowly-but not so to an eternal God. Time is something very different to Him than it is to us. We often hate to wait to trust Him. But we really have no choice. We can either wait on

Him and have peace or push ahead and force something ugly and hurtful- losing our peace and joy in the process.

Ask Jesus to change you today. Surrender to Him your skills and time. See what happens. "Come, follow me, Jesus said, and I will make you fishers of men" (Mk 1:17 - NIV). He will change you into something beautiful and enduring. How? By fellowship with Himself! "And we all...are being transformed into the same image from one degree of glory to another. For this comes from the Lord, who is the Spirit" (2 Cor 3:18). We truly cannot imagine the changes ahead of us. "(The Lord Jesus Christ) who, by the power that enables him to transform everything under his control, will transform our lowly bodies so that they will be like his glorious body" (Phil 3:21 - NIV).

Response

I thank you God for showing me _____

_____.

STRATEGY

Follow Jesus today, remembering His power to transform anything, as seen in **John 2:1-11**(Read now)

As I follow Jesus today I will remember _____

OBEDIENCE (I will statement)

The Spirit is convicting or leading me today to do or stop doing:

_____

_____.

PETITIONS (Following your reciting of The Lord's Prayer)

I pray for these scheduled meetings today:
I pray also for these pressing needs of myself, my family, my church, my disciples,[22] my world:

CONFESSION and REPENTANCE

---

[22] Those whom you are discipling may be considered "your" disciples in the same way Paul meant when he told the Corinthians, "Be imitators of me as I am of Christ" (1 Cor 11:1)

I confess these, my sins with every intention to never repeat them, but rather to live as Jesus would live, by Your enabling grace and Spirit ...
*Never confess without a faith that looks to the cross of Christ, where the guilt and penalty of all our sins was paid!

WALK (Think about the following hymn)

Power for Service

1) Spirit of power, anoint me for service,
Spirit of holiness, cleanse Thou my heart;
Give to my soul of Thyself a new vision,
And a new measure of power impart.

*Fill me with power for service and use me;
Is there not some work my weak hands can do?
Make me a channel of life and of blessing,
And with the Spirit anoint me anew.*

2) Not one lost soul have I won for Thy kingdom,
All my life has been fruitless and waste;
Others have joy for the jewels ingathered;
May not my soul of this joy have a taste?

3) Never before has my soul so a hungered
For Thy infilling, O Spirit of love!
Come to the throne, be my Master and Ruler,
Reign Thou and draw my affections above.

4) Myself I yield in complete consecration,
Body and spirit and soul to be Thine;
Spirit of power, regard Thou my yearnings,
And fill Thou me with Thy fullness divine.
(Elisha A Hoffman, 1839-1929)

Response

Help me Jesus, to _____

_____.

VICTORY

Memorize *Acts 1:8* by reading it in sections 5 times, reciting (without looking) 5 times and repeating it throughout the day 5 times (at least at 9AM, 12 noon and 3PM when you STOP the day to worship and talk to God).

"Freely you have received, freely give" (NIV-Matt 10:8) – Remind yourself to speak peace (Luke 10:5) wherever you go and to whomever you speak, and always be ready to share something of the Word if the person is receptive and has time to listen. Be prepared to ask, "the person of peace question" (PoP) to anyone who seems ready and willing to be discipled.[23]

Be prepared for opposition (spiritual warfare) and expect victory in Jesus' name.

Write down the name (s) of those with whom you shared today and pray for them. _____

_____.

____ Check when the day is completed, never beating yourself up if you did not finish; but, just asking Jesus to help you next day!

---

[23] PoP question: "Would you like to discover for yourself what God is like and how God wants you to live?"

Day Seven

God - The Judge

ADORATION

In court cases, it is the function of a judge to reach a just verdict after contemplating all the evidence. Though often forsaken in this life, when true justice is accomplished, the guilty are fairly punished and the innocent acquitted. So, when the Scripture declares, "God is a righteous judge, a God who feels indignation every day." (Ps 7:11), it is stating an awesome and fearful fact. God is just. So, evil must be punished and good rewarded. How do we fare as humans under the gaze of a holy Judge?

"The Lord looks down from heaven...to see if there are any who understand, who seek God. They have all turned aside, together they have become corrupt; there is none who does good." (Ps 14:2-3). Our sin must be punished, as He promised (Gen 2:17), by death. (Rom 6:23).

God cannot simply ignore sin or have His love trump it and remove it. If a single sin could go without His justly punishing it, He would cease to be perfectly just, holy and fair. Abraham knew this and asked, "Will not the Judge of all the earth do what is just?" (Gen 18:25). Of course, He will. "The adversaries of the Lord shall be broken to pieces. Against them he will thunder in heaven; the Lord will judge the ends of the earth." (1 Sam 2:10).

If we are all guilty, how then can anyone be pardoned by a holy Judge? It would be impossible if God, Himself, did not intervene for us. He sent His Eternal Son, perfect and holy, to become our sin offering. The Lamb of God came to offer His own life as punishment for our sin. "God made him who had no sin to be sin for us, so that in him we might become the righteousness of God" (2 Cor 5:21 - NIV). Infinite love filled the Triune God and satisfied the demands of His perfect justice! "By this we know love, that he laid down his life for us" (1 John 3:16.) But, God's love does not displace or remove justice. That could not be, or God would cease to be God. His love made a way for sinners to be justly saved through Jesus Christ! Disciples follow Jesus out of gratitude and love for providing this one way to be saved.

The day of judgment is coming! "He will judge the world in righteousness; he will govern the peoples with justice" (Ps 9:8 - NIV). But how will this be accomplished? "The Father judges no one, but has given all judgment to the Son" (John 5:22). "This will take place on the day when God will judge men's secrets through Jesus Christ." (Rom 2:16 - NIV). "For we must all appear before the judgment seat of Christ, so that each one may receive what is due for what he has done while in the body, whether good or evil." (2 Cor 5:10). Jesus will judge the world at that time, not before. For a while evil can occur and the wicked often seem to go unpunished. But not forever!

The thought of judgment is a fearful thing. Be careful not to wish it upon others. When we judge the hearts of others, we wrongly usurp Christ's sole role. "There is only one lawgiver and judge, he who is able to save and destroy. But who are you to judge your neighbor?" (James 4:12). Human judges may "carry out God's wrath on the wrongdoer" (Rom 13:4), when certain of their guilt. But true justice will occur only when Jesus comes. For now, we should patiently follow Jesus by faith, knowing that "the Judge is standing at the door!" (James 5:9).

Response

I thank you God for showing me _____

_____.

STRATEGY

Follow Jesus today, remembering that your life should be greatly impacted by the fact of His Coming Glory, as seen in Philippians **2:1-11**(Read now)

As I follow Jesus today I will remember _____

_____.

OBEDIENCE (I will statement)

The Spirit is convicting or leading me today to do or stop doing: _____

_____.

PETITIONS (Following your reciting of The Lord's Prayer)

I pray for these scheduled meetings today:

I pray also for these pressing needs of myself, my family, my church, my disciples,[24] my world:

---

[24] Those whom you are discipling may be considered "your" disciples in the same way Paul meant when he told the Corinthians, "Be imitators of me as I am of Christ" (1 Cor 11:1)

CONFESSION and REPENTANCE

I confess these, my sins with every intention to never repeat them, but rather to live as Jesus would live, by Your enabling grace and Spirit ...

*Never confess without a faith that looks to the cross of Christ, where the guilt and penalty of all our sins was paid!

WALK (Think about the following hymn)

Day of Judgment, Day of Wonders!

1) Day of judgment, day of wonders!
Hark! the trumpet's awful sound,
Louder than a thousand thunders,
Shakes the vast creation round!
How the summons
Will the sinner's heart confound!

2) See the Judge our nature wearing,
Clothed in majesty divine!
You who long for his appearing
Then shall say, "This God is mine!"
Gracious Savior,
Own me on that day for thine!

3) At his call the dead awaken,
Rise to life from earth and sea;
All the powers of nature shaken
By his look, prepare to flee:
Careless sinner,
What will then become of thee?

4) Horrors past imagination,
Will surprise your trembling heart,
When you hear your condemnation,
"Hence, accursed wretch departs!
Thou with Satan
And his angels, have thy part!"

5) Satan, who now tries to please you,
Lest you timely warning take,
When that word is past, will seize you,
Plunge you in the burning lake:

> Think, poor sinner,
> Thy eternal all's at stake!
>
> 6) But to those who have confessed,
> Loved, and served the Lord below;
> He will say, "Come near ye blessed,
> See the kingdom I bestow:
> You for ever
> Shall my love and glory know."
>
> 7) Under sorrows and reproaches,
> May this thing your courage raise!
> Swiftly God's great day approaches,
> Sighs shall then be changed to praise:
> We shall triumph
> When the world is in a blaze.
> (John Newton, 1725-1807)

Response

Help me Jesus, to _____

_____.

VICTORY

Memorize *2 Corinthians 5:10*

Be prepared for opposition (spiritual warfare) and expect victory in Jesus' name

Write down the name (s) of those with whom you shared today and pray for them. _____

_____.

____ Check when the day is completed, never beating yourself up if you did not finish; but, just asking Jesus to help you next day!

Day Eight

God - The Destroyer

ADORATION

    We will often be surprised by these brief portrayals of the amazing nature of God as revealed in Scripture. But we have not often been shocked. This study may startle you, causing you to adjust your view of God so that you may more reverently embrace Him. God is a destroyer. We so often peg the devil as 'the destroyer," the feared wrecker of this world, that God-in contrast- is viewed only as the Life Giver. One, not to fear, but to love. The Bible reveals that He is that; but, He is more. Many give lip service to "the fear of God" and the "judgment of God;" but, often without a shudder or a second thought. In this, I believe, we seriously and dangerously err.

    The OT represents God as a destroyer hundreds of times. We could limit our study to a handful of these texts with great edification. Instead, to emphasize my point, I will focus on God as Destroyer only in the NT. In the full light of the gospel of God's grace! He does not change. He has ever been a God of Love and He, alike, has always been a Destroyer!

    We rightly rejoice that Jesus has destroyed and will bring destruction on death, Satan and his kingdom. "Christ Jesus, who abolished death and brought life and immortality to light through the gospel" (2 Tim 1:10b). "He too shared in their humanity so that by his death he might destroy him who holds the power of death-that is, the devil-and free those who all their lives were held in slavery by their fear of death" (Heb 2:14 - NIV; also 1 Cor 15:24-25; 2 Thess 2:8; 1 John 3:8). But the NT writers do not use God's nature as a Destroyer only to warn and move unbelievers. There is much here to motivate disciples in their walk with Christ.

    As Jesus sent out His 12 apostles on a discipling mission, He said, "And do not fear those who kill the body but cannot kill the soul. Rather, fear him who can destroy both soul and body in hell" (Matt 10:28). To the disciples at Corinth, Paul warned, "Do you not know that you are God's temple and that God's Spirit lives in you? If anyone destroys God temple, God will destroy him: for God's temple is holy, and you are that temple" (1 Cor 3:16-17). He later was more explicit, "Do you not know that your bodies are members of Christ? Flee from sexual immorality...Or do you not know that your body is a temple of the Holy Spirit, within you, whom you have from God? You are not your own" (1 Cor 6:15, 18-19).

James reminded his believing readers, "There is only one Lawgiver and Judge, the one who is able to save and destroy. But you-who are you to judge your neighbor?" (James 4:12 - NIV). And Peter solemnly added, "But the day of the Lord will come like a thief, and then the heavens will pass away with a roar; and the heavenly bodies will be burned up and dissolved, and the earth and the works that are done on it will be exposed. Since all these things are thus to be dissolved, what sort of people ought you to be in lives of holiness and godliness, waiting for and hastening the coming of the day of God, because of which the heavens will be set on fire and destroyed...." (2 Pet 3:10- 12). All these NT leaders, by these many verses in God's Word, warn us that, however far we might advance in our conceptions of grace, believers must never forget to "worship God acceptably with reverence and awe, for our God is a consuming fire" (Heb 12:28b-29).

Response

I thank you God for showing me _____

STRATEGY

Follow Jesus today, remembering His power to transform anything, as seen in **Matthew 21:18-22**(Read now).

As I follow Jesus today I will remember _____

_____.

OBEDIENCE (I will statement)

The Spirit is convicting or leading me today to do or stop doing:

_____

_____.

PETITIONS (Following your reciting of The Lord's Prayer)

I pray for these scheduled meetings today:

I pray also for these pressing needs of myself, my family, my church, my disciples,[25] my world:

CONFESSION and REPENTANCE

I confess these, my sins with every intention to never repeat them, but rather to live as Jesus would live, by Your enabling grace and Spirit …

*Never confess without a faith that looks to the cross of Christ, where the guilt and penalty of all our sins was paid!

WALK (Think about the following hymn)

Psalm One – The Blessed One

1) That man is blest who, fearing God
From sin restrains his feet,
Who will not stand with wicked men,
Who shuns the scorners' seat.

2) Yea, blest is he who makes God's law
His portion and delight,
And meditates upon that law
With gladness day and night.

3) That man is nourished like a tree
Set by the river's side;
Its leaf is green, its fruit is sure
And thus his works abider

4) The wicked like the driven chaff
Are swept from off the land;
They shall not gather with the just
Nor in the judgment stand.

(5) The Lord will guard the righteous well,
Their way to Him is known;
The way of sinners, far from God,
Shall surely be o'erthrown.!
(English rendition of King David 11th century BC))

---

[25] Those whom you are discipling may be considered "your" disciples in the same way Paul meant when he told the Corinthians, "Be imitators of me as I am of Christ" (1 Cor 11:1)

Response

Help me Jesus, to _____

_____.

VICTORY

Memorize *2 Thessalonians 1:6-7* by reading it in sections 5 times, reciting (without looking) 5 times and repeating it throughout the day 5 times (at least at 9AM, 12 noon and 3PM when you STOP the day to worship and talk to God).

"Freely you have received, freely give" (NIV-Matt 10:8) – Remind yourself to speak peace (Luke 10:5) wherever you go and to whomever you speak, and always be ready to share something of the Word if the person is receptive and has time to listen. Be prepared to ask, "the person of peace question" (PoP) to anyone who seems ready and willing to be discipled.[26]

Be prepared for opposition (spiritual warfare) and expect victory in Jesus' name Write down the name (s) of those with whom you shared today and pray for them_____

_____.

____ Check when the day is completed, never beating yourself up if you did not finish; but, just asking Jesus to help you next day!

---

[26] PoP question: "Would you like to discover for yourself what God is like and how God wants you to live?"

Day Nine

God - The Fire

ADORATION

To help us better understand his nature, God often likens Himself to physical objects. But, we must remember that there is not an exact correlation between God and any object. When Scripture affirms, "our God is a consuming fire" (Heb 12:29), it is likening God to an inextinguishable blaze. Whenever such comparisons are made, we make proper conclusions about God only if we do the following: (1) Discern the obvious and chief characteristics of the object mentioned, (2) Ascribe them to God without any taint of sin, limitation or imperfection, and (3) Praise Him for eternally being such a great God.

Fire chiefly reveals brightness, heat, cleansing or destruction. Each passage must be examined to discern which of the characteristics of fire are being ascribed to God. When Christ is viewed in His glory, it is said, "his eyes were like blazing fire" (Rev 1:14; 19:12 – NIV). So, Jesus' understanding of us (eyesight) involves an infinite brightness that penetrates all the secrets and darkness of our hearts. Therefore, let's not delude ourselves by trying to get away with sin! Paul warns that the day is coming when "the Lord Jesus is revealed from heaven with his mighty angels in flaming fire, inflicting vengeance on those who do not know God and on those who do not obey the gospel of our Lord Jesus." (2 Thes 1:7). Here, His infinite and perfect justice is likened to a fire that will consume His enemies. So, warn non-Christians of their danger. And remember Peter said, "Since everything will be destroyed [by fire] what kind of people ought you to be? You ought to live holy and godly lives (2 Pet 3:11,12 - NIV).

The work of the Holy Spirit is likened to "tongues as of fire" in Acts 2:3. The Spirit often inflames believers to share the Word of God boldly (cf. Acts 4:31b). God asked, "Is not my word like fire?" (Jer 23:29). When we speak it, great good can come as the Spirit uses it to burn down idols, spark repentance or ignite devotion in the listeners. So, share the Truth often and listen carefully when others share it with you. We would do well ever to obey God's command. "Do not put out the Spirit's fire" (1 Thes 5:19 - NIV) by sinful silence or sinful indulgence.

Let's remember that nothing we do apart from faith in Christ can endure God's judgment. On that Day, "the fire will test the quality of each man 's work." And "no one can lay any foundation other than...Jesus Christ"

(1 Cor. 3:11-13*)*. So, the Spirit would have us often ask ourselves today and every day, **"Is my life at this moment truly built on Christ, by my exhibiting a faith that is working through love?**

Response

I thank you God for showing me _____

_____.

STRATEGY

Follow Jesus today, remembering His power to transform anything, as seen in **Matthew 17:1-8**(Read now)

As I follow Jesus today I will remember _____

_____.

OBEDIENCE (I will statement)

The Spirit is convicting or leading me today to do or stop doing: _____

_____.

PETITIONS (Following your reciting of <u>The Lord's Prayer</u>)

I pray for these scheduled meetings today:

I pray also for these pressing needs of myself, my family, my church, my disciples,[27] my world:

CONFESSION and REPENTANCE

I confess these, my sins with every intention to never repeat them, but rather to live as Jesus would live, by Your enabling grace and Spirit …

---

[27] Those whom you are discipling may be considered "your" disciples in the same way Paul meant when he told the Corinthians, "Be imitators of me as I am of Christ" (1 Cor 11:1)

*Never confess without a faith that looks to the cross of Christ, where the guilt and penalty of all our sins was paid!

WALK (Think about the following hymn)

Lo, He Comes with Clouds Descending

1) Lo! He comes, with clouds descending,
once for our salvation slain;
thousand thousand saints attending
swell the triumph of His train.
Alleluia! Alleluia! Alleluia!
God appears on earth to reign.

2) Ev'ry eye shall now behold Him,
robed in dreadful majesty;
those who set at naught and sold Him,
pierced, and nailed Him to the tree,
deeply wailing, deeply wailing,
shall the true Messiah see.

3) Every island, sea, and mountain,
heav'n and earth, shall flee away;
all who hate Him must, confounded,
hear the trump proclaim the day:
Come to judgment! Come to judgment!
Come to judgment, come away!

4) Now redemption, long expected,
see in solemn pomp appear!
And His saints, by men rejected,
coming with Him in the air.
Alleluia! Alleluia! Alleluia!
See the day of God appear!

5) Yea, amen! Let all adore Thee,
high on Thine eternal throne;
Savior, take the pow'r and glory,
claim the kingdom for Thine own:
O come quickly, O come quickly,
Alleluia! Come, Lord, come!
(Charles Wesley, 1707-1788)

Response

Help me Jesus, to _____

_____.

VICTORY

Memorize *Matthew 3:11*

Be prepared for opposition (spiritual warfare) and expect victory in Jesus' name.

Write down the name (s) of those with whom you shared today and pray for them. _____

_____.

____ Check when the day is completed, never beating yourself up if you did not finish; but, just asking Jesus to help you next day!

Day Ten

God - The Renewer

ADORATION

"Oh, if I could just go back and start over again!" But time rolls on. Are there, then, no second chances? Satan says no and breathes his deadening chill into every soul that is open to his lies. Defeated ones often lament, "Restore us to yourself, O Lord, renew our days as of old" (Lam 5:21). "Lord I have heard of your fame; I stand in awe of your deeds, O Lord. Renew them in our day, in our time; make them known: in wrath remember mercy" (Hab 3:2 - NIV). But will He? Can He reverse time and restore what we have wasted? He can and does!

He promises, "they who hope in the Lord will renew their strength; they will...run and not grow weary, they will walk and not faint" (Isa 40:31). After adultery and murder, David could humbly pray, "Create in me a clean heart, O Lord, and renew a right spirit within me" (Ps 51:10). And Paul, "the chief of sinners" says, "So we do not lose heart. Though our outward self is wasting away, yet our inward self is being renewed day by day" (2 Cor 4:16). God's grace and power turn murderers into great kings and apostles! Certainly, He can help you! He helped Naomi when all she had was poverty and sorrow. God gave her life back to her. "The women said to Naomi: 'Blessed be the Lord...He shall be to you a restorer of life and a nourisher of your old age" (Ruth 4:14-15).

God's mercy allows for renewal. "When you send your Spirit they are created, and you renew the face of the earth" (Ps 104:30 - NIV). What He does every Spring, in nature, He does in the springtime of our lives when we are born again. "He saved us, not because of works done by us in righteousness, but according to his own mercy, by the washing of regeneration and renewal of the Holy Spirit" (Titus 3:5). Are you sure that you have been born again? Turn from sin to Christ by faith and be renewed!

The Christian, by faith, has "put on the new self, which is being renewed in knowledge after the image of its Creator" (Col 3:10). God is removing the habits of sin and replacing lies with both true knowledge and true living. He is showing us that Christ is truth and life - the center of everything. "Do not be conformed to this world but be transformed by the renewing of your mind" (Rom 12:2). And however bleak it seems, dear believer, trust like Job, "All the days of my hard service I will wait for my renewal to come. You will call, and I will answer you; you will long for the creature you have made" (Job 14:14b-15 - NIV). He loves you and has not forgotten you. Your day is coming.

"Jesus said... at the renewal of all things, when the Son of Man sits on his glorious throne...everyone who has left houses or brothers or sisters or father or mother or children or fields for my sake will receive a hundred times as much and will inherit eternal life. But many who are first will be last, and many who are last will be first" (Matt 19:28-30 - NIV). Be a disciple and do not give up. Jesus has won and will lead you into victory! God will fully and finally win, renewing the entire world.

Response

I thank you God for showing me _____

_____.

STRATEGY

Follow Jesus today, remembering His power to renew, as seen in **Mark 5:1-13** (Read now)

As I follow Jesus today I will remember _____

_____.

OBEDIENCE (I will statement)

The Spirit is convicting or leading me today to do or stop doing: _____

_____.

PETITIONS (Following your reciting of The Lord's Prayer)

I pray for these scheduled meetings today:

I pray also for these pressing needs of myself, my family, my church, my disciples,[28] my world:

---

[28] Those whom you are discipling may be considered "your" disciples in the same way Paul meant when he told the Corinthians, "Be imitators of me as I am of Christ" (1 Cor 11:1)

CONFESSION and REPENTANCE

I confess these, my sins with every intention to never repeat them, but rather to live as Jesus would live, by Your enabling grace and Spirit …

*Never confess without a faith that looks to the cross of Christ, where the guilt and penalty of all our sins was paid!

WALK (Think about the following hymn)

Revive thy Work, O Lord

1) Revive Thy work, O Lord!
Now to Thy saints appear!
Oh, speak with power to every soul,
And let Thy people hear!

Revive Thy work, O Lord!
While here to Thee we bow;
Descend, O gracious Lord, descend!
Oh, come, and bless us now!

2) Revive Thy work, O Lord!
And every soul inspire;
Oh, kindle in each heart, we pray,
The Pentecostal fire!

3) Revive Thy work, O Lord!
Exalt Thy precious name!
And may Thy love in every heart
Be kindled to a flame!

4) Revive Thy work, O Lord!
And bless to all Thy Word!
And may its pure and sacred truth
In living faith be heard!

5) Revive Thy work, O Lord!
And make Thy servants bold;
Convict of sin and work once more
As in the days of old.

6) Revive Thy work, O Lord!
Give Pentecostal showers!
Be Thine the glory, Thine alone!
The blessing, Lord, be ours!
(Albert Midlane, 1825-1909)

Response

Help me Jesus, to _____

_____.

VICTORY

Memorize *2 Corinthians 5:17*

Be prepared for opposition (spiritual warfare) and expect victory in Jesus' name.

Write down the name (s) of those with whom you shared today and pray for them. _____

_____.

____ Check when the day is completed, never beating yourself up if you did not finish; but, just asking Jesus to help you next day!

10-Day Period 2

Discipleship and our Believing

**Begin by reading Appendix Two – A Faith that does NOT Save

As you begin your second week, it is important that you continue to focus your faith on the reality of Jesus' presence with you. This is a different type of faith than what many Christians actually possess. Christians are told what to believe about Jesus from the Bible. But few today seem to actually walk with Him as a daily Leader. They only know Him as their Savior. One who merely saves us from sins' penalty, and who actually has little to do with how we live daily! We need to have faith for today. Not only faith to save us from hell, as wonderful as that is. But a faith that saves us from the power of sin in our lives right now, so we can reach out and make other disciples, as Christ commanded.

What we need is a present TRUST, because that is what saving faith actually is: a deep trust in Jesus as revealed to us in the holy Scriptures and in our daily lives. All biblically literate Christians know Hebrews 11 is "the great faith chapter." Read it over again and ask yourself, "Is this the type of faith I have?" For, you will see, the faith of Hebrews 11 is always a *faith in action*. "By faith Abel offered (v.4) … by faith Noah constructed an ark (v. 7) … by faith Abraham obeyed (v. 8) …." The inward belief is always proven real by the outward act. You will see this throughout Hebrews 11. But, the chapter ends with these amazing words, "All of these, though commended through their faith, did not receive what was promised., since … apart from us they should not be made perfect" (39-40). We are linked together with them. We are one people of God. We share true faith and it leads us to a shared destiny with God.

So, Hebrews 12 shocks us by telling us that they are watching us, calling them a "great cloud of witnesses" (12:1). As they watch YOU live your life, are they cheering, crying or booing? That is a most serious question that Hebrews' author wants us to consider as a motivation to do one main thing: "fix your eyes on Jesus" as we "throw off everything that hinders, and the sin that so easily entangles, and … run with perseverance the race marked out for us" (12:1-2 - NIV). That is simple discipleship—making Jesus your constant fixation. Holy Spirit help us!

Day Eleven

God – The I AM

ADORATION

We live in a world of constant change. Data deemed vital a short time ago is discarded as irrelevant today. This dizzying speed of change involves not only news, weather and political revelations. Older bastions of morality are being scrapped, too. Some preachers and many politicians today seem to choose their positions and strategies more from polls and surveys than from long held moral convictions. Many leaders seem more interested in winning than in warning and guiding.

Into this growing moral lethargy, God speaks. He gives solid truth that will, no doubt, endure the test of time because He transcends time. And the greatest, most practical truth He offers us is the revelation of who He is, for He is truth. All that He has revealed Himself to be, He will always be. All that He has ever blessed and favored, He will always bless and favor. The earth and its leaders, with their popular social theories, will all perish. He, however, will remain. "Of old you laid the foundation of the earth, and the heavens are the work of your hands. They will perish, but you will remain; they will all wear out like a garment ... but you are the same, and your years have no end. (Psalm 102:25-27). God is always what matters most.

In a dark day that needed brave leadership, God called Moses. But He was scared to step forward against Egypt's sorcerers and political power without some word from God. So, he asked the Lord, "Suppose I go to the Israelites and say to them, 'The God of your fathers has sent me to you, and they ask me, what is his name? Then what shall I tell them?'" It was then and there that God told Moses all he would ever need to know. He said to Moses, "I AM WHO I AM." This is what you are to say to the Israelites: I AM has sent me to you" (Ex. 3:13-14)

Moses' strength and confidence were based on the simple and awesome fact that GOD IS. All that He ever was, He still is. All that He has ever done, He can match with equal power again, at any time. Moses must believe that the wisdom and power needed to create the universe in its infinite diversity and symmetry IS with Him. He would lead Moses wisely and powerfully. And so, He will us, for He is in all His glorious nature the Great I AM! The biblical writer described Jesus as "the radiance of the glory of God and the exact imprint of his nature" (Heb 1:3). And then he assured the persecuted and doubting Hebrew believers, "Jesus Christ is the same yesterday and today and forever" (Heb 13:8). That was what Moses and the early disciples needed to hear. Dear friend, never forget, the Great I AM being with you, too. Today. Right now. Ready to both hinder evil doers and help the righteous. Just as Jesus assured His enemies and followers, "before Abraham was, I am" (John 8:58), all who follow Him, live in the center of His very real and present existence.

So, don't give up! He only waits if it best serves His wise plan and His Son's glory. Don't allow yourselves to be "children tossed to and fro by the waves and carried about by every wind of doctrine, by human cunning, by craftiness in deceitful schemes" (Eph 4:14). Be grounded by the timeless truth that God is forever God. He will have the last word and His truth will be vindicated.

Response

I thank you God for showing me _____

_____.

STRATEGY

Follow Jesus today, who used "I am" statements about Himself numerous times, as seen in **John 10:7-21** (Read now)

As I follow Jesus today I will remember _____

_____.

OBEDIENCE (I will statement)

The Spirit is convicting or leading me today to do or stop doing: _____

_____.

PETITIONS (Following your reciting of The Lord's Prayer)

I pray for these scheduled meetings today:

I pray also for these pressing needs of myself, my family, my church, my disciples, my world:

CONFESSION and REPENTANCE

I confess these, my sins with every intention to never repeat them, but rather to live as Jesus would live, by Your enabling grace and Spirit …

*Never confess without a faith that looks to the cross of Christ, where the guilt and penalty of all our sins was paid!

WALK (Think about and listen to the following hymn on YOUTUBE for a heavenly tune)

I am the Bread of Life

1) I am the Bread of life,
He who comes to Me shall not hunger,
He who believes in Me shall not thirst.
No one can come to Me
Unless the Father draw him.

And I will raise him up,
And I will raise him up,
And I will raise him up on the last day.

2) The bread that I will give
Is My flesh for the life of the world,
And he who eats of this bread,
He shall live forever,
He shall live forever.

3) Unless you eat
Of the flesh of the Son of Man
And drink of His blood,
And drink of His blood,
You shall not have life within you.

4) I am the Resurrection,
I am the Life,
He who believes in Me
Even if he die,
He shall live forever.
(Suzanne Toolan, b. 1927)

Response

Help me Jesus, to _____

_____.

VICTORY

Memorize *John 6:35* by reading it in sections 5 times, reciting (without looking) 5 times and repeating it throughout the day 5 times (at least at 9AM, 12 noon and 3PM when you STOP the day to worship and talk to God).

"Freely you have received, freely give" (NIV-Matt 10:8) – Remind yourself to speak peace (Luke 10:5) wherever you go and to whomever you speak, and always be ready to share something of the Word if the person is receptive and has time to listen. Be prepared to ask, "the person of peace question" (PoP) to anyone who seems ready and willing to be discipled.

Be prepared for opposition (spiritual warfare) and expect victory in Jesus' name.

Write down the name (s) of those with whom you shared today _____

_____.

____ Check when the day is completed, never beating yourself up if you did not finish; but, just asking Jesus to help you next day!

Day Twelve

God – The Personal One

ADORATION

  Jesus said, "God is spirit, and those who worship him must worship in spirit and in truth" (John 4:24). God is not merely an awesome Power or a life-preserving Force. He is a being with personality, for that is what a "spirit" is—one possessing understanding, emotions and will. Angels and demons are spirits though they have no permanent physical bodies. We are spirits joined with a physical body. All of these possess the characteristics of personhood: we think, we feel, and we act. So, does God, but in an infinite and eternal way.

  God is love. He loves the world. When His people don't return that love, He says, "I have been grieved by their adulterous hearts, which have turned away from me, and by their eyes, which have lusted after their idols" (Eze. 6:9-NIV). But when His people walk or constantly fellowship with Him, God is "pleased" (Gen 5:24; Heb 11:5). We even read that God "will rejoice over you with gladness; he will quiet you by his love; he will exult over you with loud singing" (Zeph. 3:17). It is never right to conceive of God as a cold, unemotional—as impersonal. Therefore, we should never speak to (pray/worship) or about Him in a cold, distant, detached or irreverent way (See Ex 20:7; Matt 10:32). He wants our hearts (Deut 6:5; Prov 23:26) and takes it personally whenever we thoughtlessly "run through the motions" of worship. Often ask yourself, "Am I NOW acting as one should while in the presence of God?"

  God is called "the Father of spirits" (Heb 12:9) and the "God of the spirits of all flesh" (Numb16:22). At death our body "returns to the ground it came from and the spirit returns to the God who gave it" (Ecc 12:7-NIV). At a funeral we look on the dead body of a friend and weep. That which gave him his personality and life has departed. His spirit is no longer with us even though his body is. So, remember that our spirits are the most basic and important aspect of who we are. Every human, despite race, class, gender, age or health, has dignity being a spirit made in the image of God—the Greatest Spirit.

  Here's a list of practical inferences we can draw from all of this. Since God is a Person, we can have a personal relationship with Him through Christ. And since our spiritual side is more basic or enduring than our physical side. What really matters most is what we <u>are</u> rather than what we possess. Your body will decay, but your spirit will never die! We should spend more time cultivating our spirits than our bodies. We ought to honor every person as a uniquely created and beloved being despite their appearance. We're created to love and to be loved, so let's work hard to build relationships and preserve the ones we now have. Since Jesus is "the radiance of God's glory and the exact representation of his being" (Be. 1:3), let us recognize Him as the perfect human and the best man. His personality is all that God is and all that humans want to be. Dying to self and living in, through and for Him will be US AT OUR BEST!

Response

I thank you God for showing me _____

_____.

STRATEGY

Follow Jesus today, who "spoke as no other man", as seen in **John 4:7-26** **(**Read now)

As I follow Jesus today I will remember _____

_____.

OBEDIENCE (I will statement)

The Spirit is convicting or leading me today to do or stop doing: _____

_____.

PETITIONS (Following your reciting of The Lord's Prayer)

I pray for these scheduled meetings today:

I pray also for these pressing needs of myself, my family, my church, my disciples my world:

CONFESSION and REPENTANCE

I confess these, my sins with every intention to never repeat them, but rather to live as Jesus would live, by Your enabling grace and Spirit …
*Never confess without a faith that looks to the cross of Christ, where the guilt and penalty of all our sins was paid!

WALK (Think about the following hymn)

More Love to Thee

More love to Thee, O Christ, more love to Thee!
Hear Thou the prayer I make on bended knee.
This is my earnest plea: More love, O Christ, to Thee;
More love to Thee, more love to Thee!

Once earthly joy I craved, sought peace and rest;
Now Thee alone I seek, give what is best.
This all my prayer shall be: More love, O Christ to Thee;
More love to Thee, more love to Thee!

Let sorrow do its work, come grief or pain;
Sweet are Thy messengers, sweet their refrain,
When they can sing with me: More love, O Christ, to Thee;
More love to Thee, more love to Thee!

Then shall my latest breath whisper Thy praise;
This be the parting cry my heart shall raise;
This still its prayer shall be: More love, O Christ to Thee;
More love to Thee, more love to Thee!
(Elizabeth P Prentiss, (1818-1878)

Response

Help me Jesus, to _____

_____.

VICTORY

Memorize *John 4:24*

Be prepared for opposition (spiritual warfare) and expect victory in Jesus' name.

Write down the name (s) of those with whom you shared today and pray for them. _____

_____.

_____ Check when the day is completed, never beating yourself up if you did not finish; but, just asking Jesus to help you next day!

Day Thirteen

God – The Knowable One

ADORATION

    Can we be sure about God? His existence? His nature? The skeptic affirms, you cannot know for sure. No one knows for sure. Funny, he can boldly say what cannot be known by anyone! How, then, can the skeptic be so sure and know everyone else and their experiences? Do skeptics appreciate the nature of faith and the certainty that faith brings? "Now faith is the assurance of things hoped for, the conviction of things not seen (Heb 11:1). The real problem is NOT that God cannot be known. It is that the skeptic does not have faith. Millions of believers affirm that God most certainly may be known.

    He can be known because He wants to be known. "The heavens declare the glory of God… night to night reveals knowledge" (Psalm 19:1-2). However, when sin entered humanity through Adam and corrupted us all, we humans did not like what we saw of God. He is so different from us. Too different. "…What may be known about God is plain to them because God has made it plain to them. … God's invisible qualities … have been clearly seen, being understood from what has been made, so that men are without excuse. For although they knew God, they neither glorified him as God nor gave thanks to him, but their thinking became futile and their foolish hearts were darkened … Furthermore, since they did not think it worthwhile to retain the knowledge of God, he gave them over to a depraved mind, to do what ought not to be done" (Rom 1:19-21, 28 – NIV). But God did not give up on us!

    He sent Jesus to make Himself known. "No one has ever seen God, the only God, who is at the Father's side, he has made him known" (John 1:18). Jesus said, "He who has sent me is true, and him you do not know. I know him, for I come from him, and he sent me" (John 7:28b-29). And He prayed, "Now this is eternal life; that they may know you, the only true God, and Jesus Christ, whom you have sent…. I have made you known to them and will continue to make you known in order that the love you have for me may be in them, and that I myself may be in them" (John 17:3,26-NIV).

    And Jesus authorized His apostles to do the same. So, John wrote, "We (apostles) are from God. Whoever knows God listens to us; whoever is not from God does not listen to us. By this we know the Spirit of truth and the spirit of error" (1 John 4:6-8). The knowledge of God is the greatest gift we can have. By His grace, we who wanted to be left alone in our sin, have been pursued and given His knowledge. And some day, when Christ returns, "…the earth shall be full of the knowledge of the Lord as the waters cover the sea" (Isa 11:9). Be thankful you know God. Let everything else go for this priceless treasure. As Jeremiah wrote, "This is what the Lord says, Let not the wise man boast of his wisdom, or the strong man boast of his strength or the rich man boast of his riches, but let him who boasts boast in this: that he understands and knows me, that I am the Lord who exercises kindness, justice and righteousness on earth, for in these things I delight, declares the Lord" (Jer 9:23-24).

Response

I thank you God for showing me _____

_____.

STRATEGY

Follow Jesus today, who spoke to the Father as One who knew Him in **John 17:1-19** (Read now)

As I follow Jesus today I will remember _____

_____.

OBEDIENCE (I will statement)

The Spirit is convicting or leading me today to do or stop doing: _____

_____.

PETITIONS (Following your reciting of <u>The Lord's Prayer</u>)

I pray for these scheduled meetings today:

I pray also for these pressing needs of myself, my family, my church, my disciples my world:

CONFESSION and REPENTANCE

I confess these, my sins with every intention to never repeat them, but rather to live as Jesus would live, by Your enabling grace and Spirit ...

*Never confess without a faith that looks to the cross of Christ, where the guilt and penalty of all our sins was paid!

WALK (Think about the following hymn)

I Know Whom I Have Believed

1) I know not why God's wondrous grace
To me He hath made known,
Nor why, unworthy, Christ in love
Redeemed me for His own.

*But "I know Whom I have believed,
And am persuaded that He is able
To keep that which I've committed
Unto Him against that day."*

2) I know not how this saving faith
To me He did impart,
Nor how believing in His Word
Wrought peace within my heart.

3) I know not how the Spirit moves,
Convincing men of sin,
Revealing Jesus through the Word,
Creating faith in them.

4) I know not what of good or ill
May be reserved for me,
Of weary ways or golden days,
Before His face I see.

5) I know not when my Lord may come,
At night or noonday fair,
Nor if I walk the vale with Him,
Or meet Him in the air.
(Daniel Webster Whittle, 1840-1901)

Response

Help me Jesus, to _____

_____.

VICTORY

Memorize *Philippians 3:7-8*

Be prepared for opposition (spiritual warfare) and expect victory in Jesus' name.

Write down the name (s) of those with whom you shared today _____

_____.

____ Check when the day is completed, never beating yourself up if you did not finish; but, just asking Jesus to help you next day!

Day Fourteen

God – The Promising One

ADORATION

All society is based on making promises to others and keeping them. When a mother holds an infant and whispers, "I love you," she is doing more than expressing a passing emotion. She is pledging that she will constantly cherish and continually care for her baby—for that is what love does. Love makes promises and tries hard to keep them. Our marriages, our jobs, our purchases and our spiritual relationships with God and one another are all based on promises. Sometimes they are called covenants, contracts, agreements, pledges or vows. Without them life unravels. Truthfulness, faithfulness, courage and love support promise keeping.

But we often fail to do what we have promised, sometimes utterly. Humans everywhere are known for this kind of unfaithfulness, as Moses said, "God is not a man that he should lie, nor a son of man that he should change his mind ... Does he promise and not fulfill? (Num 23:19-NIV). You see, He is very unlike us. And we can totally trust Him to do as He has said. "The Lord is faithful to all his promises" (Psa 145:18-NIV).

This faithfulness of God made the Levites and all Israel sing, "you have kept your promise, for you are righteous" (Neh. 9:8b). Hebrew Christians were encouraged, "Let us hold fast the confession of our hope without wavering, for he who promised is faithful" (Heb 10:23). When one discovers that God can be trusted, completely trusted, then a great weight of worry and fear is lifted.

Look throughout the Word and at all history. Can't you say, "Your promises have been thoroughly tested, and your servant loves them" (Ps 119:140). When you have acted in faith and obedience, have you ever seen God fail to bless you? Try it and you will begin to join David in singing, "I rejoice in your promise like one who finds great spoil" (Ps 119:162-NIV). Read His Word and keep abiding in it and you will find that it is a treasure filled with amazing promises. As Peter said, "He has granted to us his precious and very great promises" (2 Pet 1:4).

However, God rarely does what we want when we want it. This does not mean that God is indifferent to our feelings. Rather, He is wise, working all things perfectly together to accomplish His will in us all simultaneously. When I am exasperated at someone's slow speed of development, He reminds me, "The Lord is not slow concerning his promise ... He is patient

….." (2 Pet 3:9). Trust Him, like our father Abraham, who "did not waver through unbelief regarding the promise of God but was strengthened in his faith and gave glory to God" (Rom 4:20-NIV).

We do this by keeping our eyes on Christ and holding His hand by faith. When you sin and break your promise to God or others, look quickly to the One who is leading you. Jesus – who never broke His promise and in whose perfect faithfulness you stand. Our hope is not in our promise keeping alone, but rather in His! "For no matter how many promises God has made, they are 'Yes' in Christ" (2 Cor 1:20-NIV).

When you get tired of life here and now. Of the struggle against sin. Remember, "this is the promise he made to us – eternal life" (1 John 2:25). Christ is coming back, and everything will then be as it should be!

Response

I thank you God for showing me _____

_____.

STRATEGY

Follow Jesus today, and trust His wisdom in how He fulfills His promise as seen in **John 11:1-44 (**Read now)

As I follow Jesus today I will remember _____

_____.

OBEDIENCE (I will statement)

The Spirit is convicting or leading me today to do or stop doing: _____

_____.

PETITIONS (Following your reciting of The Lord's Prayer)

I pray for these scheduled meetings today:

I pray also for these pressing needs of myself, my family, my church, my disciples, my world:

CONFESSION and REPENTANCE

I confess these, my sins with every intention to never repeat them, but rather to live as Jesus would live, by Your enabling grace and Spirit …

*Never confess without a faith that looks to the cross of Christ, where the guilt and penalty of all our sins was paid!

WALK (Think about the following hymn)

Standing on the Promises

(1) Standing on the promises of Christ my King,
Through eternal ages let His praises ring,
Glory in the highest, I will shout and sing,
Standing on the promises of God.

Standing, standing,
Standing on the promises of God my Savior;
Standing, standing,
I'm standing on the promises of God.

(2) Standing on the promises that cannot fail,
When the howling storms of doubt and fear assail,
By the living Word of God I shall prevail,
Standing on the promises of God.

(3) Standing on the promises I now can see
Perfect, present cleansing in the blood for me;
Standing in the liberty where Christ makes free,
Standing on the promises of God.

(4) Standing on the promises of Christ the Lord,
Bound to Him eternally by love's strong cord,
Overcoming daily with the Spirit's sword,
Standing on the promises of God.

(5) Standing on the promises I cannot fall,
List'ning every moment to the Spirit's call,
Resting in my Savior as my all in all,
Standing on the promises of God.
(Russell K Carter, 1849-1928)

Response

Help me Jesus, to _____

_____.

VICTORY

Memorize *Hebrews 10:23*

Be prepared for opposition (spiritual warfare) and expect victory in Jesus' name Write down the name (s) of those with whom you shared today and pray for them._____

_____.

_____ Check when the day is completed, never beating yourself up if you did not finish; but, just asking Jesus to help you next day!

Day Fifteen

God – The Believable One

ADORATION

It is a horrible thing not to be trusted. Teens repeat these words to restrictive parents, "Why won't you trust me?" Of course, the reason is, we have been there before. We know the nature of temptation and the weakness of human nature at that age. We believe, and trust is based on evidence. One must prove himself reliable and responsible before full confidence occurs.

So why do we NOT fully believe God? Has He not proven Himself? "The Lord said to Moses, 'How long will they not believe in me, despite all the signs that I have done among them?'" (Num 14:11). Maybe our problem is NOT one of evidence. Could it be that we do not want to believe? Perhaps we are so weak and corrupt that we would rather actually sin and die than believe and be saved! Maybe we are not really all that different from the rebelling Israelites of old. "For they did not believe in God or trust in his deliverance ... Despite all this they kept on sinning, despite his wonders, they did not believe" (Ps 78:22,32).

Perhaps our pride is so pervasive that His grace is repulsive to us. We must be able to do this for ourselves. We can't be that bad, that weak, that we need Him for everything, could we? We aren't infants, but grown-ups! "There you saw how the Lord your God carried you as a father carries his son ... despite this, you did not trust in the Lord your God" (Deut 1:31b-32-NIV). Was David right when he said, "there is none who does good, not even one" (Psa 14:3b)? Or Isaiah, "all our righteous acts are like filthy rags" (Isa 64:6b-NIV)? Or Jesus, "apart from me you can do nothing" (John 15:5b)? At our best moments, we know they spoke the hard, cold truth about all of us.

We must recognize that believing God, especially what He says about us, is so hard to swallow that no one would do so if God did not give us the gift of faith. He must enable us to believe. As Paul wrote, "Let God be true, though everyone were a liar" (Rom 3:4b). Our reasoning and intuition and opinions are all wrong concerning our need of God. It is total and complete. We are like sheep, like infants—helpless against the pull of pride, selfishness and hate.

So, let us not hesitate to trust in Him! He has proven Himself to be trustworthy. His Word is truth. "... Scripture cannot be broken" (John 10:35b). "O Sovereign Lord, you are God! Your words are trustworthy ...."

(2 Sam 7:28a). "The statutes of the Lord are trustworthy making wise the simple" (Psa 19:7b-NIV).

He sent His Son to reveal Himself and to save us from unbelief. His miracles, words and life all established His credibility as the One and Only Son of God. "Jesus said, 'You believe because I told you I saw you under the fig tree. You shall see greater things that that" (John 1:50-NIV). The Samaritans confessed, "It is no longer because of what you said that we believe; for we have heard for ourselves, and we know that this is the Savior of the world": (John 4:42).

Jesus pleaded, "Believe me when I say that I am in the Father and the Father is in me; or at least believe on the evidence of the miracles themselves" (John 14:11-NIV). His resurrection removed all doubt for, he "was declared with power to be the Son of God by his resurrection from the dead" (Rom 1:4b-NIV). So, let us believe in the One who, alone, is completely believable. And, so let us "walk by faith, not by sight" (2 Cor 5:7) down every step of today's path. The evidence is complete, and the verdict is in. Only believe!

Response

I thank you God for showing me _____

_____.

STRATEGY

Follow Jesus today, and "only believe" as He commanded in **Luke 8:40-56** (Read now)

As I follow Jesus today I will remember _____

_____.

OBEDIENCE (I will statement)

The Spirit is convicting or leading me today to do or stop doing: _____

_____.

PETITIONS   (Following your reciting of <u>The Lord's Prayer</u>)

I pray for these scheduled meetings today:

I pray also for these pressing needs of myself, my family, my church, my disciples, my world:

CONFESSION and REPENTANCE

I confess these, my sins with every intention to never repeat them, but rather to live as   Jesus would live, by Your enabling grace and Spirit ...

*Never confess without a faith that looks to the cross of Christ, where the guilt and penalty of all our sins was paid!

WALK (Think about the following hymn)

Only Believe

1) Fear not, little flock, from the cross to the throne,
From death into life He went for His own;
All power in earth, all power above,
Is given to Him for the flock of His love.

Only believe, only believe;
All things are possible, only believe,
Only believe, only believe;
All things are possible, only believe.

2) Fear not, little flock, He goeth ahead,
Your Shepherd selecteth the path you must tread;
The waters of Marah He'll sweeten for thee,
He drank all the bitter in Gethsemane.

3) Fear not, little flock, whatever your lot,
He enters all rooms, "the doors being shut,"
He never forsakes; He never is gone,
So count on His presence in darkness and dawn.
(Paul Rader, 1878-1938)

Response

Help me Jesus, to _____

_____.

VICTORY

Memorize Acts _16:31_

Be prepared for opposition (spiritual warfare) and expect victory in Jesus' name.

Write down the name (s) of those with whom you shared today _____

_____.

____ Check when the day is completed, never beating yourself up if you did not finish; but, just asking Jesus to help you next day!

Day Sixteen

God – The True One

ADORATION

Truth is the opposite of falsehood and error. What is true is real. It can be relied on and will not disappoint legitimate expectations. Lies are like dreams, without a lasting foundation. Error will ultimately disappoint those relying on it. Paul was right when he affirmed, "For we cannot do anything against the truth, but only for the truth" (2 Cor 13:8). The old saying, "Truth will out," is, well, the truth. It will eventually have its day and will win. How can we be so sure of this?

Because God is a God of truth and He reigns over heaven and earth. He, alone, is "the God of truth" (Isa 65:16). As Jeremiah also declared, "But the Lord is the true God; he is the living God and the everlasting King" (Jer 10:10). He tells the truth and supports the truth. "For the word of the Lord is right and true" (Psa 33:4, 119:160 – NIV). Joshua testified, "…every good promise of the Lord your God has come true" (Josh 23:15-NIV).

Even when the Lord allows the truth of His existence and love to be trampled down and nearly lost, He remains unchangeably devoted to the truth and will, in His perfect time, exalt and establish it. "For a long time, Israel was without the true God" (2 Chron 15:3). It got so bad that God said, "Go up and down the streets of Jerusalem … search through her squares. If you can find but one person who deals honestly and seeks the truth, I will forgive this city …. The prophets prophesy lies … and my people love it this way. But what will you do in the end?" (Jer. 5:1,31-NIV). Yes, even when all around looks bleak, and error is advancing, trust God. He, alone, does not deceive and can be relied on forever. You will surely win if you trust in and follow Him.

When Christ came, he was "the true light" (John 1:9), "the true vine" (John 15:1), in contrast with the cunning and convincing counterfeits of Satan. John declared Him to be "full of grace and truth" (John 1:14). He was and is, perfectly, always and in everything—the Revealer of truth. "For the law was given through Moses; grace and truth came through Jesus Christ" (John 1:17). His love is true love. His patience, true patience. And so, His gentleness, anger, justice and mercy were all what they should be in all of us. When Jesus said, "I am the truth," (John 14:6), He meant in everything and in every way. So, He often began His teaching with, "Verily, verily" or "I tell you the truth" (Matt 5:18, etc). Do we live as though we believe His assertions that all others must be compared with Him to test their authenticity? He is the model and mold of truth in every way!

So, Jesus can help us to be truly honest. And this is vital in our relationship with our God of truth because, "Behold you delight in truth in the inward being" (Psa 51:6). So, let us, "Buy the truth and do not sell it" (Prov 23:23), resisting the strong pull to "suppress" and "exchange the truth about God for a lie" (Rom 1:18, 25). Let no lie live in your hearts! Believe Christ's promise: If you abide in my word, you are truly my disciples, and you will know the truth and the truth, and the truth will set you free" (John 8:31-32). Live in the freedom of Christ and His soul-saving truth.

Response

I thank you God for showing me _____

_____.

STRATEGY

Follow Jesus today, and understand His claim on being the true vine, as taught in John **15:1-16** (Read now)

As I follow Jesus today I will remember _____

_____.

OBEDIENCE (I will statement)

The Spirit is convicting or leading me today to do or stop doing: _____

_____.

PETITIONS   (Following your reciting of The Lord's Prayer)

I pray for these scheduled meetings today:

I pray also for these pressing needs of myself, my family, my church, my disciples, my world:

CONFESSION and REPENTANCE

I confess these, my sins with every intention to never repeat them, but rather to live as Jesus would live, by Your enabling grace and Spirit …

*Never confess without a faith that looks to the cross of Christ, where the guilt and penalty of all our sins was paid!

WALK (Think about the following hymn)

The Light of Truth

(1) The light of truth is burning
Along our homeward way;
The wanderer returning
Beholds its golden ray;
It points to paths of duty
Where Christ would have us go,
Its radiance and beauty
None but God's children know.

*The light of truth seems dearer
When we to Christ belong;
The light of truth shines clearer
When we in Christ grow strong.
God's works of love proclaim,
This light will fail us never;
When lab'ring "In His name.*

(2) The light of truth's revealing
God's miracles of grace;
His wondrous pow'r of healing
That man can never trace,
This light new hope is giving,
inspiring us to tell
Of Him in Whom we're living--
Our Christ, Immanuel.

(3) The light of truth is guiding
The lowly contrite heart;
To Him whose word abiding
Bids Satan's hosts depart;
This light, that shines forever,
God's works of love proclaim,
This light will fail us never
When lab'ring "In His name."
(Lavinia Brauff, 1851-1920)

Response

Help me Jesus, to _____

_____.

VICTORY

Memorize *2 Corinthians 13:8*

Be prepared for opposition (spiritual warfare) and expect victory in Jesus' name.

Write down the name (s) of those with whom you shared today and pray for them. _____

_____.

_____ Check when the day is completed, never beating yourself up if you did not finish; but, just asking Jesus to help you next day!

Day Seventeen

God – The Faithful One

ADORATION

Do any of you feel good after being deceived or snookered? Of course not! We are wired to love truth. A healthy society and family depend on its members keeping their word. We all benefit when we follow the nature of God as the source of all true life. Just as He gives life, so His attributes are the natural outflow of real life. That which comes from Him should strive to be like Him. And just as He is a faithful, promise keeper, so we should keep our word and our contracts. "Know therefore that the Lord your God is God; the faithful God, who keeps covenant and steadfast love with those who love him and keep his commandments to a thousand generations" (Deut 7:9).

God does just what He says He will do. "I will remember my covenant between me and you and all living creatures of every kind. Never again will the waters become a flood to destroy all life" (Gen 9:15-NIV). He does not promise an end to all floods and tsunamis which destroy many people and devastate much property. God's promise means what it says and applies to all with whom it was made.

To Abraham and to his descendants, the Lord said, "I will confirm my covenant between me and you and will greatly increase your numbers … I will establish my covenant as an everlasting covenant between me and you and your descendants after you … to be your God and the God of your descendants after you" (Gen 17:2, 7-NIV). Paul called all New Testament (NT) believers "Abraham's offspring, heirs according to the promise" (Gal 3:29). Disciples today draw great hope from God's promise to our father Abraham (see Rom 4:11).

God promises to help His children through every tough day. "God is faithful, and he will not let you be tempted beyond your ability, but with the temptation he will also provide the way of escape, that you may be able to endure it" (1 Cor 10:13). He promises neither an easy way nor few trials. "Therefore, let those who suffer according to God's will entrust their souls to a faithful Creator while doing good" (1 Pet 4:19).

Both Daniel and Nehemiah prayed, "O Lord, the great and awesome God, who keeps his covenant of love with all who love him and obey his commands, we have sinned and done wrong" (Dan 9:4; Neh 1:5-NIV). He is the faithful One. We are unfaithful, untruthful, covenant breakers.

Thankfully, our salvation rests solely on His grace, depending on Him keeping His word perfectly, not on us keeping ours perfectly! "If we are faithless, he remains faithful-- for he cannot deny himself" (2 Tim 3:13).

When Jesus returns, all will recognize that, although He has been patient to enact justice and punish evil, the day of vengeance has come! "I saw heaven standing open and there before me was a white horse, whose rider is called Faithful and True. With justice he judges and makes war ... He treads the winepress of the fury of the wrath of God Almighty" (Rev 19:11-15-NIV). What a faithful God! True to all His holy words and promises concerning life and death!

Until then, "let us hold unswervingly to the hope we profess, for he who promised is faithful" (Heb 10:23-NIV). Remember, it is "because of the Lord's great love we are not consumed, for his compassions never fail. They are new every morning; great is your faithfulness" (Lam 3:22-23-NIV).

Response

I thank you God for showing me _____

_____.

STRATEGY

Follow Jesus today faithfully, working His will as He did the Father's will and warned us to always do, as seen in Matt **25:14-30 (**Read now)

As I follow Jesus today I will remember _____

_____.

OBEDIENCE (I will statement)

The Spirit is convicting or leading me today to do or stop doing: _____

_____.

PETITIONS (Following your reciting of <u>The Lord's Prayer</u>)

I pray for these scheduled meetings today:

I pray also for these pressing needs of myself, my family, my church, my disciples, my world:

CONFESSION and REPENTANCE

I confess these, my sins with every intention to never repeat them, but rather to live as Jesus would live, by Your enabling grace and Spirit ...

*Never confess without a faith that looks to the cross of Christ, where the guilt and penalty of all our sins was paid!

WALK (Think about the following hymn)

Great is Thy Faithfulness

(1) Great is Thy faithfulness, O God my Father;
There is no shadow of turning with Thee,
Thou changest not, Thy compassions they fail not,
As Thou hast been, Thou forever wilt be.

Great is Thy faithfulness!
Great is Thy faithfulness!
Morning by morning new mercies I see
All I have needed Thy hand hath provided
Great is Thy faithfulness, Lord unto me!

(2) Summer and winter and springtime and harvest,
Sun, moon, and stars in their courses above;
Join with all nature in manifold witness,
To Thy great faithfulness, mercy, and love.

(3) Pardon for sin and a peace that endureth,
Thine own dear presence to cheer and to guide;
Strength for today, and bright hope for tomorrow
Blessings all mine, with ten thousand beside.
(Thomas O Chisholm, 1866-1960)

Response

Help me Jesus, to _____

VICTORY

Memorize *Lamentations 3:22-23* by reading it in sections 5 times, reciting (without looking) 5 times and repeating it throughout the day 5 times (at least at 9AM, 12 noon and 3PM when you STOP the day to worship and talk to God).

"Freely you have received, freely give" (NIV-Matt 10:8) – Remind yourself to speak peace (Luke 10:5) wherever you go and to whomever you speak, and always be ready to share something of the Word if the person is receptive and has time to listen. Be prepared to ask, "the person of peace question" (PoP) to anyone who seems ready and willing to be discipled.

Be prepared for opposition (spiritual warfare) and expect victory in Jesus' name.

Write down the name (s) of those with whom you shared today _____
_____.

____ Check when the day is completed, never beating yourself up if you did not finish; but, just asking Jesus to help you next day!

Day Eighteen

God – The Living One

ADORATION

I think that everyone deeply within "thirsts for God, for the living God" (Psa 42:2). Life and death are absolute opposites. The one delights and refreshes, while the other repulses and destroys. Life is real, true existence. Death is nothing—the end of existence. So, **no mistake could be as fatal and harmful as this: to trust death to help you, to fulfill you, to save you.** This happened whenever one trusts in "worthless idols" rather than in "the Lord (who) is the true God ... the living God and the everlasting King (Jer 10:10) But, idols do not have to be carved out of wood or stone. "Greed ... is idolatry" (Col 3:5-NIV). Whatever and whomever you crave MORE than God is your idol at that moment. And all idols are deadly! To fondle them is to play with stinking, wretched death. We are warned by Paul to "Turn from these worthless things to the living God, who made heaven and earth" (Acts 14:15-NIV).

It should not surprise us that the living God does not look lightly on those who turn from life to death. Turning from what He promotes to what He condemns. This insanity is heightened to its most absurd expression when desperate, perishing sinners turn away from Jesus. He is the water of life, the bread of life, the light of life (see John 4:14; 6:35; 8:12). In fact, Jesus simply is life itself (John 14:6). He and His ways totally oppose death, as He is always greater than death. "I am the resurrection and the life. He who believes in me will live, even though he dies" (John 11:25-NIV).

We can insult others with few consequences; but not the living God. King Sennacherib spoke "to mock the living God" (2 Kgs 19:16). If someone does not do what I want them to do, so what? But, not so for those who disregard the true God because "it is a fearful thing to fall into the hands of the living God" (Heb 10:31). It is absolute insanity to turn away from the living and loving God who long ago said, "As I live, declares the Lord God, I have no pleasure in the death of the wicked, but that the wicked turn from his way and live. Turn back! Turn back from your evil ways, for why will you die O house of Israel?" (Eze 33:11).

Faith and courage grow when we know that the living God is with us. David cries out, "The Lord lives, and blessed be my rock, and exalted be the God of my salvation!" (Psa 18:46). So, he wondered, "Who is this uncircumcised Philistine that he should defy the armies of the living God?" (2 Sam 17:26-NIV). Daniel knew God was alive and obeyed Him at great risk. Causing a pagan king to write, "I issue a decree that in every part of my kingdom people must fear and reverence the God of Daniel for he is the living God and ... his kingdom will never be destroyed ... He rescues and saves ... He has rescued Daniel from the power of the lions" (Dan 6:26-28-NIV).

Through faith in Jesus, we have become temples of the living God! "For we are the temple of the living God" (2 Cor 6:16). We have "turned to God from idols, to serve the living and true God" (1 Thes 1:9). And our new family is among "God's household, which is the church of the living God" (1 Tim 3:15). We have been graced to truly live by Jesus! So, enjoy and share the life that the LIVING GOD has given you today!

Response

I thank you God for showing me _____

_____.

STRATEGY

Follow Jesus today and live by faith, as He taught Nicodemus in **John 3:1-21** (Read now)

As I follow Jesus today I will remember _____

_____.

OBEDIENCE (I will statement)

The Spirit is convicting or leading me today to do or stop doing: _____

_____.

PETITIONS (Following your reciting of <u>The Lord's Prayer</u>)

I pray for these scheduled meetings today:

I pray also for these pressing needs of myself, my family, my church, my disciples, my world:

CONFESSION and REPENTANCE

I confess these, my sins with every intention to never repeat them, but rather to live as Jesus would live, by Your enabling grace and Spirit ...

*Never confess without a faith that looks to the cross of Christ, where the guilt and penalty of all our sins was paid!

WALK (Think about the following hymn)

He LIVES!

1) I serve a risen Saviour, He's in the world today
I know that He is living, whatever men may say
I see His hand of mercy, I hear His voice of cheer
And just the time I need Him He's always near

He lives (He lives), He lives (He lives), Christ Jesus lives today
He walks with me and talks with me
Along life's narrow way
He lives (He lives), He lives (He lives), Salvation to impart
You ask me how I know He lives?
He lives within my heart

2) In all the world around, me I see His loving care
And though my heart grows weary I never will despair
I know that He is leading, through all the stormy blast
The day of His appearing will come at last

3) Rejoice, rejoice, O Christian Lift up your voice and sing
Eternal hallelujahs to Jesus Christ, the King
The Hope of all who seek Him, the Help of all who find
None other is so loving, so good and kind
(Alfred H. Ackley, 1887-1960)

Response

Help me Jesus, to _____

_____.

VICTORY

Memorize *Matthew 10:39*

Be prepared for opposition (spiritual warfare) and expect victory in Jesus' name.

Write down the name (s) of those with whom you shared today _____
_____.

____ Check when the day is completed, never beating yourself up if you did not finish; but, just asking Jesus to help you next day!

Day Nineteen

God – The Real One

ADORATION

When we see something that we have longed for, but have doubt that it will ever happen, we sometimes rub our eyes and say, "I don't believe my eyes—Is that for real?" We do not want to rush into believing it is real—just to be disappointed. So, we are often cautiously optimistic at best. We test it out before trusting it. We do not want to be hurt by trusting in a fantasy or mirage. Believing a lie can be more than just embarrassing. It can be disastrous!

God is real. He is an Object worth knowing, trusting in and relying on. He is much more than simply one of many realities. He is the Ultimate Reality.

John spoke of the Holy Spirit in this way, "But as his anointing teaches you about all things, and as that anointing is real, not counterfeit—just as it has taught you, remain in him" (1 John 2:27-NIV). The Spirit teaches us to remain focused on following Jesus Christ. The early Gnostics (whom John opposed) promised a deep connection with God through their mysterious training and rites. Yes, they experienced something—but it was a powerful counterfeit, not the true God.

Paul spoke of Christ in this way, too. "These are a shadow of the things that are to come; the reality, however, is found in Christ" (Col 2:17-NIV). All the OT ways of worship were designed to lead to Jesus, not replace Him. He is the substance. They are ae shadows. At best, just reflections. Why grab on to the shadows and focus on the reflections when you can access the REAL THING—God, Himself?

Jesus warned us that this will be an issue throughout the last times, "For false Christs and false prophets will arise and perform great signs and wonders, to lead astray, if possible, even the elect" (Matt 24:24). There is only one true God. There is only one true Christ. He said, "For my flesh is real food and my blood is real drink" (John 6:55-NIV). When we are personally united or connected with Him in His death on the cross, we will be nourished and satisfied in the truest way. Death will no longer have a lasting hold on us! All that we want to feed our souls with may be found only in union with the real, Jesus of history. And your daily walk with Him will produce objective, obvious results—because you are in the presence of the one true and living God!

Cars and jobs are real. Human relationships are real So, why not trust in them? Because they last for only awhile and then are gone. They are not real for long. So, all created things will disappoint all who focus their lives on them as if they were the greatest reality. This is what God meant when He told Moses to tell the children of Israel that "I AM has sent me to you" (Ex 3:14). There is no one compared to Him.

To know God is to know the One whom we must know. The One we cannot do without knowing. The One who IS and won't change. He is the only real Helper and Savior, as the Samaritans once realized, "we know that this man is really the Savior of the world" (John 4:42-NIV). Union with Him will save you and all who do the same. The Bible predicts that the time will come when everyone will bow and acknowledge Him as the peerless God and Creator. "At the name of Jesus every knee shall bow" (Phil 2:10). Let us show those around us that we have found God by bowing in submission to Jesus. No more walking in the shadows when we can walk with God!

Response

I thank you God for showing me _____

_____.

STRATEGY

Follow Jesus today with total faith in His life after death as Thomas learned in John **20:24-29 (**Read now)

As I follow Jesus today I will remember _____

_____.

OBEDIENCE (I will statement)

The Spirit is convicting or leading me today to do or stop doing: _____

_____

PETITIONS (Following your reciting of The Lord's Prayer)

I pray for these scheduled meetings today:

I pray also for these pressing needs of myself, my family, my church, my disciples, my world:

CONFESSION and REPENTANCE

I confess these, my sins with every intention to never repeat them, but rather to live as Jesus would live, by Your enabling grace and Spirit …

*Never confess without a faith that looks to the cross of Christ, where the guilt and penalty of all our sins was paid!

WALK (Think about the following hymn)

Be Thou My Vision

1) Be Thou my Vision, O Lord of my heart;
Naught be all else to me, save that Thou art
Thou my best Thought, by day or by night,
Waking or sleeping, Thy presence my light.

2) Be Thou my Wisdom, and Thou my true Word;
I ever with Thee and Thou with me, Lord;
Thou my great Father, I Thy true son;
Thou in me dwelling, and I with Thee one.

3) Be Thou my battle Shield, Sword for the fight;
Be Thou my Dignity, Thou my Delight;
Thou my soul's Shelter, Thou my high Tower:
Raise Thou me heavenward, O Power of my power.

4) Riches I heed not, nor man's empty praise,
Thou mine Inheritance, now and always:
Thou and Thou only, first in my heart,
High King of Heaven, my Treasure Thou art.

5) High King of Heaven, my victory won,
May I reach Heaven's joys, O bright Heaven's Sun!
Heart of my own heart, whatever befall,
Still be my Vision, O Ruler of all.
(Originally 6th century Irish Saint Dallán Forgaill from a 5th c. hymn by Saint Patrick called Patrick's Breastplate)

Response

Help me Jesus, to _____

_____.

VICTORY

Memorize *John 17:3* by reading it in sections 5 times, reciting (without looking) 5 times and repeating it throughout the day 5 times (at least at 9AM, 12 noon and 3PM when you STOP the day to worship and talk to God).

"Freely you have received, freely give" (NIV-Matt 10:8) – Remind yourself to speak peace (Luke 10:5) wherever you go and to whomever you speak, and always be ready to share something of the Word if the person is receptive and has time to listen. Be prepared to ask, "the person of peace question" (PoP) to anyone who seems ready and willing to be discipled.

Be prepared for opposition (spiritual warfare) and expect victory in Jesus' name.

Write down the name (s) of those with whom you shared today _____

_____.

_____ Check when the day is completed, never beating yourself up if you did not finish; but, just asking Jesus to help you next day!

Day Twenty

God – The Good One

ADORATION

That which is good is what truly benefits, helps or nurtures us. Something is bad if it has an ultimately negative effect on us. Medicine is good, assisting our health. Evil, though, is like a disease, a plague. It breaks you down and leads you astray. It's not always easy to immediately tell if something is good or bad. Will those clouds yield a nice, gentle rain or a devastating flood?

We too often define good by our feelings. Not everything that hurts is bad. The surgeon's scalpel removes disease. The operation, though painful, was good. Likewise, not everything that feels great is good for us. When good things like sleep, food, sexuality, entertainment, etc. become excessive or selfish, they prove to be extremely harmful and destructive. Isaiah warns, "Woe to those who call evil good and good evil" (Isa 5:20). People and nations can lose their way by defining "good" as that which immediately increases their wealth, status, power or prospects. But God's Word states, "let no one seek his own good, but the good of others" (1 Cor 10:24).

When we affirm that God is good, we declare that all He is and all He does is ultimately helpful and positive. David said, "You are good; and do good" (Psa 119:68). His way (Matt 7:13-14), His laws (Rom 7:12,16) and His will (Rom 12:2) are declared to be good. Every good gift is from Him (James 1:17). Even the trials He allows to come our way are good (Psa 119:71) and are designed, like all things, to work together for our good (Rom 8:28; Gen 50:20). Think of something you enjoy—the sunrise, a cold drink, a tasty meal or a warm smile. None of these good things lasts long. But goodness with God never ends! He is nothing but good. He cannot be evil—even for a moment. "For he is good; for his steadfast love endures forever" (2 Chr 7:3).

Jesus declared, "No one is good—except God alone" (Mk 10:18). Since God is thoroughly or completely good, we best understand goodness by observing Him not others. Goodness is what God is and all He does. Our good God is constantly teaching us through life's experiences what is truly good—like justice, mercy and prayer (Micah 6:8).

Since God is good, we know that evil cannot win. It may have its day or epoch, but it cannot triumph! This gives us great hope and a determination to do good regardless of results (Gal 6:7-8). We were created in Christ Jesus to do good works (Eph 2:10). To overcome evil by good (Rom 12:21), following the way of our good Lord Jesus, whom Peter described as One who "went around doing good and healing all those who were under the power of the devil because God was with him" (Acts 10:38). Follow Him and do good today everywhere you go.

Response

I thank you God for showing me _____

_____.

STRATEGY

Follow Jesus today and do good even if it will entrap you, as He did in **Luke 6:1-11 (**Read now**)**

As I follow Jesus today I will remember _____

_____.

OBEDIENCE (I will statement)

The Spirit is convicting or leading me today to do or stop doing: _____

_____.

PETITIONS (Following your reciting of The Lord's Prayer)

I pray for these scheduled meetings today:

I pray also for these pressing needs of myself, my family, my church, my disciples, my world:

CONFESSION and REPENTANCE

I confess these, my sins with every intention to never repeat them, but rather to live as Jesus would live, by Your enabling grace and Spirit …

*Never confess without a faith that looks to the cross of Christ, where the guilt and penalty of all our sins was paid!
WALK (Think about the following hymn)

Somebody did a Golden Deed

1) Somebody did a golden deed,
Proving himself a friend in need;
Somebody sang a cheerful song,
Brightening the sky the whole day long,
Was that somebody you?
Was that somebody you!

2) Somebody thought 'tis sweet to live,
Willingly said, "I'm glad to give;"
Somebody fought a valiant fight,
Bravely he lives to shield the right,
Was that somebody you?
Was that somebody you!

3) Somebody made a loving gift,
Cheerfully tried a load to lift;
Somebody told the love of Christ,
Told how His will was sacrificed,
Was that somebody you?
Was that somebody you!

4) Somebody filled the days with light,
Constantly chased away the night;
Somebody's work bore joy and peace,
Surely his life shall never cease,
Was that somebody you?
Was that somebody you!
(John R Clements, 1868-1946)

Response

Help me Jesus, to _____

_____.

VICTORY

Memorize *Ephesians 2:10* by reading it in sections 5 times, reciting (without looking) 5 times and repeating it throughout the day 5 times (at least at 9AM, 12 noon and 3PM when you STOP the day to worship and talk to God).

"Freely you have received, freely give" (NIV-Matt 10:8) – Remind yourself to speak peace (Luke 10:5) wherever you go and to whomever you speak, and always be ready to share something of the Word if the person is receptive and has time to listen. Be prepared to ask, "the person of peace question" (PoP) to anyone who seems ready and willing to be discipled.

Be prepared for opposition (spiritual warfare) and expect victory in Jesus' name.

Write down the name (s) of those with whom you shared today and pray for them.
_____
_____.

_____ Check when the day is completed, never beating yourself up if you did not finish; but, just asking Jesus to help you next day!

10-Day Period 3

Discipleship and our Following Jesus

**Begin by reading Appendix Three – *Is Total Submission Too Radical for You?*

We think that "follow the leader" is a child's game. But really, we all need to be far better followers as adults. Soldiers know, when walking through a mine field, that one misstep, one moment straying from precisely following in the steps of the one ahead of them, might result in their death. The reality of present danger heightens our willingness to listen and follow the advice of others.

So, during this period, our aim is to become convinced that we are in peril in this world unless we lean each moment on the presence and protection of Jesus. It would serve you well to read the ancient classic, Pilgrim's Progress, by John Bunyan. In it, the way of biblical discipleship is clearly and powerfully portrayed.

We must believe the Scripture texts that speak of the believer's danger. Satan is depicted as a roaring lion seeking someone to devour. We are warned not to turn to the right or to the left, lest we stray off the path and into destruction. We are told to live like soldiers under the command of an officer. Spiritual warfare is everywhere pictured as a daily reality. His fiery darts and subtle temptations are directed against us, to defile and destroy us. Yes. We live in a highly scientific age—but within that sphere, Satan and his forces are still arrayed against us. Spirit help us, daily, to never let anyone or anything between us and Jesus!

Day Twenty-one

God - the All-Seeing One

ADORATION

The Bible often portrays God as the all-knowing One. He is omniscient. Nothing takes Him by surprise. The Scriptures, however, go to great lengths to personalize God's knowledge. He is not to be considered as a superpower, coldly controlling nations and individuals like so many puppets. Rather, He is seen as an intimate Insider, whose heart is touched by the world He so completely understands, and, yet, so deeply loves. God not only knows, He sees.

Hagar was "mistreated" by Sarai and fled for her life. During this time of isolation and abandonment, "the angel of the Lord found Hagar near a spring in the desert" (Gen 16:7-NIV). Moses calls this angel, "The Lord" (16:13), thus indicating that this was one of those times the Son of God was sent by the Father to earth before coming as the Messiah. After His caring words and reassuring promises, Hagar said to the Son, "You are the God who sees me." And "I have now seen the One who sees me" (16:13-NIV).

David often was refreshed in his trials by the certainty that God saw him. Even when he was too burdened to speak, David knew, "you perceive my thoughts from afar" (Ps 139:2-NIV). Though surrounded by darkness, as we all sometimes are, we may join David in the assurance that, "even the dark is not dark to you; the night is bright as the day, for darkness is as light with you" (Ps 139:12). When injustice, oppression and intimidation seem to rule, we are comforted by the thought. "Does He who formed the eye not see?" (Ps 94:9b-NIV).

One day Jesus met a sad funeral procession of "the only son of his mother, and she was a widow" (Lk 7:12). She had lost her husband and now had gone through the sorrow of seeing her only son die. "And when the Lord saw her, he had compassion on her and said to her, 'Do not weep.'" (7:13). God in flesh did not see a traffic problem, he saw a brokenhearted woman. He stopped, He healed her son and "gave him to his mother."

What is true then remains true today. "Your Father, who sees what is done in secret, will reward you" (Matt 6:4,6-NIV). Since God sees you, never give up to despair and never give in to sin's temptations. Ask and He will help you, "For the eyes of the Lord range throughout the earth to strengthen those whose hearts are fully committed to him" (2 Chron 16:9a-NIV). Remember, "The Lord does not look at the things man looks at. Man looks at the outward appearance, but the Lord looks at the heart" (1 Sam 16:7b-NIV). Trust in the God who, though He sees your heart at its best and its worst, still delights in you because He always sees you "in Christ!"

Response

I thank you God for showing me _____

_____.

STRATEGY

Follow Jesus today, remembering His power, as incarnate God to see what others could not see, as seen in **John 1:43-51 (**Read now)

As I follow Jesus today I will remember _____

_____.

OBEDIENCE (I will statement)

The Spirit is convicting or leading me today to do or stop doing: _____

_____.

PETITIONS (Following your reciting of The Lord's Prayer)

I pray for these scheduled meetings today:

I pray also for these pressing needs of myself, my family, my church, my disciples,[29] my world:

CONFESSION and REPENTANCE

I confess these, my sins, with every intention to never repeat them, but rather to live as Jesus would live, by Your enabling grace and Spirit ...

---

[29] Those whom you are discipling may be considered "your" disciples in the same way Paul meant when he told the Corinthians, "Be imitators of me as I am of Christ" (1 Cor 11:1)

*Never confess without a faith that looks to the cross of Christ, where the guilt and penalty of all our sins was paid!

WALK (Think about the following hymn)

I Know Who Holds Tomorrow

1) I don't know about tomorrow;
I just live from day to day.
I don't borrow from its sunshine
For its skies may turn to grey.

I don't worry o'er the future,
For I know what Jesus said.
And today I'll walk beside Him,
For He knows what is ahead.

*Many things about tomorrow
I don't seem to understand
But I know who holds tomorrow
And I know who holds my hand.*

2) Every step is getting brighter
As the golden stairs I climb;
Every burden's getting lighter,
Every cloud is silver-lined.

There the sun is always shining,
There no tear will dim the eye;
At the ending of the rainbow
Where the mountains touch the sky.

3) I don't know about tomorrow;
It may bring me poverty.
But the one who feeds the sparrow,
Is the one who stands by me.

And the path that is my portion
May be through the flame or flood;
But His presence goes before me
And I'm covered with His blood.

Response

Help me Jesus, to _____

_____.

VICTORY

Memorize *Hebrews 13:5*

Be prepared for opposition (spiritual warfare) and expect victory in Jesus' name.

Write down the name (s) of those with whom you shared today and pray for them. _____

_____.

_____ Check when the day is completed, never beating yourself up if you did not finish; but, just asking Jesus to help you next day!

Day Twenty-two

God - the Caller

ADORATION

    The name "church" means called-out ones. Every believer has been called out of the world like Lazarus was called out of the cave in which he was entombed. We who are saved have been "called out of darkness into his marvelous light" (1 Pet 2:9). It is irresistible when God so calls. "And those whom he predestined he also called" (Rom 8:30). This is termed "effectual calling" because it always produces a positive spiritual response. No one hangs up on God when He calls with the immediate purpose to save us. At that moment He speaks to us personally. "He calls his own sheep by name and leads them out" (John 10:3).

    What kind of people does God most often call? Not those we would highlight in our little black books. "Brothers, think of what you were when you were called. Not many of you were wise...influential...of noble birth. But God chose the foolish things of the world to shame the wise; the weak things of the world to shame the strong. He chose the lowly...and despised things...so that no one may boast before him." (1 Cor 1:26-29-NIV). Jesus said plainly, "It is not the healthy who need a doctor, but the sick. I have not come to call the righteous, but sinners" (Mark 2:17). Is your heart like God's? Whom do you call and invite to dinner or to church, hoping they will respond? Whom do you omit?

    Some of God's calls are general invitations, left up to the hearer to respond as he wishes. Often at these times we foolishly hang up on Him! "When Israel was a child I loved him, and out of Egypt I called my son. The more they were called, the more they went away" (Hos 11:1-2a). He interrupts us when we are relishing our sin, and we ignore Him. How stupid to ignore the call of God! When Ed McMahon and Publisher's Clearinghouse calls at one's door, the person does not grumble and slam the door. They know they have won something BIG. All of God's calls are good. Don't slam the door on Him. He is offering you a gift of immeasurable value.

    Christian, He has called you to be holy (1 Cor 1:2; 2 Tim 1:9), to live in peace (1 Cor 7:15), to be free (Gal 5:13), full of hope (Eph 1:18), and peace (Col 3:15), to share in the glory of our Lord Jesus Christ (2 Thes 2:14), to eternal life (1 Tim 6:12), and to eternal glory (2 Pet 5:10). Don't hang up! Rather, "walk in a manner worthy of the calling to which you have been called" (Eph 4:1). Don't plug your ears and run away. Be patient and remember "we know that in all things God works for the good of those who love him, who have been called according to his purpose" (Rom 8:28-NIV).

Do not think that God would be more pleased with YOU if you were like someone else. It was your name He called. He wants YOUR heart and love just as YOU are and where He has put YOU. "Only let each person lead the life that the Lord has assigned to him and to which God has called him. This is my rule in all the churches" (1 Cor 7:17). "For the gifts and the calling of God are irrevocable" (Rom 11:29). Serve Christ right now, where you are, for "you also are among those who are called to belong to Jesus Christ" (Rom 1:6-NIV).

Response

I thank you God for showing me _____

_____.

STRATEGY

Follow Jesus today, remembering the solemn parable He taught in **Matt 22:1-14**(Read now)

As I follow Jesus today I will remember _____

_____.

OBEDIENCE (I will statement)

The Spirit is convicting or leading me today to do or stop doing: _____

_____.

PETITIONS (Following your reciting of The Lord's Prayer)

I pray for these scheduled meetings today:

I pray also for these pressing needs of myself, my family, my church, my disciples my world:

CONFESSION and REPENTANCE

I confess these, my sins, with every intention to never repeat them, but rather to live as Jesus would live, by Your enabling grace and Spirit ...

*Never confess without a faith that looks to the cross of Christ, where the guilt and penalty of all our sins was paid!

WALK (Think about the following hymn)

Jesus Call Us

1) Jesus calls us o'er the tumult
of our life's wild, restless sea;
day by day his sweet voice soundeth,
saying, "Christian, follow me!"

2) As of old the apostles heard it
by the Galilean lake,
turned from home and toil and kindred,
leaving all for Jesus' sake.

3) Jesus calls us from the worship
of the vain world's golden store,
from each idol that would keep us,
saying, "Christian, love me more!"

4) In our joys and in our sorrows,
days of toil and hours of ease,
still he calls, in cares and pleasures,
"Christian, love me more than these!"

5) Jesus calls us! By thy mercies,
Savior, may we hear thy call,
give our hearts to thine obedience,
serve and love thee best of all.
(Cecil Frances Alexander, 1818-1895)

Response

Help me Jesus, to _____

_____.

VICTORY

Memorize *Psalm 50:15*

Be prepared for opposition (spiritual warfare) and expect victory in Jesus' name.

Write down the name (s) of those with whom you shared today _____
_____.

____ Check when the day is completed, never beating yourself up if you did not finish; but, just asking Jesus to help you next day!

Day Twenty-three

God - the Ever Present One

ADORATION

How every person answers the question, "Is there a God?" reveals the center of their world view. Nearly every culture has concluded that God exists; but wrong ideas about His nature always lead to unfortunate consequences. People have been and are willing to do horrible things to others in the name of their God. Belief in God's omnipresence is, perhaps, the most relevant and practical of all aspects of God's nature, for if we believe He is always present-that will greatly affect how we act.

The Bible clearly teaches that God is always present. "Where shall I go from your Spirit? Or where can I flee from your presence?" (Ps 139:7). "For a man's ways are before the eyes of the Lord, and he ponders all his paths" (Prov 5:21). "He is actually not far from each one of us, for in him we live and move and have our being" (Acts 17:27b-28a).

Millions rightly believe that God is everywhere, who wrongly conclude that He is everything. They exalt God's omnipresence, but deny his personality as a separate being, distinct from His creation. This is called Pantheism. Another error to avoid, when thinking of God's presence, is that He is somehow extended throughout creation, with part of Him here and part there. No, God is fully everywhere. The earth is full of His presence and glory (Isa. 6:3). Remember, too that God is everywhere present without being changed by the environment. He is not defiled by being in the worst places any more than the sun's rays are defiled when they shine on a rubbish heap. Jesus did not absorb sin and imperfection by being "the friend of tax collectors and sinners" (Matt 11:19). Even in the awful darkness and suffering of hell, God is present-preserving the lives of those who continually hate and despise Him.

Since God is everywhere, nothing escapes His notice. Ultimately, no wrong shall go unpunished and no good unrewarded. Every person is, therefore, known completely by Him. He is able to judge rightly, and He shall. So, do not be a fake. Be open and honest. Sincerely look to Jesus as your perfect Savior and Helper. Those who trust in Him should be greatly encouraged by this doctrine of God's omnipresence! "Be strong and courageous. Do not be afraid or terrified...for the Lord your God goes with you; he will never leave you nor forsake you" (Deut 31:6; Heb 13:5-NIV).

Since God is always present, we should honor and exalt Him constantly. Reject everything that deflects from His glory and exalt everything that honors Him. He told Abraham, "I am the Lord Almighty; walk before me and be blameless" (Gen 17:1b). Walk or live as one in the presence of God. Practice the presence of God. He told Israel, "My presence will go with you, and I will give you rest" (Ex 33:14). By the power of the Spirit abandon whatever displeases God. Selfishness, pride, anger, greed and fear are all unworthy of one who believes that God is present. "Blessed are those who have learned to acclaim you, who walk in the light of your presence, O Lord" (Ps 89:15-NIV). Never lose hope, for God is near!

Response

I thank you God for showing me _____

_____.

STRATEGY

Follow Jesus today, remembering the promise He gave to every disciple as they lived to make other disciples as seen in **Matt 28:16-20** (Read now)

As I follow Jesus today I will remember _____

_____.

OBEDIENCE (I will statement)

The Spirit is convicting or leading me today to do or stop doing: _____

_____.

PETITIONS Following your reciting of <u>The Lord's Prayer</u>)

I pray for these scheduled meetings today:

I pray also for these pressing needs of myself, my family, my church, my disciples, my world:

CONFESSION and REPENTANCE

I confess these, my sins, with every intention to never repeat them, but rather to live as Jesus would live, by Your enabling grace and Spirit …

*Never confess without a faith that looks to the cross of Christ, where the guilt and penalty of all our sins was paid!

WALK (Think about the following hymn)

Anywhere with Jesus

1) Anywhere with Jesus I can safely go,
Anywhere He leads me in this world below;
Anywhere without Him dearest joys would fade;
Anywhere with Jesus I am not afraid.

*Anywhere, anywhere! Fear I cannot know;
Anywhere with Jesus I can safely go.*

2) Anywhere with Jesus I am not alone;
Other friends may fail me, He is still my own;
Though His hand may lead me over dreary ways,
Anywhere with Jesus is a house of praise.

3) Anywhere with Jesus, over land and sea,
Telling souls in darkness of salvation free;
Ready as He summons me to go or stay,
Anywhere with Jesus when He points the way.

4) Anywhere with Jesus I can go to sleep,
When the darkening shadows round about me creep,
Knowing I shall waken nevermore to roam;
Anywhere with Jesus will be home, sweet home.
(Jessie B Pounds, 1861-1921)

Response

Help me Jesus, to _____

_____.

VICTORY

Memorize *Proverbs 3:5-6*

Be prepared for opposition (spiritual warfare) and expect victory in Jesus' name.

Write down the name (s) of those with whom you shared today _____
_____.

_____ Check when the day is completed, never beating yourself up if you did not finish; but, just asking Jesus to help you next day!

Day Twenty-four

God – the Example

ADORATION

We are nothing in comparison with God. He is infinite, eternal and unchangeable. We are finite, mortal and ever changing. Nevertheless, we have been made in His image. There are ways in which we are to keep Him before our minds, to reflect Him, to follow His example. No pursuit on earth is a more worthy one than to so love and desire Him that we set our minds and lives on following Him wholeheartedly.

"Not a man of this evil generation shall see the good land I swore to give your forefathers, except Caleb...because he followed the Lord wholeheartedly" (Deut 1:35-36-NIV). "So, Solomon did what was evil in the sight of the Lord and did not wholly follow the Lord, as David his father had done" (1 Kgs 11:6). Do not be surprised that David is mentioned as one who followed the Lord completely. Repentance removes the stain of sin! When one truly humbles himself in confession and rejection of his sin, God no longer holds that person guilty. Incomplete obedience is removed by the obedience and cross of Christ! "Josiah removed all the detestable idols from all the territory belonging to the Israelites... As long as he lived, they did not fail to follow the Lord, the God of their fathers" (2 Chron 34:33-NIV).

Jesus Christ is both the Savior and the Example of His people. "I am the light of the world. Whoever follows me will not walk in darkness, but will have the light of life" (John 8:12b). "My sheep hear my voice; and I know them, and they follow me" (John 10:27). "If anyone serves me, he must follow me; and where I am, there will my servant be also. If anyone serves me, the Father wall honor him" (John 12:26).

Think of It! God is filled with delight when He sees us desire His Son. When one, by faith, steps out from the mass of men pleasers to please Jesus, alone. Even though that path leads to great self-denial, shame and even death, it is one worth taking. "I have set you an example that you should do as I have done for you. I tell you the truth, no servant is greater than his master...Now that you know these things, you will be blessed if you do them" (John 13:15-17-NIV). "A new command I give you: Love one another. As I have loved you, so you must love one another. By this all men will know that you are my disciples, if you love one another." (John 13:34-NIV).

The Apostles imitated Christ. Paul said, "Follow my example as I follow the example of Christ" (1 Cor 11:1-NIV). THAT was and is the great standard. If our words and behavior do NOT reflect the Lord's, no one should follow what we say or do. But if they are in line with the clear teaching and life of Jesus, then step in line. Peter reminded believers, "...If you suffer for doing good and you endure it, this is commendable before God. To this you were called, because Christ suffered for you, leaving you an example, that you should follow in his steps". (1 Pet 2:20-21-NIV). The great book, "In His Steps" by Charles Sheldon, tells what happened when a few Christians in a small city decided to "follow in his steps." Read it and, by a faith filled with love, do it! Great reward awaits those who "follow the Lamb wherever he goes." (Rev 14:4b).

Response

I thank you God for showing me _____

_____.

STRATEGY

Follow Jesus today, remembering the demand He placed on all believers, in **Luke 9:18-26 (**Read now)

As I follow Jesus today I will remember _____

_____.

OBEDIENCE (I will statement)

The Spirit is convicting or leading me today to do or stop doing: _____

_____.

PETITIONS (Following your reciting of The Lord's Prayer)

I pray for these scheduled meetings today:

I pray also for these pressing needs of myself, my family, my church, my disciples, my world:

CONFESSION and REPENTANCE

I confess these, my sins, with every intention to never repeat them, but rather to live as Jesus would live, by Your enabling grace and Spirit …

*Never confess without a faith that looks to the cross of Christ, where the guilt and penalty of all our sins was paid!

WALK (Think about the following hymn)

Footsteps of Jesus

1) Sweetly, Lord, have we heard Thee calling,
Come, follow Me!
And we see where Thy footprints falling
Lead us to Thee.

*Footprints of Jesus,
That make the pathway glow;
We will follow the steps of Jesus
Where'er they go.*

2) Though they lead o'er the cold, dark mountains,
Seeking His sheep;
Or along by Siloam's fountains,
Helping the weak

3) If they lead through the temple holy,
Preaching the Word;
Or in homes of the poor and lowly,
Serving the Lord.

4) Though, dear Lord, in Thy pathway keeping,
We follow Thee;
Through the gloom of that place of weeping,
Gethsemane!

5) If Thy way and its sorrows bearing,
We go again,
Up the slope of the hillside, bearing
Our cross of pain.

6) By and by, through the shining portals,
Turning our feet,
We shall walk, with the glad immortals,
Heav'n's golden street.

7) Then, at last, when on high He sees us,
Our journey done,
We will rest where the steps of Jesus
End at His throne.
(Mary BC Slade, 1826-1882)

Response

Help me Jesus, to _____

_____.

VICTORY

Memorize *1 Corinthians 11:1* by reading it in sections 5 times, reciting (without looking) 5 times and repeating it throughout the day 5 times (at least at 9AM, 12 noon and 3 PM when you STOP the day to worship and talk to God).

Be prepared for opposition (spiritual warfare) and expect victory in Jesus' name.

Write down the name (s) of those with whom you shared today and pray for them. _____

_____.

____ Check when the day is completed, never beating yourself up if you did not finish; but, just asking Jesus to help you next day!

Day Twenty-five

God – the Inviting One

ADORATION

It's nice to receive a personal invitation to a friend's party. But have you ever received one from a celebrity? They get framed and put on the wall! Do you realize that God has given you many such invitations? "Come to me all who labor and are heavy laden, and I will give you rest" (Matt 11:28). Incline your ear and come to me; hear, that your soul may live" (Isa 55:3). Quite an invitation! What happens if we disregard it? If we do not RSVP God? Listen to the answer as told by Jesus:

"A certain man was preparing a great banquet and invited many guests. At the time of the banquet he sent his servant to tell those who had been invited, 'Come, for everything is now ready.' But they alike began to make excuses. The first said, 'I have just bought a field, and I must go and see it. Please excuse me.' Another said, '1have just bought five yokes of oxen, and I'm on my way to try them out. Please excuse me.' Still another said, '1 just got married, so I can't come.' The servant came back and reported this to his master. Then the owner of the house became angry and ordered his servant, 'Go out quickly into the streets and alleys of the town and bring in the poor, the crippled, the blind and the lame.' 'Sir,' the servant said, 'what you ordered has been done, but there is still room.' Then the master told his servant, 'Go out to the roads and country lanes and make them come in, so that my house will be full. I tell you, not one of those men who were invited will get a taste of my banquet.' "(Luke 14:16-24-NIV).

When God invites you, go! Whatever He invites you to is good. It will be much better than anything that you are having to leave. He met fisherman and said, "Come, follow me, Jesus said, and I will make you fishers of men" (Matt 4:19-NIV). Quite a gamble wasn't it? Leave one's family business, security, relatives! But did they choose unwisely? Of course not. Peter asked, "See we have left everything and followed you! What then will we have?" (Matt 19:27). Jesus answered, "I tell you the truth, no one who has left home or brothers or sisters or mother or father or children or fields for me and the gospel will fail to receive a hundred times as much in the present age...and in the age to come, eternal life" (Mk 10:29-30-NIV). When he saw Jesus walking on water, Peter said, "Lord, if it is you, command me to come to you on the water. He said, 'Come' (Matt 14:28-29). You will never know what you have missed by not answering the invitation of Christ!

"Come, everyone who thirsts, come to the waters; and he who has no money, come buy and eat! Come, buy wine and milk without money and without price" (Isa 55:1). But, when you come to God, come sincerely as He is playing no games. And He knows what is compelling you to come. Whether it is faith driven by love or mere greed and selfishness "The Lord says, these people come near to me with their mouth and honor me with their lips, but their hearts are far from me" (Isa 29:13-NIV). He wants your heart and He must have it. "Come near to God and he will come near to you" (James 4:8-NIV). Can you trust Him? Will He have you? Jesus promised, "Whoever comes to me I will never cast out!" (John 6:37). Believe and come today. The door is open.

Response

I thank you God for showing me _____

_____.

STRATEGY

Follow Jesus today, remembering the compassion behind His invitations, as seen in **Matt 9:35-10:15** (Read now).

As I follow Jesus today I will remember _____

_____.

OBEDIENCE (I will statement)

The Spirit is convicting or leading me today to do or stop doing: _____

_____.

PETITIONS   (Following your reciting of The Lord's Prayer)

I pray for these scheduled meetings today:

I pray also for these pressing needs of myself, my family, my church, my disciples, my world:

CONFESSION and REPENTANCE

I confess these, my sins, with every intention to never repeat them, but rather to live as Jesus would live, by Your enabling grace and Spirit …

*Never confess without a faith that looks to the cross of Christ, where the guilt and penalty of all our sins was paid!

WALK (Think about the following hymn)

Our Great Savior!

1) Jesus! what a Friend for sinners!
Jesus! Lover of my soul;
Friends may fail me, foes assail me,
He, my Savior, makes me whole.

Hallelujah! what a Savior!
Hallelujah! what a Friend!
Saving, helping, keeping, loving,
He is with me to the end.

2) Jesus! what a Strength in weakness!
Let me hide myself in Him;
Tempted, tried, in Him confiding,
He, my Strength, my vict'ry wins.

3) Jesus! what a Help in sorrow!
While the billows o'er me roll,
Even when my heart is breaking,
He, my Comfort, helps my soul.

4) Jesus! what a Guide and Keeper!
While the tempest still is high,
Storms about me, night o'ertakes me,
He, my Pilot, hears my cry.

5) Jesus! I do now receive Him,
More than all in Him I find;
Christ in me, the Hope of glory,
I am His, and He is mine.
(J. Wilbur Chapman, 1859-1918)

Response

Help me Jesus, to _____

_____.

VICTORY

Memorize *Revelation 22:17*

Be prepared for opposition (spiritual warfare) and expect victory in Jesus' name.

Write down the name (s) of those with whom you shared today _____

_____.

____ Check when the day is completed, never beating yourself up if you did not finish; but, just asking Jesus to help you next day!

Day Twenty-six

God – the Leader

ADORATION

When we are confused or lost, we need a guide or leader. Someone who knows the way and can create safety by going before us. "I will lead them beside streams of water, on a level path where they will not stumble" (Jer 31:9-NIV). Sometimes everything is so dark before us that we dare not take a step. We cry, "Give ear, O Shepherd of Israel, you who lead Joseph like a flock ... shine forth" (Ps 80:1). And He promises, "And I will lead the blind in a way that they do not know...I will turn the darkness before them into light (Isa 42:16). Those who believe can always say, "God is with us. He is our leader" (2 Chron 13:12-NIV).

If God is our Leader, our Shepherd, then we are His followers, His sheep. "We are his people and the sheep of his pasture" (Ps 100:3). But are we following Him? Are we consciously and willingly walking in His way, right behind Him? Or are we enamored by the sideway glances and constantly detouring from His Word and Spirit onto our ill-conceived shortcuts? Let us repent of not following Him, not walking with Him step by step.

God's kind guidance of His people has taken many forms. During the exodus, "In the daytime he led them with the cloud, and all the night with a fiery light" (Ps 78:14). He used Moses, Joshua, Samuel and David as faithful but imperfect leaders. Their leadership all pointed to David's greatest Son, whom God promised to make "a leader and commander for the peoples" (Isa 55:4). He would not be a harsh leader; but, one who "will tend his flock like a shepherd...he will gather the lambs in his arms...and gently lead those that are with young" (Isa 40:11). Christ "the Lamb ... will be their Shepherd; he will lead them to springs of living water" (Rev 7:17-NIV). Because "the Lord (Jesus) is our Shepherd we shall not be in want" (Ps 23:1-NIV). We can't claim the promises of Psalm 23 without committing to follow Jesus, like sheep do their shepherd.

It is through His Word and Spirit, that the Lord leads us. "Let your good Spirit lead me on level ground" (Ps 143:10). "When the Helper comes...He will bear witness about me...the Spirit of truth...will guide you into all the truth" (John 15:26; 16:13). So, it is our great duty to submit to the Spirit's teaching, the Word of truth, and to "keep in step with the Spirit" (Gal 5:25).

Since God is our Leader, in full control and assuring victory to His followers, FOLLOW HIM! Walk by faith not by sight. Trust like children.

Since we are followers of Christ, see how the Son of Man responded to life's challenges and follow Him. By the power of the Spirit, follow Jesus into a life of loving service to God and others, today!

Response

I thank you God for showing me _____

_____.

STRATEGY

Follow Jesus today, remembering that He has a unique path for you, as He taught Peter in **John 21:15-23** (Read now).

As I follow Jesus today I will remember _____

_____.

OBEDIENCE (I will statement)

The Spirit is convicting or leading me today to do or stop doing: _____

_____.

PETITIONS (Following your reciting of The Lord's Prayer)

I pray for these scheduled meetings today:

I pray also for these pressing needs of myself, my family, my church, my disciples, my world:

CONFESSION and REPENTANCE

I confess these, my sins, with every intention to never repeat them, but rather to live as Jesus would live, by Your enabling grace and Spirit …

*Never confess without a faith that looks to the cross of Christ, where the guilt and penalty of all our sins was paid!

WALK (Think about the following hymn)

Follow On

1) Down in the valley with my Savior I would go,
Where the flowers are blooming and the sweet waters flow;
Everywhere He leads me I would follow, follow on,
Walking in His footsteps till the crown be won.

Follow! follow! I would follow Jesus!
Anywhere, everywhere, I would follow on!
Follow! follow! I would follow Jesus!
Everywhere He leads me I would follow on!

2) Down in the valley with my Savior I would go,
Where the storms are sweeping and the dark waters flow;
With His hand to lead me I will never, never fear,
Danger cannot fright me if my Lord is near.

3) Down in the valley, or upon the mountain steep,
Close beside my Savior would my soul ever keep;
He will lead me safely in the path that He has trod,
Up to where they gather on the hills of God.
(William O Cushing, 1823-1902)

Help me Jesus, to _____

_____.

VICTORY

Memorize *Luke 9:57-58* by reading it in sections 5 times, reciting (without looking) 5 times and repeating it 5 times.

Be prepared for opposition (spiritual warfare) and expect victory in Jesus' name.

Write down the name (s) of those with whom you shared today _____

_____.

____ Check when the day is completed, never beating yourself up if you did not finish; but, just asking Jesus to help you next day!

Day Twenty-seven

God – the Marvelous One

ADORATION

When our eyes behold something extraordinary, perhaps that we have never seen before, we cannot but gaze at it. It is a marvel to us. For a while we stop mid whatever we are doing because our minds are captured. This can happen to any of our senses. They can be thrilled and marvel at sounds, smells, tastes, touches. But in this world, such moments quickly end, and the marvel and wonder are gone, leaving us longing for another bite or sight or note or aroma.

One reason such marvels end, is because they were never intended to last forever. They were designed to lead us on. To create longing that they cannot satisfy. They are tools in the hands of a marvelous God who, alone, can thrill and awe us endlessly. In a culture that tries to thrill and capture our hearts, it is good to be aware of this fact: our hearts were made for an eternity of marveling, not for a moment of exhilaration. "Praise be to the Lord God, the God of Israel, who alone does marvelous deeds." (Ps 72:18-NIV). God and God alone marvels us in all He does. All His works are carefully planned and performed, leaving us wanting to compose songs about Him and sing them forever. "O Lord you are my God; I will exalt you and praise your name, for in perfect faithfulness you have done marvelous things, things planned long ago" (Isa. 25:1-NIV)."Oh sing to the Lord a new song, for he has done marvelous things; his right hand and his holy arm have worked salvation for him" (Ps 98:1).

Those who do not submit to God, begin to hate His marvelous nature and works. They want to be like Him. To take His place and to be admired, praised and marveled at. This was true of Satan and Adam. And it is true of you and me. So, when the Son of God came, He came as a marvel in every way. His birth, miracles, words, life. The crowds stared and stayed if He satisfied their senses. But when He challenged their hearts. Their way of life. Then they rejected and killed Him. And He saw it all coming. "And all were astonished at the majesty of God. But while they were all marveling at everything that he was doing, Jesus said to his disciples, 'Let these words sink into your ears: The Son of Man is about to be delivered into the hands of men" (Luke 9:43-44). Yet this was the greatest marvel of all. His rejection and death were part of the marvelous plan of salvation. So, it was prophesied long before He came, "The stone that the builders rejected has become the cornerstone; this is the Lord's doing; it is marvelous in our eyes" (Ps 118:22-23). Jesus claimed this verse as His own (Mart 21:42).

Our greatest thrill now is to marvel at Him by faith. To walk as one happy with His plan and in love with Him. Soon the senses will forever peak, "On the day he comes to be glorified in his holy people and to be marveled at among all those who have believed" (2 Thes 1:10-NIV). Then, we will join the heavenly ones who sing, "Great and marvelous are your deeds, Lord God Almighty. Just and true are your ways, King of the ages. Who will not fear you, O Lord, and bring glory to your name? For you alone are holy." (Rev 15:3b-4-NIV). Even so come, Lord Jesus!

Response

I thank you God for showing me _____

_____.

STRATEGY

Follow Jesus today, remembering the marvel He was, is and ever will be as it was recorded in John 7:32-39 **(Read now)**

As I follow Jesus today I will remember _____

_____.

OBEDIENCE (I will statement)

The Spirit is convicting or leading me today to do or stop doing: _____

_____.

PETITIONS (Following your reciting of The Lord's Prayer)

I pray for these scheduled meetings today:

I pray also for these pressing needs of myself, my family, my church, my disciples my world:

CONFESSION and REPENTANCE

I confess these, my sins, with every intention to never repeat them, but rather to live as Jesus would live, by Your enabling grace and Spirit ...

*Never confess without a faith that looks to the cross of Christ, where the guilt and penalty of all our sins was paid!

WALK (Think about the following hymn)

I Stand Amazed

1) I stand amazed in the presence
Of Jesus the Nazarene,
And wonder how He could love me,
A sinner condemned, unclean.

How marvelous! How wonderful!
And my song shall ever be:
How marvelous! How wonderful!
Is my Savior's love for me!

2) For me it was in the garden,
He prayed: "Not my will, but Thine."
He had no tears for His own griefs,
But sweat-drops of blood for mine.

3) In pity angels beheld Him,
And came from the world of light
To strengthen Him in the sorrows
He bore for my soul that night.

4) He took my sins and my sorrows,
He made them His very own;
He bore the burden to Calv'ry,
And suffered and died alone.

5) When with the ransomed in glory
His face I at last shall see,
'Twill be my joy through the ages
To sing of His love for me.
(Charles H Gabriel, 1856-1932)

Response

Help me Jesus, to _____

_____.

VICTORY

Memorize <u>Revelation 5:13</u>

Be prepared for opposition (spiritual warfare) and expect victory in Jesus' name.

Write down the name (s) of those with whom you shared today _____

_____.

____ Check when the day is completed, never beating yourself up if you did not finish; but, just asking Jesus to help you next day!

Day Twenty-eight

God – the Shepherd

ADORATION

During biblical times, sheep and lambs could represent a significant part of a family's wealth. So, their care was very important. Small shepherding tasks were assigned to teenagers. Men would at times shepherd larger flocks. When God chose to liken Himself to a shepherd, he chose a cultural role very dear to the lives of most Near Eastern families.

Early in the Scriptures, Jacob spoke of "the God who has been my shepherd all my life long to this day" (Gen 48:15). And David's most famous psalm begins, "The Lord is my shepherd, I shall not want" (Ps 23:1). God was perfectly and endlessly caring for them, in ways that human shepherds imperfectly and occasionally cared for their flocks. And so, God keeps you, if you are one of His sheep. Rejoice that you have such a Shepherd!

When the children of Israel were being overlooked by their pastors (spiritual shepherds), the Lord promised that He would intervene. "As a shepherd looks after his scattered flock when he is with them, so will I look after my sheep. I will rescue them from all the places where they were scattered on a day of clouds and darkness. I will bring them into their own land. I will pasture them...I will tend them...I myself will tend my sheep and have them lie down, declares the Sovereign Lord. I will search for the lost and bring back the strays. I will bind up the injured and strengthen the weak...." (Ezekiel. 34:11-16-NIV). Take each of those verbs of pastoral care and apply them to yourself, dear disciple, as a promise from the Lord, for He will do this and more for you! Indeed, Jesus, the Chief Shepherd (1 Pet 5:4), said, "I am the good shepherd. The good shepherd lays down his life for the sheep" (John 10:11). He has died your death and saved you by His life! "For you were straying like sheep but have now returned to the Shepherd and Overseer of your souls" (1 Pet 2:25).

This is a favorite theme of those who spoke of Messiah Jesus and His love for us. "He will tend his flock like a shepherd; He will gather his lambs in his arms; he will carry them in his bosom; and gently lead those who are with young" (Is 40:11). How much closer could you be than "in His bosom?" He loves you immensely. Trust His love and care. When in need, cry out with the psalmist, "O save your people and bless your heritage! Be their shepherd and carry them forever" (Ps 28:9). And then, with fullness of faith, receive His reassurance, "Fear not, little flock, for it is your Father's good pleasure to give you the kingdom" (Lk 12:32). You might be insignificant and opposed NOW, but that is not for long! "For the Lamb at the center of the throne will be (your) shepherd; he will lead (you) to springs of living water." (Rev 7:17-NIV).

Response

I thank you God for showing me _____

_____.

STRATEGY

Follow Jesus today, remembering the tender care with which He deals with all His people, as seen in **Matt 11:25-30 (**Read now**)**

As I follow Jesus today I will remember _____

_____.

OBEDIENCE (I will statement)

The Spirit is convicting or leading me today to do or stop doing: _____

_____.

PETITIONS (Following your reciting of The Lord's Prayer)

I pray for these scheduled meetings today:

I pray also for these pressing needs of myself, my family, my church, my disciples, my world:

CONFESSION and REPENTANCE

I confess these, my sins, with every intention to never repeat them, but rather to live as Jesus would live, by Your enabling grace and Spirit …

*Never confess without a faith that looks to the cross of Christ, where the guilt and penalty of all our sins was paid!

WALK (Think about the following hymn)

The King of Love My Shepherd is

1) The King of love my shepherd is,
whose goodness faileth never.
I nothing lack if I am his,
and he is mine forever.

2) Where streams of living water flow,
my ransomed soul he leadeth;
and where the verdant pastures grow,
with food celestial feedeth.

3) Perverse and foolish, oft I strayed,
but yet in love he sought me;
and on his shoulder gently laid,
and home, rejoicing, brought me.

4) In death's dark vale I fear no ill,
with thee, dear Lord, beside me;
thy rod and staff my comfort still,
thy cross before to guide me.

5) Thou spreadst a table in my sight;
thy unction grace bestoweth;
and oh, what transport of delight
from thy pure chalice floweth!

6) And so, through all the length of days,
thy goodness faileth never;
Good Shepherd, may I sing thy praise
within thy house forever.
(Reproduction of Psalm 23, Henry W Baker, 1821-1877)

Response

Help me Jesus, to _____

_____.

VICTORY

Memorize *John 10:11*

Be prepared for opposition (spiritual warfare) and expect victory in Jesus' name.

Write down the name (s) of those with whom you shared today _____
_____.

_____ Check when the day is completed, never beating yourself up if you did not finish; but, just asking Jesus to help you next day!

Day Twenty-nine

God – the Friend

ADORATION

We get a kind of buzz from rubbing shoulders with celebrities. And we feel especially thrilled when a friendship develops with them. But infinitely greater is the marvel that our Creator, the Lord God Almighty, is One who wants to walk with us and befriend us (Gen3:8)! He is greatly pleased by our walking with Him (Gen 5:22-24; Heb 11:5). God not only connects with us; but, He actually delights in us. He calls us His friends and acts towards us like friends! "...Your offspring of Abraham my friend" (Is 41:8). "Abraham believed God, and it was counted to him as righteousness-- and he was called a friend of God" (James 2:23; see 2 Chron 20:7). Faith made Abraham a friend of God. Abraham trusted His friend, and followed His God away from his family, his culture, his gods. And found God to be "a friend who sticks closer than a brother" (Prov 18:24).

"Thus, the Lord used to speak with Moses face to face, as a man speaks to his friend" (Ex 33:11). Even when God gave His Holy Law, He showed His mind-boggling desire to fellowship with us and save us (Gen 3:15; 15:6; Gal. 3:6-9). Job realized it when he declared, "Even now my witness is in heaven; my advocate is on high. My intercessor is my friend...on behalf of a man he pleads with God as a man pleads for his friend" (Job 16:19-21-NIV). Jesus was "the Lamb that was slain from the creation of the world" (Rev 13:9-NIV), for through faith in His perfect life and sin-bearing death all sinners of all ages are saved.

When on earth, Jesus quoted a verse which underlines the fact that He was the closest friend of The Father. "Awake, O sword, against my shepherd, against the man who is close to me, declares the Lord Almighty. Strike the shepherd and the sheep will be scattered...." (Zech 13:7-NIV).

So, He who knew perfect friendship said, "No longer do I call you servants, for the servant does not know what his master is doing, but I have called you friends, for all that I have heard from my Father I have made known to you" (John 15:15). Faith transforms our relationship from outsiders (servants) into insiders (friends) with God. But remember, faith that does not act is not a living faith. Jesus reminds us all, "You are my friends if you do what I command you" (John 15:14). Friendship with God has its demands. "...Don't you know that friendship with the world is hatred toward God. Anyone who chooses to be a friend of the world becomes an enemy of

God" (James 4:4-NIV). No earthly friendship should be closer than our walk with Jesus, who was belittled as a friend of tax collectors and sinners" (Matt 11:19). Follow your Friend for true life now and forever!

Response

I thank you God for showing me _____

_____.

STRATEGY

Follow Jesus today, remembering what a friend He was to His disciples, as seen in His prayer in John 17:1-11 (Read now)

As I follow Jesus today I will remember _____

_____.

OBEDIENCE (I will statement)

The Spirit is convicting or leading me today to do or stop doing: _____

_____.

PETITIONS (Following your reciting of The Lord's Prayer)

I pray for these scheduled meetings today:

I pray also for these pressing needs of myself, my family, my church, my disciples, my world:

CONFESSION and REPENTANCE

I confess these, my sins, with every intention to never repeat them, but rather to live as Jesus would live, by Your enabling grace and Spirit ...

*Never confess without a faith that looks to the cross of Christ, where the guilt and penalty of all our sins was paid!

WALK (Think about the following hymn)

I've Found a Friend

1) I've found a Friend, O such a friend! He loved me ere I knew Him;
He drew me with the cords of love, and thus He bound me to Him;
And round my heart still closely twine those ties which naught can sever,
For I am His, and He is mine, forever and forever.

2) I've found a Friend, O such a friend! He bled, He died to save me;
And not alone the gift of life, but His Own Self He gave me!
Naught that I have mine own I call, I'll hold it for the Giver,
My heart, my strength, my life, my all are His, and His forever.

3) I've found a Friend, O such a friend! All pow'r to Him is given,
To guard me on my onward course, and bring me safe to heaven.
The eternal glories gleam afar, to nerve my faint endeavor,
So now to watch, to work, to war, and then to rest forever.

4) I've found a Friend, O such a friend! So kind and true and tender,
So wise a Counselor and Guide, so mighty a Defender!
From Him who loves me now so well what power my soul can sever?
Shall life or death, shall earth or hell? No! I am His forever.
(James G Small, 1817-1888)

Response

Help me Jesus, to _____

_____.

VICTORY

Memorize *John 15:14*

Be prepared for opposition (spiritual warfare) and expect victory in Jesus' name.

Write down the name (s) of those with whom you shared today and pray for them. _____

_____.

____ Check when the day is completed, never beating yourself up if you did not finish; but, just asking Jesus to help you next day!

Day Thirty

God – the Indwelling One

ADORATION

God loves us. He loved to walk and talk with Adam and Eve in the garden (Gen 3:8) and missed them when they ran off, calling, "Where are you?" (3:9). Sin separated them from Him, just as sin can "separate" us from acknowledging and living in His presence (1 Jn 1:3-7). We can hardly fathom His closeness to and delight in us. But let's try.

OT believers knew that God was near to them. Moses wrote, "For what great nation is there that has a god so near to it as the Lord our God is to us whenever we call upon him? (Deut 4:7). And that Divine Presence was known to be near, especially in the Temple. Following Solomon's prayer, "fire came down from heaven and consumed the burnt offering and the sacrifices, and the glory of the Lord filled the temple" (2 Chron 7:2). David sang, "the Lord is in his holy temple" (Ps 11:4) and the prophet echoed, "But the Lord is in his holy temple; let all the earth keep silence before him" (Hab 2:20). So, OT believers said, from His temple, God hears (Ps 18:6); may be gazed upon (27:4), and there prayed to (Jonah 2: 7). They knew that God was near them all the time, but especially in His temple. Though some conceived of God being "within" them (Ps 51:11), His nearness around them and in His temple sufficed.

It is in this regard, especially, that the Word reveals a colossal change following the coming of Christ. He aimed at dwelling within us as His temple through His Spirit. He spoke of "the Spirit of truth...[who] dwells with you and will be in you" (John 14:17). John writes, "By this he meant the Spirit, whom those who believed in him were later to receive. Up to that time the Spirit had not been given, since Jesus had not yet been glorified." (See Jn 7:38-39-NIV). God is not only now near us. He is within us!

"Do you not know that your body is a temple of the Holy Spirit within you, whom you have from God? You are not your own; you were bought with a price. So glorify God with your body." (1 Cor 6:19-20; also, Rom 8:9-11). "If anyone loves me, he will keep my word, and my Father will love him, and we will come to him and make our home with him" (John 14:23). The aged Apostle John would later echo Jesus and write, "Those who obey his commands live in him, and he in them" (1 John 3:24-NIV). Believer, live like God is within you, directing you, sanctifying you--for He is! Follow Him.

The mystery of God indwelling our body, though, has not all been told. The omnipresent God is not only within us all, individually. He is within us corporately or universally. NT believers together are Christ's Body. "In him the whole building is joined together and rises to become a holy temple in the Lord. And in him you too are being built together to become a dwelling in which God lives by His Spirit" (Eph 2:21-22-NIV).[30] By promoting Christian unity, you are enhancing His fullness on earth (Eph 3:16-18). Experience Him when you meet together, even in the smallest groups, because Jesus said, "For where two or three are gathered in my name, there am I among them" (Matt 18:20).

Response

I thank you God for showing me _____

_____.

STRATEGY

Follow Jesus today, remembering His promised presence within us as seen in **John 16:16-24** (Read now)

As I follow Jesus today I will remember _____

_____.

OBEDIENCE (I will statement)

The Spirit is convicting or leading me today to do or stop doing: _____

_____.

PETITIONS (Following your reciting of The Lord's Prayer)

I pray for these scheduled meetings today:

I pray also for these pressing needs of myself, my family, my church, my disciples my world:

---

[30] See also Cs Lewis' Mere Christianity 64-65.

CONFESSION and REPENTANCE

I confess these, my sins, with every intention to never repeat them, but rather to live as Jesus would live, by Your enabling grace and Spirit …

*Never confess without a faith that looks to the cross of Christ, where the guilt and penalty of all our sins was paid!

WALK (Think about the following hymn)

May the Mind of Christ my Savior

1) May the mind of Christ my Savior
Live in me from day to day,
By His love and pow'r controlling
All I do and say.

2) May the Word of Christ dwell richly
In my heart from hour to hour,
So that all may see I triumph
Only through His pow'r.

3) May the peace of Christ my Savior
Rule my life in everything,
That I may be calm to comfort
Sick and sorrowing.

4) May the love of Jesus fill me,
As the waters fill the sea;
Him exalting, self-abasing,
This is victory.

5) May I run the race before me,
Strong and brave to face the foe,
Looking only unto Jesus
As I onward go.

6) May His beauty rest upon me
As I seek the lost to win,
And may they forget the channel,
Seeing only Him.
(Kate B Wilkinson, 1859-1928)

Response

Help me Jesus, to _____

_____.

VICTORY

Memorize *Galatians 2:20*

Be prepared for opposition (spiritual warfare) and expect victory in Jesus' name.

Write down the name (s) of those with whom you shared today _____

_____.

_____ Check when the day is completed, never beating yourself up if you did not finish; but, just asking Jesus to help you next day!

10-Day Period 4

Discipleship and our Obeying Jesus

**Begin by reading Appendix Four – Following Jesus and Obedience

During the next ten days our overarching focus is on learning what surrendering to Jesus first feels like and then looks like. This is going to be extremely difficult for most Western Christians. We have been conditioned to think that only losers surrender. We should realize that submitting ourselves totally to the triune God of the Bible leads to life, not to denigration, depression and death! We are freed only when we surrender to the Great Liberator! Disciples obey! The Gospel of Mark repeatedly shows their quick or immediate obedience.

That kind of response often strikes us as dehumanizing. Please recognize that democracy, though ancient in its origin, was not often the governing model practiced for most of human history. Kings ruled, and citizens submitted. Jesus is our King. He is not a public servant whom we elected! He does not have a four-year term. When we pledge ourselves to follow Him, it cannot be with the underlying thought of replacing Him if we dislike the way He rules.

Thinking of obedience apart from political nuances, and in line with how many of us work at our jobs, we run into another set of problems. We like to think for ourselves. To have a say in the process. To freely disagree and even walk off and go on strike when our employers do not deliver what we think is fair. The NT disciples were professional workers, yet they surrendered this to do what Jesus said to do—and just how He said to do it. He told fishermen where to fish! He told successful businessmen what to do with their money. He demanded each disciple to forsake his or her sense of time management. He demanded all and He gave real life and joy in exchange. Holy Spirit help us to utterly follow Him and when our weakness makes that hard—help our unbelief!!

Day Thirty-one

God – The King

ADORATION

To say that God is king is to affirm that God is sovereign. Webster's defines "sovereign" as "above or superior to all others; chief greatest, supreme." If God is a King, we must understand the scope of His kingdom. The Bible answers, "Our God is in the heavens; he does all that he chooses" (Ps 115:3; 135:6). "How awesome is the Lord Most High, the great King over all the earth" (Ps 47:2-NIV). "...His dominion is an eternal dominion; his kingdom endures from generation to generation. All the peoples of the earth are regarded as nothing. He does as he pleases with the powers of heaven and the peoples of the earth. No one can hold back his hand or say to him: 'What have you done?'" (Dan 4:34-35-NIV).

Throughout Scripture God's reign is depicted as universal or total. It is over all His creatures in heaven and on earth: great and small, angels and men, lions and lambs, Satan and demons. This rule of God is not merely general but specific, including in its scope all His creatures and all their activities, from the falling of the sparrow to the decisions of a king, to the evil activities of the prince of darkness (Matt 10:29; Prov 21:1; John 19:11; Job 1:8-12; cf I Chr 21:1 with 2 Sam 24:1). God is in ultimate control of life and death (Deut 32:39; Rev 1:17-18), health and sickness (1 Sam 2:6-7; John 9:1-3; 2 Cot 12:7-9), wealth and poverty (1Chr 29:11-12; Is 45:7; Hag 2:8). Yet His decisions are never arbitrary or malicious. He is loving and kind, willing far sooner and more often to exalt His grace than His judgment (Ex 20:4-6; Ez 18:23; 2 Pet 3:9). God is not like a volcano, or "the perfect storm" —uncontrollable forces which overcome everything in their course. Though God is an absolute, eternal and unchanging King, His rule is based on a perfect goodness, wisdom, love and justice, which, while permitting wrong, does no wrong (Gen 18:25; James 1:13).

Since God is King our relation to Him is forever that of inferiority (Is 40:25-28) and dependency (Ps 145:15-16). It is insanity to rebel against Him and want to rule ourselves or make a name for ourselves that rivals His (Ps 10:4; 12:4; Gen 11:4). Or to depend on creatures and things rather than on the Creator (Ps 20:7). Since God is King, the ultimate reason for all events is known (Mart 11:25-26). God "works out everything in conformity with the purpose of his will" (Eph 1:11b-NIV). Therefore, we should not complain, but rather be optimistic and full of praise as we declare Him to be Lord of our money, time, speech—our all.

On earth all types of people rule: harsh and gentle, evil and kind. No one in their right mind, given the opportunity to choose, would select for a leader a Hitler over a Mandela or an Idi Amin over an Abraham Lincoln. People want a fair, wise, patient and kind leader. Jesus came, not only to die as our Savior but to be raised and enthroned as our King. When He returns all creation will sing, "Hallelujah! For our Lord God Almighty reigns" (Rev 19:6). The wise now surrender to Him, for all will bow ultimately before Him and confess that He is Lord (Phil 2:10-11). The foolish cling to the god of their own freedom, not knowing that "when the Son sets you free, you will be free indeed" (John 8:36).

Response

I thank you God for showing me _____

_____.

STRATEGY

Follow Jesus today as your King, thinking about His words in **Luke 19:11-27** (Read now)

As I follow Jesus today I will remember _____

_____.

OBEDIENCE (I will statement)

The Spirit is convicting or leading me today to do or stop doing: _____

_____.

PETITIONS (Following your reciting of The Lord's Prayer)

I pray for these scheduled meetings today:

I pray also for these pressing needs of myself, my family, my church, my disciples,[31] my world:

CONFESSION and REPENTANCE

I confess these, my sins with every intention to never repeat them, but rather to live as Jesus would live, by Your enabling grace and Spirit …
*Never confess without a faith that looks to the cross of Christ, where the guilt and penalty of all our sins was paid!

WALK (Think about the following hymn)

Rejoice the Lord is King!

1) Rejoice, the Lord is King!
Your Lord and King adore;
Rejoice give thanks and sing, and triumph evermore;
Lift up your heart, lift up your voice;
Rejoice, again I say, rejoice!

2) Jesus, the Savior, reigns, the God of truth and love;
When He had purged our stains He took His seat above:
Lift up your heart, lift up your voice;
Rejoice, again I say, rejoice!

3) His kingdom cannot fail, He rules o'er earth and Heav'n,
The keys of death and hell are to our Jesus giv'n;
Lift up your heart, lift up your voice;
Rejoice, again I say, rejoice!

4) He sits at God's right hand till all His foes submit,
And bow to His command, and fall beneath His feet:
Lift up your heart, lift up your voice;
Rejoice, again I say, rejoice!

5) He all His foes shall quell, shall all our sins destroy,
And every bosom swell with pure seraphic joy;
Lift up your heart, lift up your voice,
Rejoice, again I say, rejoice!

---

[31] Those whom you are discipling may be considered "your" disciples in the same way Paul meant when he told the Corinthians, "Be imitators of me as I am of Christ" (1 Cor 11:1)

> 6) Rejoice in glorious hope! Jesus the Judge shall come,
> And take His servants up to their eternal home.
> We soon shall hear th'archangel's voice;
> The trump of God shall sound, rejoice!
> (Charles Wesley, 1707-1788)

Response

Help me Jesus, to _____

_____.

VICTORY

Memorize *Psalm 2:1-3* by reading it 5 times, reciting (without looking) 5 times and repeating it throughout the day 5 times (at least at 9AM, 12 noon and 3PM when you STOP the day to worship and talk to God).

Be prepared to ask, "the person of peace question" (PoP) to anyone who seems ready and willing to be discipled.[32]

Be prepared for opposition (spiritual warfare) and expect victory in Jesus' name.

Write down the name (s) of those with whom you shared today and pray for them_____

_____.

____ Check when the day is completed with praise and glory to God, alone!

---

[32] PoP question: "Would you like to discover for yourself what God is like and how God wants you to live?"

Day Thirty-two

God – The Father

ADORATION

What do you think of when you hear the word--father? When a human term is used of God, we take the core of that term—what it basically stands for—and strip it of all imperfection, sin and limitation. Only then may it rightly reflect God. And even then, it captures only a small glimpse of who He is. Though God has revealed Himself through many terms, Jesus clearly identified one title as His favorite. "Pray then like this: Our Father in heaven..." (Matt 6:9). Fatherhood at its core is strength, dependability, courage and love. God is our perfect and unchanging Father in all these and many more ways. He is "one God and Father of all, who is over all and through all and in all" (Eph 4:6).

Though Fatherhood uniquely represents the Father's relationship with the Son, the basic features of fatherhood are equally shared by each Person of the Trinity. So, it could be said of the coming Messiah, "For to us a child is born, to us a son is given...and he will be called ... Everlasting Father" (Isaiah 9:6). In prayer, the Spirit leads us to cry, "Abba! Father!" (Rom 8:15). Jesus and the Spirit, too, are always like a perfect father to us.

Fatherhood also speaks of origins. A father produces children. Our identity is linked in special ways with our fathers. "You deserted the Rock, who fathered you; you forgot the God who gave you birth" (Deut 32:18-NIV). God relentlessly reminds believers that He will be our Father and we will be His sons (2 Sam 7:14; 2 Cor 6:18; Rev 21:3). He will not give over His beloved children to sin and Satan, however much we might, in times of weakness, desire it (see Hosea). "No one is able to snatch them out of the Father's hand" (John 10:29)." Where are your zeal and your might? The stirring of your inner parts and your compassion are held back from me. For you are our Father, though Abraham does not know us, and Israel does not acknowledge us; you, O Lord, are our Father, our Redeemer from of old is your name" (Isa 63:15-16). He will not disown His children.

The Prodigal Son was not thinking soundly when he left his loving father to live in sin. When he came to his senses, he returned to his father and found him to be what he always was: forgiving and full of love. How much more foolish are we whenever we stray from our Heavenly Father? "...You saw how the Lord your God carried you as a father carries his son" (Deut 1:31-NIV). "Besides this, we have had human fathers who disciplined us and we respected them. Shall we not much more be subject the Father of spirits and live!" (Heb 12:9). Fools leave a good father in the pursuit of "life." True life is walking with our ever-good heavenly Father.

Response

I thank you God for showing me _____

_____.

STRATEGY

Follow Jesus today, remembering His declared relationship of total submission to His Father's will, as seen in **Matt 26:36-46** (Read now)

As I follow Jesus today I will remember _____

_____.

OBEDIENCE (I will statement)

The Spirit is convicting or leading me today to do or stop doing: _____

_____.

PETITIONS (Following your reciting of The Lord's Prayer)

I pray for these scheduled meetings today:
I pray also for these pressing needs of myself, my family, my church, my disciples my world:

CONFESSION and REPENTANCE

I confess these, my sins, with every intention to never repeat them, but rather to live as Jesus would live, by Your enabling grace and Spirit …

*Never confess without a faith that looks to the cross of Christ, where the guilt and penalty of all our sins was paid!

WALK (Think about the following hymn)

This is My Father's World

1) This is my Father's world, and to my listening ears
All nature sings, and round me rings the music of the spheres.
This is my Father's world: I rest me in the thought
Of rocks and trees, of skies and seas;
His hand the wonders wrought.

2) This is my Father's world, the birds their carols raise,
The morning light, the lily white, declare their Maker's praise.
This is my Father's world: He shines in all that's fair;
In the rustling grass I hear Him pass;
He speaks to me everywhere.

3) This is my Father's world. O let me ne'er forget
That though the wrong seems oft so strong, God is the ruler yet.
This is my Father's world: the battle is not done:
Jesus Who died shall be satisfied,
And earth and Heav'n be one.

4) This is my Father's world, dreaming, I see His face.
I open my eyes, and in glad surprise cry, "The Lord is in this place."
This is my Father's world, from the shining courts above,
The Beloved One, His Only Son,
Came—a pledge of deathless love.

5) This is my Father's world, should my heart be ever sad?
The Lord is King—let the heavens ring. God reigns—let the earth be glad.
This is my Father's world. Now closer to Heaven bound,
For dear to God is the earth Christ trod.
No place but is holy ground.

6) This is my Father's world. I walk a desert lone.
In a bush ablaze to my wondering gaze God makes His glory known.
This is my Father's world, a wanderer I may roam
Whate'er my lot, it matters not,
My heart is still at home.
(Maltbie Babcock, 1858—1901)

Response

Help me Jesus, to _____

_____.

VICTORY

Memorize *Luke 11:13*

Be prepared for opposition (spiritual warfare) and expect victory in Jesus' name.

Write down the name (s) of those with whom you shared today _____

_____.

____ Check when the day is completed, never beating yourself up if you did not finish; but, just asking Jesus to help you next day!

Day Thirty-three

God – The Commander

ADORATION

When we think of a commander, we usually think in military terms. A commander is a leader who directs a group of soldiers. He issues commands and they obey. Submission to his authority is key. Even in times of mortal danger, a soldier is trained to think, "My commander has better information and more experience, so his orders are better than my feelings about it." How often do we think of our relationship to Jesus in this way?

The coming Messiah would be "a witness to the peoples, a leader and commander for the peoples" (Isa 55:4). He appeared to Joshua, as follows: "... Joshua went up to him and asked, Are you for us or for our enemies? Neither, he replied, but as commander of the army of the Lord I have now come. Then Joshua fell face-down to the ground in reverence, and asked him, What message does my Lord have for his servant? The commander of the Lord's army replied, Take off your sandals, for the place where you are standing is holy." (Josh 5:13-15-NIV). Paul taught Timothy that serving Jesus was like a soldier under a commander. "No one serving as a soldier gets involved in civilian affairs—he wants to please his commanding officer." (2 Tim 2:4-NIV).

However, it is NOT so much as a General that the Bible speaks of God as Commander. Rather it is as our Sovereign, our King. The One who has the right to issue commands and have them obeyed by all in His kingdom. He created Adam and Eve and commanded them, "you must not eat from the tree of the knowledge of good and evil, for when you eat of it you will surely die" (Gen 2:17-NIV). He reveals himself as the God who is "... showing steadfast love to the thousandth generation of those who love me and keep my commandments" (Ex 20:6). He is a Commander who ought to be loved for all He orders us to do. He commands nothing of us that is impossible to do, by His grace. "Now what I am commanding you today is not too difficult for you or beyond your reach ... It is not up in heaven ... nor is it beyond the sea ... No, the word is very near you; it is in your mouth and in your heart, so you may obey it." (Deut 30:11-14-NIV). Every command is good and lovely, as commanded by a good God. So, John would say, "For this is the love for God: to obey his commands. And his commands are not burdensome" (1 John 5:3-NIV). Are they your burden or blessing?

Jesus is our King. As He commanded mighty winds to cease and evil spirits to leave their victims (Luke 8:25, 29), so He commands us. In fact, obedience to Him is made an evidence of true salvation. "If you obey my commands, you will remain in my love, just as I have obeyed my Father's commands and remain in his love" (John 15:10-NIV). "Those who obey commands live in Him, and He in them." (1 John 3:24-NIV). Believers are "those who keep the commandments of God and hold to the testimony of Jesus." (Rev 12:17). Commanders are obeyed. And there has never been such a wise, good, powerful and loving Commander as Jesus!

Response

I thank you God for showing me _____

_____.

STRATEGY

Follow Jesus today, remembering His ability to command even nature as seen in **Matt 8:23-27** (Read now)

As I follow Jesus today I will remember _____

_____.

OBEDIENCE (I will statement)

The Spirit is convicting or leading me today to do or stop doing: _____

_____.

PETITIONS (Following your reciting of The Lord's Prayer)

I pray for these scheduled meetings today:

I pray also for these pressing needs of myself, my family, my church, my disciples my world:

CONFESSION and REPENTANCE

I confess these, my sins, with every intention to never repeat them, but rather to live as Jesus would live, by Your enabling grace and Spirit ...

*Never confess without a faith that looks to the cross of Christ, where the guilt and penalty of all our sins was paid!

WALK (Think about the following hymn)

Master the Tempest is Raging

1) Master, the tempest is raging!
The billows are tossing high!
The sky is o'ershadowed with blackness,
No shelter or help is nigh;
Carest Thou not that we perish?
How canst Thou lie asleep,
When each moment so madly is threat'ning
A grave in the angry deep?

The winds and the waves shall obey Thy will,
Peace, be still!
Whether the wrath of the storm-tossed sea,
Or demons or men, or whatever it be,
No waters can swallow the ship where lies
The Master of ocean, and earth, and skies;
They all shall sweetly obey Thy will,
Peace, be still! Peace, be still!
They all shall sweetly obey Thy will,
Peace, peace, be still!

2) Master, with anguish of spirit
I bow in my grief today;
The depths of my sad heart are troubled—
Oh, waken and save, I pray!
Torrents of sin and of anguish
Sweep o'er my sinking soul;
And I perish! I perish! dear Master—
Oh, hasten, and take control.

> 3) Master, the terror is over,
> The elements sweetly rest;
> Earth's sun in the calm lake is mirrored,
> And heaven's within my breast;
> Linger, O blessed Redeemer!
> Leave me alone no more;
> And with joy I shall make the blest harbor,
> And rest on the blissful shore.
> (Mary Baker, 1883-1921)

Response

Help me Jesus, to _____

_____.

VICTORY

Memorize *1 John 3:23*

Be prepared for opposition (spiritual warfare) and expect victory in Jesus' name.

Write down the name (s) of those with whom you shared today _____

_____.

____ Check when the day is completed, never beating yourself up if you did not finish; but, just asking Jesus to help you next day!

Day Thirty-four

God – The Covenant Maker

ADORATION

  Living in a culture that routinely sees the breaking of contracts as no big thing, creates dangerous thought patterns within the Christian. Promise keeping is important. God is trustworthy, human nature is not. But our nature can be changed. The world of the Bible helped people keep their promises by making covenants, which were seriously made agreements. Since He wants to be understood by us humans, God often reveals Himself in common ways we can grasp. So, the Bible speaks of Him as entering covenants with individuals and larger groups. You can be sure God will keep His part in a covenant. "He remembers his covenant forever, the word that he commanded for a thousand generations, the covenant that he made with Abraham, his sworn promise to Isaac" (Ps 105:8-9). As His children, we should also keep our promises (Ps 15:1-4; 66:13-14; 116:14).

  Covenants often had threats attached to them, warning of the consequences of being unfaithful to the covenant. Some covenants were one sided—or unconditional—with God, assuring those in the covenant that He would fulfill it. This followed the royal grant covenants that kings often made when granting land to faithful subjects. Most covenants demanded something of both parties, and so, were conditional. Instead of merely shaking hands to "seal the deal," blood was often used, with birds or animals cut in two and the people in covenant would look at or walk between them repeating their part and responsibilities. This ceremony warned that what happened to the sacrificed animals would happen to them if they broke their part of the agreement. (See Gen 15:6-19 of God entering an unconditional covenant and Gen 17:1-14 of a conditional covenant.) Circumcision was the ceremonial sign of a covenant, which said very graphically, "May what happened to my son's cut off flesh happen to him if he grows up and breaks this covenant!" (Gen 17:7,10). So, the Hebrew word for "making" a covenant was literally "cutting" a covenant. Israel's social order was preserved by assuring that consequences could be expected to fall on all covenant breakers. (Jer 34:18-20 cf. Gal 6:7-8.)

  The Old Covenant made with Israel at Sinai promised life to all who perfectly kept the Law. Because they were sinful, as we are, Israel could not keep this covenant and had to be punished for breaking the covenant or else have someone provided to keep it for them. Jesus came to be the Covenant

Keeper who would give them and us His righteousness (perfect obedience) upon our believing (See Rom 1:17; Phil 3:9). He was the promised Messiah who would be given as a "covenant for the people and a light for the Gentiles" (Isa 42:6), the "messenger of the covenant" (Mal 3:1). He is "the mediator of a new covenant" (Heb 9:15) and, so, pastors today are "made...ministers of a new covenant—not of the letter but of the Spirit; for the letter kills, but the Spirit gives life" (2 Cor 3:6). By grace, we are God's people. Promise keepers not liars, followers of Christ not Adam. Ask the Spirit to help you keep your word to both God and man. And when you don't—praise Him for the Good News of Jesus Christ!

Response

I thank you God for showing me _____

_____.

STRATEGY

Follow Jesus today, remembering His solemn commencement of the New Covenant at the Last Supper as seen in Luke 22:7-23 (Read now)

As I follow Jesus today I will remember _____

_____.

OBEDIENCE (I will statement)

The Spirit is convicting or leading me today to do or stop doing: _____

_____.

PETITIONS (Following your reciting of The Lord's Prayer)

I pray for these scheduled meetings today:

I pray also for these pressing needs of myself, my family, my church, my disciples my world:

CONFESSION and REPENTANCE

I confess these, my sins, with every intention to never repeat them, but rather to live as Jesus would live, by Your enabling grace and Spirit ...

*Never confess without a faith that looks to the cross of Christ, where the guilt and penalty of all our sins was paid!

WALK (Think about the following Sovereign Grace praise song)

Covenant of Grace

1) I only want to serve you
Bring honor to Your name
Though often I have failed You
Your faithfulness remains
I'll glory in my weakness
That I might know Your strength
I will live my life at the Cross of Christ
And raise a banner to proclaim

The wonder of Your Mercy Lord
The beauty of Your grace
That You would even pardon me
And bring me to this place
I stand before Your holiness
I can only stand amazed
The sinless Savior died to make
A covenant of grace

2) You welcome us before You
Into this holy place
The brilliance of Your glory
Demands our endless praise
The One the only Savior
Has opened heaven's doors
We can enter in free from all our sin
By Your cleansing sacrifice.
(Don Wallace, 1997)

Response

Help me Jesus, to _____

_____.

VICTORY

Memorize *Luke 22:20*

Be prepared for opposition (spiritual warfare) and expect victory in Jesus' name.

Write down the name (s) of those with whom you shared today _____

_____.

____ Check when the day is completed, never beating yourself up if you did not finish; but, just asking Jesus to help you next day!

Day Thirty-five

God – The Just One

ADORATION

"This is what the Lord says, 'You have abandoned me; therefore, I now abandon you to Shishak." So, "The leaders of Israel and the king humbled themselves and said, 'The Lord is just.'" (2 Chr 12:5b-6-NIV). To be just is to be fair. It is to pay what is owed, to give what is deserved. God is perfectly and unchangeably just. Even Nebuchadnezzar confessed, "all his works are right, and his ways are just" (Dan 4:37). The Judge of the whole earth will do what is right (Gen 18:25).

Some think that because evil is not immediately punished there must not be a just God ruling the universe. As Solomon noted, "Because the sentence against an evil deed is not executed speedily, the heart of the children of man is fully set to do evil" (Ecc 8:11). But God's justice is perfectly linked with His mercy and patience. He will punish wrong and reward good in His own perfect time (Luke 18:7-8; Rev 6:10). So, "Do not be deceived: God cannot be mocked. A man reaps what he sows" (Gal 6:7). Although God does not delight in bringing "affliction or grief to the children of men" (Lam 3:32-33), there comes a time when His patience ends and "The Lord of hosts is exalted in justice" (Isa 5:16). Belief in God's justice helps us endure and accept all of life's present inequalities. However, we often now see that, "God is not unjust to overlook your work and the love that you have shown for his name in serving the saints, as you still do" (Heb 6:10).

Let us remember, since God is just, that injustice and oppression cannot ultimately win! Jesus promised, "a time is coming when all. will hear his voice and come out—those who have done good will rise to live, and those who have done evil will rise to be condemned" (John 5:28-29-NIV). Since injustice cannot finally win, let us constantly promote fairness in all we do. And since everyone will justly reap what they have sown, let us see the foolishness of sin and forsake it, while we see the wisdom of holiness, obedience and faith, embracing them! "And be sure that your sin will find you out" (Num 32:23). Let us run to Christ for safety because "God is just…He will punish those who do not know God and obey the gospel of our Lord Jesus. They will be punished with everlasting destruction and shut out from the presence of the Lord" (2 Thes 1:6,8-9-NIV). Though we sinners are helpless to save ourselves from judgment, "at the right time Christ died for the ungodly" (Rom 5:6). What God's justice demanded, God's grace provided! So, we can join David and "sing of your love and your justice" (Ps 101:1-NIV). That which we once could only fear, we can truly joyfully celebrate and absolutely adore!

Response

I thank you God for showing me _____

_____.

STRATEGY

Follow Jesus today, remembering His powerful warning for the Pharisees about doing justice, as seen in **Luke 11:42-43** (Read now)

As I follow Jesus today I will remember _____

_____.

OBEDIENCE (I will statement)

The Spirit is convicting or leading me today to do or stop doing: _____

_____.

PETITIONS (Following your reciting of The Lord's Prayer)

I pray for these scheduled meetings today:

I pray also for these pressing needs of myself, my family, my church, my disciples my world:

CONFESSION and REPENTANCE

I confess these, my sins, with every intention to never repeat them, but rather to live as Jesus would live, by Your enabling grace and Spirit …

*Never confess without a faith that looks to the cross of Christ, where the guilt and penalty of all our sins was paid!

WALK (Think about the following hymn)

Let us love and sing and wonder

1) Let us love and sing and wonder
Let us praise the Savior's name
He has hushed the law's loud thunder
He has quenched Mount Sinai's flame
He has washed us with His blood
He has washed us with His blood
He has washed us with His blood
He has brought us nigh to God

2) Let us love the Lord Who bought us
Pitied us when enemies
Called us by His grace and taught us
Gave us ears and gave us eyes
He has washed us with His blood
He has washed us with His blood
He has washed us with His blood
He presents our souls to God

3) Let us sing though fierce temptation
Threatens hard to bear us down
For the Lord, our strong salvation,
Holds in view the conqu'ror's crown
He, Who washed us with His blood,
He, Who washed us with His blood,
He, Who washed us with His blood,
Soon will bring us home to God

4) Let us wonder grace and justice
Join and point to mercy's store
When through grace in Christ our trust is
Justice smiles and asks no more
He Who washed us with His blood
He Who washed us with His blood
He Who washed us with His blood
Has secured our way to God

5) Let us praise and join the chorus
Of the saints enthroned on high
Here they trusted Him before us
Now their praises fill the sky
Thou hast washed us with Thy blood
Thou hast washed us with Thy blood
Thou hast washed us with Thy blood
Thou art worthy Lamb of God

6. Yes, we praise Thee, gracious Saviour
Wonder, love, and bless Thy Name.
Pardon, Lord our poor endeavor
Pity for Thou knowest our frame
Wash our souls and songs with blood
Wash our souls and songs with blood
Wash our souls and songs with blood
For by Thee, we come to God

Response

Help me Jesus, to _____

_____.

VICTORY

Memorize *Proverbs 21:15*

Be prepared for opposition (spiritual warfare) and expect victory in Jesus' name.

Write down the name (s) of those with whom you shared today _____

_____.

_____ Check when the day is completed, never beating yourself up if you did not finish; but, just asking Jesus to help you next day!

Day Thirty-six

God – The Gracious One

ADORATION

Grace is a special type of love. It is love expressed to those who do not deserve it. A truly free love. When God "came down" on Mount Sinai and "proclaimed his name" to Moses, His first words of self-description were, "The Lord, the Lord, a God merciful and gracious, slow to anger, and abounding in steadfast love and faithfulness" (Ex. 34:6). The constant blessing that His priests were to give included, "the Lord ... be gracious unto you" (Num 6:25). As none could keep His Law, all needed His grace. In the OT Scriptures, God's grace was sometimes suppressed, and Israel had to experience that He is also just. He cannot simply ignore sin. Jonah learned this and declared, "Those who cling to worthless idols, forfeit the grace that could be theirs." (Jonah 2:8-NIV). Our idols cost us much more and deliver much less than we realize. Even when Israel was deservedly to be punished, Isaiah revealed, "Yet the Lord longs to be gracious unto you, he rises to show you compassion" (Isa 30:18-NIV). Grace might be called God's chief instinct, as Jeremiah declared, "Though he brings grief, he will show compassion, so great is his unfailing love, for he does not willingly bring affliction or grief to the children of men" (Lam. 3:32-33-NIV). He is "the God of all grace" (1 Pet 5:10).

The Father sent the Son into the world with a plan of salvation designed to be "to the praise of his glorious grace" (Eph 1:6). Through Jesus, God transformed the sinner's relationship to Himself from one of fear and judgment into a relationship where "grace also might reign" (Rom 5:21). "God made him who had no sin to be sin for us, so that in him we might become the righteousness of God" (2 Cor 5:21-NIV). Jesus turned God's judgment throne into "the throne of his grace" (Heb 4:16) for all those saved by faith. And the Bible, through Christ, is transformed into "the word of his grace" (Acts 20:32) rather than His "law" in the NT. For, through Jesus, we are "not under law but under grace" (Rom 6:14). What hangs over the believer's head is not the sword of God's threatening wrath, but the bright shining sun of His glorious grace!

All believers should "Be strengthened by the grace that is in Christ" (2 Tim 2:1). Grace is the first word of NT Christianity, (see 1 Cor 1:3; 16:24, etc). So, every Christian's "speech should always be gracious" (Col 4:6). Let us be on the guard to never "change" or "fall away" (Gal 5:4; Jude 4) from this gift of God's grace. By grace we are saved (Eph 2:5,8)! Live like real followers of Jesus--graciously. Do good to others just for love's sake. And never lose your marvel and love for such a God who has opened heaven and eternal life to you by Sovereign, unchanging and unconquerable grace!

Response

I thank you God for showing me _____

_____.

STRATEGY

Follow Jesus today, remembering His gracious manner as seen in **Luke 7:36-50** (Read now)

As I follow Jesus today I will remember _____

_____.

OBEDIENCE (I will statement)

The Spirit is convicting or leading me today to do or stop doing: _____

_____.

PETITIONS (Following your reciting of The Lord's Prayer)

I pray for these scheduled meetings today:

I pray also for these pressing needs of myself, my family, my church, my disciples my world:

CONFESSION and REPENTANCE

I confess these, my sins, with every intention to never repeat them, but rather to live as Jesus would live, by Your enabling grace and Spirit …

*Never confess without a faith that looks to the cross of Christ, where the guilt and penalty of all our sins was paid!

WALK (Think about the following, maybe most- famous of all hymns)

Amazing Grace

1) Amazing grace! how sweet the sound,
That saved a wretch; like me!
I once was lost, but now am found,
Was blind, but now I see.

2)'Twas grace that taught my heart to fear,
And grace my fears relieved;
How precious did that grace appear
The hour I first believed!

3) The Lord hath promised good to me,
His word my hope secures;
He will my shield and portion be
As long as life endures.

4) When we've been there ten thousand years,
Bright shining as the sun,
We've no less days to sing God's praise
Than when we first begun..
(John Newton, 1725-1807)

Response

Help me Jesus, to _____

VICTORY

Memorize *John 1:17*

Be prepared for opposition (spiritual warfare) and expect victory in Jesus' name.

Write down the name (s) of those with whom you shared today _____

_____.

____ Check when the day is completed, never beating yourself up if you did not finish; but, just asking Jesus to help you next day!

Day Thirty-seven

God – The Lawgiver

ADORATION

    Most normal people are not exhilarated when the sailboat they are in is being tossed and driven, out of control, by an unexpected, raging storm. So, they factor in the weather, the wind and the waves, before they launch out. Because professional sailors have established the rules or laws of safe sailing, amateurs can have a good time on the water. They remain happy and peaceful if they sail within the bounds of those established laws. Overstepping those guidelines may "give a rush" for a while, but soon terror arises as the pilot loses control and the boat begins to capsize, threatening life itself. Rules do not kill us. But breaking the established boundaries may. Lawlessness kills!

    The Ten Commandments were a summary of God's will concerning our relationship with Him and with others. They are called the Law of God. He wrote these laws, Himself on stone tablets prepared by Moses (Ex 34:1). The law of God established the guidelines to be followed by His chosen people. They were the terms of His covenant with them. Obedience would bring blessing. Disobedience would result in punishment (Deut 30:11-20). The psalmist declared, "The law of the Lord is perfect, reviving the soul." (Ps 19:7a). And again, "Oh how love I your law! I meditate on it all day long" (Ps 119:97). Our good God gave laws that were good to obey. Paul summarized the law as "holy, and the commandment is holy, righteous and good" (Rom.7:12).

    Unfortunately, because of our innate imperfection, no human could keep the law and, thus, be given life. All have broken it through sin. "Sin is lawlessness" (1 John 3:4). But Jesus was sent to obey it in our behalf and, thereby, to earn a righteousness or perfect obedience for us. He succeeded! And His righteousness is given to everyone's account who, by faith, trusts in Him for salvation (Rom 1:17; Phil 3:9).

    The NT can confuse us if we forget that the moral Law is good. It becomes a bad thing only when we use it wrongly (1 Tim 1:8) to try to earn our own salvation or approval by God from it. The verses that speak of the law negatively (like Rom 10:4; Gal 3:25; Col 2:16-17; Heb 10:1) are about those who are trying to earn their way before God, apart from faith in Christ. God's moral law is still a great rule for life. When we are saved, something very special happens concerning our relationship to the Law of God. God promises, "This is the covenant I will make...I will put my law in their minds and write it on their hearts. I will be their God, and they will be my people" (Jer 31:33; cf Heb 8:10; 10:16).

The way of Jesus is more demanding than the OT law, as the Sermon on the Mount (Matt 5-7) clearly reveals. Christians have a higher law to live by. As Paul wrote, "Carry each other's burdens, and in this way, you will fulfill the law of Christ" (Gal 6:2). "I am not free from God's law but am under Christ's law" (I Cor 9:21). But we always must remember, our cause of eternal life is faith in Christ's merits, His obedience —not ours. We obey because of being saved, not to be saved.

Response

I thank you God for showing me _____

_____.

STRATEGY

Follow Jesus today, remembering His perfect obedience to the Law as seen in **Matt 4:1-11** (Read now)

As I follow Jesus today I will remember _____

_____.

OBEDIENCE (I will statement)

The Spirit is convicting or leading me today to do or stop doing: _____

_____.

PETITIONS (Following your reciting of The Lord's Prayer)

I pray for these scheduled meetings today:

I pray also for these pressing needs of myself, my family, my church, my disciples my world:

CONFESSION and REPENTANCE

I confess these, my sins, with every intention to never repeat them, but rather to live as Jesus would live, by Your enabling grace and Spirit ...

*Never confess without a faith that looks to the cross of Christ, where the guilt and penalty of all our sins was paid!

WALK (Think about the following hymn)

Most Perfect is the Law of God

1) Most perfect is the law of God,
Restoring those that stray;
His testimony is most sure,
Proclaiming wisdom's way.

2) O how love I thy law! O how love I thy law!
It is my meditation all the day.
O how love I thy law! O how love I thy law!
It is my meditation all the day.

3) The precepts of the Lord are right;
With joy they fill the heart;
The Lord's commandments all are pure,
And clearest light impart.

4) The fear of God is undefiled
And ever shall endure;
The statutes of the Lord are truth
And righteousness most pure.

5) They warn from ways of wickedness
Displeasing to the Lord,
And in the keeping of his Word
There is a great reward.

(From Psalm 19:7-11 and Psalm 119:97, David ben Jesse, ca 1050 BC)

Response

Help me Jesus, to _____

_____.

VICTORY

Memorize _Romans 3:20_

Be prepared for opposition (spiritual warfare) and expect victory in Jesus' name.

Write down the name (s) of those with whom you shared today and pray for them. _____

_____.

____ Check when the day is completed, never beating yourself up if you did not finish; but, just asking Jesus to help you next day!

Day Thirty-eight

God – The Lord of Hosts

ADORATION

A vast ocean and enormous mountains are so impressive to most people that they will plan their vacations just to be near them. At such places, we naturally contemplate the greatness of earth's Creator. But, remember, every single aspect of His nature is marked by infinite greatness! The Good News of Christ's birth was so great that it had to be declared on earth in a great way. So, God summoned a great number of heavenly creatures to herald this Great News. "And suddenly there was with the angel a great company of the heavenly host praising God and saying, Glory to God in the highest, and on earth peace…" (Lk 2:13-14). Who was this great host from heaven?

They are angels. "Praise him, all his angels, praise him, all his heavenly hosts!" (Ps 148:2). They live to serve the Lord. And His great acts demand great praise from this great host. "Praise the Lord, all his heavenly hosts, you his servants who do his will." (Ps 103:21-NIV). They surround the Lord. "I saw the Lord sitting on his throne with all the host of heaven on his right and on his left." (1 Kgs 22:11). When sent, they go forth as an army to battle evil for His glory (2 Kgs 6:17; Is 37:36; Dan 10:13,20) and to protect and serve His people (Ps 34:7; 91:11; Dan 12:1; Matt 4:11; Heb 1: 14). They are a vast host. "The chariots of God are tens of thousands and thousands of thousands" (Ps 68:17-NIV). Jesus knew that they were at His disposal and, therefore, assured His followers of victory (Matt 26:52-53).

If one of the heavenly host can slay 185,000 warriors (Is 37:36), think of their combined power! But do not stop there. Think of the power of their Commander, of the Lord—the One to whom they joyfully submit and constantly worship with great awe (Is 6:1-3), for He is infinitely greater than all of them. Over 250 times in the OT, God is called "the Lord of hosts" (also translated as "Lord Almighty"). David summoned courage to face and defeat Goliath as he knew that the Captain of the army of heaven was on his side. "You come to me with a sword and with a spear and with a javelin, but I come to you in the name of the Lord of hosts, the God of the armies of Israel, whom you have defied" (1 Sam 17:45).

The Lord of hosts (Almighty) was the favorite name of God used by many prophets. He can turn a pagan king's heart to do His will: "I will raise up Cyrus…says the Lord Almighty (Is 45:13-NIV). He who is both followed and served by the army of heaven marvels that so few on earth heed Him: "Consider…how evil and bitter it is for you when you forsake the Lord your

God and have no awe of me, declares the Lord, the Lord Almighty." (Jer 2:19-NIV). When facing insurmountable odds, we are reminded it is, "Not by might, nor by power, but by my Spirit, says the Lord of hosts." (Zech 4:6). So, we should not fear man, nor ever act as if we were alone or insignificant. Instead, we should pray for deliverance, never giving up because ours is the God whom all the heavenly host stand ready to obey. He need only speak the word.

Response

I thank you God for showing me _____

_____.

STRATEGY

Follow Jesus today, remembering what He told his disciples about the heavenly host when betrayed in the Garden of Gethsemane as seen in **Matt 26:47-56** (Read now)

As I follow Jesus today I will remember _____

_____.

OBEDIENCE (I will statement)

The Spirit is convicting or leading me today to do or stop doing: _____

_____

PETITIONS (Following your reciting of <u>The Lord's Prayer</u>)

I pray for these scheduled meetings today:

I pray also for these pressing needs of myself, my family, my church, my disciples my world:

CONFESSION and REPENTANCE

I confess these, my sins, with every intention to never repeat them, but rather to live as Jesus would live, by Your enabling grace and Spirit …

*Never confess without a faith that looks to the cross of Christ, where the guilt and penalty of all our sins was paid!

WALK (Think about the following hymn)

The Doxology

> Praise God from whom all blessings flow;
> Praise Him, all creatures here below,
> Praise Him above, ye heavenly host,
> Praise Father, Son and Holy Ghost.
> (Thomas Ken, 1637-1711)

Response

Help me Jesus, to _____

_____.

VICTORY

Memorize *Psalm 34:7*

Be prepared for opposition (spiritual warfare) and expect victory in Jesus' name.

Write down the name (s) of those with whom you shared today _____

_____.

____ Check when the day is completed, never beating yourself up if you did not finish; but, just asking Jesus to help you next day!

Day Thirty-nine

God – The Worker

ADORATION

Do you like to work? Before you answer, consider this. God loves to work. Is it possible that our dislike of work may reveal, in some subtle ways, a dislike of God? A rebellion against His nature in favor of an unproductive, idle and self-indulgent lifestyle?

From the beginning, God is revealed as a Worker. "And on the seventh day God finished his work that he had done, and he rested on the seventh from all his work that he had done" (Gen 2:2). Billions have marveled at His work. "The heavens declare the glory of God; and the sky above proclaims his handiwork" (Ps 19:1). However, all too often, that is where it ends. With a passing admiration rather than with a deep and thoughtful reflection. David says, "I will meditate on your wonderful works" (Ps 145:5-NIV). Those works include not only the work of creation but also the works of His providence. The works of God's providence include all things under God's rule, all that God is involved with. According to the Bible, that includes the growth of hair on our heads, the emergence of a lily through the soil and every political leader that rules on earth, as well as the falling of a baby bird out of its nest. God is constantly at work in all things—yet without being the Author of sin. "Jesus said to them, My Father is always at his work to this very day, and I, too, am working" (John 5:17-NIV).

A piece of work reveals thought, skill, power and perseverance. God is and shows all this and more. His plan and direction of your life is a work of art! Perfect, wise, staged according to plan. Including everything, the apparently bad or good. "And I know that in all things God works for the good of those who love him" (Rom 8:28-NIV). Not trusting in God as a Worker fills our hearts with discontentment, pressure and sadness. Let the Artist do His work and be filled with joy and peace as you wait on Him to finish what He has begun in you.

Sometimes we must wait through very hard times and incredibly trying circumstances. Like coal pressurized into a diamond, we see blessing arise out of suffering. The Psalmist captures it and says, "Come and see what God has done, how awesome his works in man's behalf! He turned the sea into dry land...kept our feet from slipping...tested us and refined us like silver...brought us into prison and laid burdens on our backs. You let men ride over our heads; we went through fire and water, but you brought us to a place of abundance" Ps 66:5-12-NIV).We don't mind it when He turns sea into dry land, but when He leads us into prison or allows chariots to run over our heads, we often cry out, "Why? Where are You? What are You doing?" He knows. He loves. Don't despair. "...work out you own salvation with fear and trembling, for it is God who works in you, both to will and to work for his good pleasure" (Phil 2:12- 13). Your life is His work. "For we are his workmanship, created in Christ Jesus for good works, which God prepared beforehand, that we should walk in them" (Eph 2:10). In everything you do, He is with you. "he who began a good work in you will bring it to completion at the day of Jesus Christ" (Phil 1:6).

Response

I thank you God for showing me _____

_____.

STRATEGY

Follow Jesus today, remembering how hard He worked and what He taught His disciples about work as seen in Matthew 9:35-37 (Read now)

As I follow Jesus today I will remember _____

_____.

OBEDIENCE (I will statement)

The Spirit is convicting or leading me today to do or stop doing: _____

_____.

PETITIONS (Following your reciting of The Lord's Prayer)

I pray for these scheduled meetings today:

I pray also for these pressing needs of myself, my family, my church, my disciples my world:

CONFESSION and REPENTANCE

I confess these, my sins, with every intention to never repeat them, but rather to live as Jesus would live, by Your enabling grace and Spirit ...

*Never confess without a faith that looks to the cross of Christ, where the guilt and penalty of all our sins was paid!

WALK (Think about the following hymn)

Work for the Night is Coming

(1) Work, for the night is coming,
Work through the morning hours;
Work while the dew is sparkling,
Work 'mid springing flowers;
Work when the day grows brighter,
Work in the glowing sun;
Work, for the night is coming,
When man's work is done.

(2) Work, for the night is coming,
Work through the sunny noon;
Fill brightest hours with labor,
Rest comes sure and soon.
Give every flying minute,
Something to keep in store;
Work, for the night is coming,
When man works no more.

(3) Work, for the night is coming,
Under the sunset skies;
While their bright tints are glowing,
Work, for daylight flies.
Work till the last beam fadeth,
Fadeth to shine no more;
Work, while the night is darkening,
When man's work is o'er.
(Anna L. Cogdill 1836-1907)

Response

Help me Jesus, to _____

_____.

VICTORY

Memorize *John 4:34*

Be prepared for opposition (spiritual warfare) and expect victory in Jesus' name.

Write down the name (s) of those with whom you shared today _____

_____.

____ Check when the day is completed, never beating yourself up if you did not finish; but, just asking Jesus to help you next day!

Day Forty

God – The Rewarder

ADORATION

Since God is just or fair in all that He does, "a man reaps what he sows" (Gal. 6:7-NIV). Paul again wrote, "The Lord will reward everyone for whatever good he does, whether he is slave or free" (Eph 6:8-NIV). But, due to His wise, patient and loving nature, rarely is the reward or punishment fully and immediately bestowed. So, God is sometimes misread as being either ambivalent or distant. We often need to be reminded, as was King Asa, "The Lord is with you when you are with him. If you seek him, he will be found by you, but if you forsake him, he will forsake you...Be strong and do not give up, for your work will be rewarded" (2 Chron 15:2,7-NIV). Or as John pled with his readers, "Watch out that you do not lose what you have worked for, but that you may be rewarded" (2 John 8-NIV). The readers of the epistle to the Hebrews were in danger of giving up, so the author wrote, "do not throw away your confidence, which has a great reward" (Heb 10:35).

God certainly blesses His people NOW; but, it is hardly comparable to what is coming! Jesus declared, "I am coming soon! My reward is with me. And I will give to everyone according to what he has done" (Rev 22:12-NIV). Often God's people suffer on earth. Jesus said specifically to them, "Rejoice and be glad, for your reward is great in heaven" (Matt 5: 12). Faith patiently believes and waits.

"Without faith it is impossible to please God because anyone who comes to him must believe that he exists and that he rewards those who earnestly seek him" (Heb 11:6-NIV). Faith looks beyond the physical realm to God. However unnoticed or unappreciated you seem to be, remember, "in the Lord your labor is not in vain" (I Cor 15:58). "Your Father, who sees what is done in secret will reward you" (Matt 6:4,6-NIV) "And if anyone gives even a cup of water to one of these little ones because he is my disciple, I tell you the truth, he will certainly not lose his reward" (Matt 10:42-NIV). So, always be kind to all. "He who is kind to the poor lends to the Lord, and he will reward him for what he has done" (Prov 19:17-NIV).

Humbly hold on to Christ as your gift of "righteousness," (Jer 23:6; 1 Cor 1:30) for apart from Him none of us are sinless in anything we do. In ourselves, we deserve no rewards, only wrath. Yes, He promises us much; but, the greatest reward will be God, Himself. He said, "I am your shield, your exceeding great reward. (Gen 15:1). An unending relationship of love with our triune Creator is both our greatest gift and reward.

Response

I thank you God for showing me _____

_____.

STRATEGY

Follow Jesus today, remembering what He told His disciples about the future day of rewards as seen in **Matt 16:24-27** (Read now)

As I follow Jesus today I will remember _____

_____.

OBEDIENCE (I will statement)

The Spirit is convicting or leading me today to do or stop doing: _____

_____.

PETITIONS (Following your reciting of The Lord's Prayer)

I pray for these scheduled meetings today:

I pray also for these pressing needs of myself, my family, my church, my disciples my world:

CONFESSION and REPENTANCE

I confess these, my sins, with every intention to never repeat them, but rather to live as Jesus would live, by Your enabling grace and Spirit …

*Never confess without a faith that looks to the cross of Christ, where the guilt and penalty of all our sins was paid!

WALK (Think about the following hymn)

Will there be any Stars in Your Crown?

1) I am thinking today of that beautiful land
I shall reach when the sun goeth down;
When through wonderful grace by my Savior I stand,
Will there be any stars in my crown?

Will there be any stars, any stars in my crown,
When at evening the sun goeth down?
When I wake with the blest in the mansions of rest,
Will there be any stars in my crown?

2) In the strength of the Lord let me labor and pray,
Let me watch as a winner of souls;
That bright stars may be mine in the glorious day,
When His praise like the sea-billow rolls.

3) Oh, what joy it will be when His face I behold,
Living gems at His feet to lay down;
It would sweeten my bliss in the city of gold,
Should there be any stars in my crown.
(Eliza E. Hewitt, 1801-1900)

Response

Help me Jesus, to _____

_____.

VICTORY

Memorize *Psalm 19:11*

Be prepared for opposition (spiritual warfare) and expect victory in Jesus' name.

Write down the name (s) of those with whom you shared today _____

_____.

____ Check when the day is completed, never beating yourself up if you did not finish; but, just asking Jesus to help you next day!

10-Day Period 5

Discipleship and our Mastering the Words of Jesus

**Begin by reading Appendix Five – Following Jesus and a Memorized Mastery of His Word

Paul commanded the Romans, living in a city he had never visited, "Do not be conformed to this world, but be transformed by the renewal of your mind" (Rom 12:2). Do you think he would expect the same of us, today? Of course, he would! That is why a daily renewal of mind is necessary to following Jesus today. Thoughts usually precede action. So, you literally become what you think about. Or as already mentioned: our behavior follows our beliefs.

We all know that God is worth thinking about! And His Word is the expression of His actual will for us. So, His words as stated in the Bible, reveal the very way we should live. His Word, in this way, can become our life.

Think of what it would be like if His Church became committed to mastering and living by His Word out of love! That is what He intended and what the Church at her best, down through world Christian history, expected her members to do—master the Word! Holy Spirit help us!

Day Forty-one

God – The Creator

ADORATION

Every rational being longs to fathom WHY we are here and HOW life came into existence. Are we an accident or the result of a plan? An evolutionary accident has no obligation to please a Maker. But if we are given life by another, we owe that One our life. "The sea is his for he made it" (Ps 95:5a). Everyone recognizes that "the builder of a house has greater honor than the house itself" (Heb 3:3). The truly blessed also humbly confess, "For every house is built by someone, but God is the builder of everything" (Heb 3:4). Without an understanding of who made us and why we are here, life is a frustrating puzzle. So, God helps us understand by speaking to us and, in the beginning of His Word, declaring, "In the beginning God created the heavens and the earth." (Gen 1:1). The Bible reveals that a Triune God: Father (Heb1:1-2), Son (John 1:3) and Spirit (Gen 1:2; Ps 104:30) created the universe. We owe Him everything.

God created all things by His infinite wisdom (Prov 3:19), power (Rom 1:20) and goodness (Gen 1:3, I Tim 4:4). He spoke the universe into existence. "By faith we understand that the universe was formed at God's command, so that what was seen was not made out of what was visible" (Heb 11:3; Gen 1; Ps 145:5). We were created in His likeness to live in joy by knowing, exalting and following our Maker. He designed that, alone, to be the path to human happiness. He spoke of those "whom I have created for my glory, whom I formed and made" (Is 43:7; Rom 11:36). It was man's sin (following Satan) that ruined the world (Gen 3; Rom 8:19-21). Sin ended man's fellowship with God (Gen 3:8-10); but God promised to send a Second Adam-Jesus (1 Cor 15:22, 45-47) to restore our fellowship by His perfect life and atoning death (Gen 3:15; Is 53; 2 Cot 5:21; I John 1:1-7). Our joy is achievable only in Jesus, "for all things were created by him and for him" (Col 1:16).

It is obviously both unwise and dangerous to forget one's Maker. Yet we all have a history of forsaking God. "Israel has forgotten his Maker (Hos 8:14). "(Gentiles) exchanged the truth of God for a lie and worshiped and served created things rather than the Creator... (Rom 1:25). Instead of following our cravings (idols) we should, by the Spirit's power, "turn from these worthless things to the living God, who made heaven and earth and sea and everything in them." (Acts 14:15). As God's new creation (2 Cor 5: 17), we should rejoice and be glad about each day as "the day the Lord has made"

(Ps 118:24), with "everything beautiful in its time (Ecc 3:11). Our Creator has "the whole world (and you and me, brother) in His hands!"

Response

I thank you God for showing me _____

STRATEGY

Follow Jesus today, remembering His part in creation as seen in **John 1:1-14** (Read now)

As I follow Jesus today I will remember _____

OBEDIENCE (I will statement)

The Spirit is convicting or leading me today to do or stop doing: _____
_____.

PETITIONS (Following your reciting of The Lord's Prayer)

I pray for these scheduled meetings today:

I pray also for these pressing needs of myself, my family, my church, my disciples my world:

CONFESSION and REPENTANCE

I confess these, my sins, with every intention to never repeat them, but rather to live as Jesus would live, by Your enabling grace and Spirit …

*Never confess without a faith that looks to the cross of Christ, where the guilt and penalty of all our sins was paid!

WALK (Think about the following hymn)

All Creatures of our God and King

1) All creatures of our God and King,
lift up your voice and with us sing
Alleluia! Alleluia!
Thou burning sun with golden beam,
thou silver moon with softer gleam,
O praise Him, O praise Him!
Alleluia! Alleluia! Alleluia!

2) Thou rushing wind that art so strong,
ye clouds that sail in heav'n along,
O praise Him! Alleluia!
Thou rising morn, in praise rejoice,
ye lights of ev'ning find a voice!
O praise Him, O praise Him!
Alleluia! Alleluia! Alleluia!

3) And all ye men of tender heart,
forgiving others, take your part,
O sing ye! Alleluia!
Ye who long pain and sorrow bear,
praise God and on Him cast your care!
O praise Him, O praise Him!
Alleluia! Alleluia! Alleluia!

4) Let all things their Creator bless
and worship Him in humbleness,
O praise Him! Alleluia!
Praise, praise the Father, praise the Son,
and praise the Spirit, Three in One:
O praise Him, O praise Him!
Alleluia! Alleluia! Alleluia!
(Francis of Assisi, 1181-1226 tr. By William H Draper)

Response

Help me Jesus, to _____

_____.

VICTORY

Memorize *1 Peter 4:19*

Be prepared for opposition (spiritual warfare) and expect victory in Jesus' name.

Write down the name (s) of those with whom you shared today and pray for them. _____

_____.

____ Check when the day is completed, never beating yourself up if you did not finish; but, just asking Jesus to help you next day!

Day Forty-two

God – The Rock

ADORATION

Jacob (Gen 49:24), Moses (Deut 32:4-37), Hannah (1 Sam 2:2), David (Ps 18:2; 144:1), Isaiah (Isa 17:10; 44:8), Paul (Rom 9:33; 1 Cor 10:4) and Peter (Acts 4:11; 1 Pet 2:8) are among those who spoke of God as "the Rock." Amazing things are revealed when God employs parts of creation to describe Himself to us. 1. When God is likened to something with which we are familiar, He wants us to know that He is near to us. 2. God wants us to know that whatever good is derived from that object (ie, a rock, a shield, a fountain, etc.), He is that to us perfectly, without limitation and forever! 3. He wants us to remember that as the Creator, every good and perfect gift comes from Him, so all good things in life are designed by Him to draw our minds and hearts to Him in worship and service.

The rocks often were good places in which to hide, formidable strongholds and safe refuges from trouble (2 Sam 22:1-3). A large rock was chosen as a stable foundation, where wise men-built houses (Matt 7:24). Just as one's home is the central place of importance to all the peoples of the earth, so its foundation is an issue of vast significance. Through this imagery, the significance of following Jesus and obeying His Word becomes apparent.

"So, this is what the Sovereign Lord says: See, I lay in Zion a tested stone, a precious cornerstone for a sure foundation; the one who trusts will never be dismayed" (Isa 28:16). Zechariah later adds, "From Judah will come the cornerstone" (Zech 10:4). During the week of His Passion, Jesus quoted the Psalmist (118:22-23) saying, "Have you never read the Scriptures, the stone the builders rejected has become the capstone; the Lord has done this, and it is marvelous in our eyes" (Matt 21:42-43). Paul calls Him the only possible foundation (I Cor 3:11), the "chief cornerstone" (Eph 2:20). Peter quotes Isaiah (8:14) and refers to Jesus as "a chosen and precious cornerstone" to those who believe. "But to those who do not believe," He becomes "a stone that causes men to stumble" (I Pet 2:6-8). Just as where one chooses to build his house will affect all who live there, so what we do with Jesus will determine our entire existence—and affect forever those surrounding us.

Since Jesus is "the rock higher than I" (Ps 61:2), place all your confidence in Him. His promises will not shift under your feet. His Word cannot fail (Matt 24:35). Let Him be your strength. And find in Him your only true refuge from sin's guilt and curse. He is no fool who sings, "Rock of Ages (Is 26:4 - KJV) cleft for me, let me hide myself in thee."

Response

I thank you God for showing me _____

_____.

STRATEGY

Follow Jesus today, remembering how He solemnly ended His Great Sermon on the Mount as seen in **Matt 7:24-29** (Read now)

As I follow Jesus today I will remember _____

_____.

OBEDIENCE (I will statement)

The Spirit is convicting or leading me today to do or stop doing: _____

_____.

PETITIONS (Following your reciting of The Lord's Prayer)

I pray for these scheduled meetings today:

I pray also for these pressing needs of myself, my family, my church, my disciples my world:

CONFESSION and REPENTANCE

I confess these, my sins, with every intention to never repeat them, but rather to live as Jesus would live, by Your enabling grace and Spirit …

*Never confess without a faith that looks to the cross of Christ, where the guilt and penalty of all our sins was paid!

WALK (Think about the following hymn)

Hiding in Thee

1) O safe to the Rock that is higher than I,
My soul in its conflicts and sorrows would fly;
So sinful, so weary, Thine, Thine, would I be;
Thou blest "Rock of Ages," I'm hiding in Thee.

*Hiding in Thee, hiding in Thee,
Thou blest "Rock of Ages,"
I'm hiding in Thee.*

2) In the calm of the noontide, in sorrow's lone hour,
In times when temptation casts o'er me its power;
In the tempests of life, on its wide, heaving sea,
Thou blest "Rock of Ages," I'm hiding in Thee.

(3) How oft in the conflict, when pressed by the foe,
I have fled to my refuge and breathed out my woe;
How often, when trials like sea billows roll,
Have I hidden in Thee, O Thou Rock of my soul.
(William O Cushing, 1823-1902)

Response

Help me Jesus, to _____

_____.

VICTORY

Memorize *Psalm 18:2*

Be prepared for opposition (spiritual warfare) and expect victory in Jesus' name.
Write down the name (s) of those with whom you shared today _____

_____.

_____ Check when the day is completed, never beating yourself up if you did not finish; but, just asking Jesus to help you next day!

Day Forty-three

God – The Near One

ADORATION

We often act strangely when we are alone. We can do things that are evil, completely selfish, self-destructive and delusional when no one is around us. So, God gives us companions in life to keep us from ourselves, from our own craziness. And He often reminds us of His close presence. "The eyes of the Lord are everywhere, keeping watch on the evil and the good" (Prov 15:3). His closeness often saves us. When we neither sense His presence nor want Him nearby, He is still there—and we are the better off for it. "For in him we live and move and have our being" (Acts 17:28a).

Those who are wise will want Him near. They will not only want His life-giving presence, they will want His loving presence—His fellowship. Though "he is not far from each one of us" (Acts 17:27), there is a special closeness that He reveals and offers to those who come near to Him through Christ in love. To those who run to Him rather than running away from Him. To those who say, "Those who are far from you will perish. ...But as for me, it is good to be near God. I have made the Sovereign Lord my refuge; I will tell of all your deeds" (Ps 73:27-28).

Think of the benefits of God's nearness! First, we are given peace when God comes near us and pardons us through Christ. We can then say, "He who vindicates me is near. Who then will bring charges against me? Let us face each other!" (Isa 50:8). Our sins are all covered. The broken Law has been paid for on the cross for us. Its condemning power is finished! From that foundation, unbelievable courage can flow from us. "The following night the Lord stood near to Paul and said, 'Take courage! As you have testified about me in Jerusalem, so you must also testify in Rome'" (Acts 23:11). And Jeremiah attested, "You came near when I called you, and you said, 'Do not fear'" (Lam 3:57). "Those who devise wicked schemes are near...Yet you are near, O Lord (Ps 119:151a).

Another benefit of God's nearness is prayer. "What other nation is so great as to have their gods near them the way the Lord our God is near us whenever we pray to him?" (Deut 4:7). "The Lord is near to all who call on him, to all who call on him in truth" (Ps 145:18). He promises us, "Come near to God and he will come near to you" (James 4:8a).

Also, the presence of the Lord means we do not need to avenge ourselves. We can be gentle peacemakers, as Paul said, "Let your gentleness be evident to all. The Lord is near" (Phil. 4:5). Live in His presence. Love His presence. It is your life. "Seek the Lord while he may be found; call on him while he is near" (Isa 55:6).

Lastly, when you are in the process of making disciples, Jesus extends a most comforting and empowering promise: "And surely, I am with you, to the very end of the age" (Matt 28:20)!

There are many who think that the truth of God's nearness (omnipresence) is the most practically helpful aspect of God's character. Live in the truth that He is always with us!

Response

I thank you God for showing me _____

_____.

STRATEGY

Follow Jesus today, remembering how Jesus wants to be near and help us as seen in His great prayer in **John 17:20-26** (Read now)

As I follow Jesus today I will remember _____

_____.

OBEDIENCE (I will statement)

The Spirit is convicting or leading me today to do or stop doing:
_____

_____.

PETITIONS (Following your reciting of The Lord's Prayer)

I pray for these scheduled meetings today:

I pray also for these pressing needs of myself, my family, my church, my disciples my world:

CONFESSION and REPENTANCE

I confess these, my sins, with every intention to never repeat them, but rather to live as Jesus would live, by Your enabling grace and Spirit ...

*Never confess without a faith that looks to the cross of Christ, where the guilt and penalty of all our sins was paid!

WALK (Think about the following hymn)

Nearer Still Nearer

1) Nearer, still nearer, close to Thy heart,
Draw me, my Savior—so precious Thou art!
Fold me, oh, fold me close to Thy breast;
Shelter me safe in that "haven of rest";
Shelter me safe in that "haven of rest."

2) Nearer, still nearer, nothing I bring,
Naught as an off'ring to Jesus, my King;
Only my sinful, now contrite heart,
Grant me the cleansing Thy blood doth impart;
Grant me the cleansing Thy blood doth impart.

3) Nearer, still nearer, Lord, to be Thine!
Sin, with its follies, I gladly resign,
All of its pleasures, pomp and its pride,
Give me but Jesus, my Lord crucified;
Give me but Jesus, my Lord crucified.

4) Nearer, still nearer, while life shall last,
Till safe in glory my anchor is cast;
Through endless ages ever to be
Nearer, my Savior, still nearer to Thee;
Nearer, my Savior, still nearer to Thee!
(Lelia Morris, 1862-1929)

Response

Help me Jesus, to _____

_____.

VICTORY

Memorize *Psalm 22:11*

Be prepared for opposition (spiritual warfare) and expect victory in Jesus' name.

Write down the name (s) of those with whom you shared today _____
_____.

_____ Check when the day is completed, never beating yourself up if you did not finish; but, just asking Jesus to help you next day!

Day Forty-four

God – The First One

ADORATION

Most cultures have their games in which those who come in first are declared 'the winners' and given some award for their accomplishment. This drive to win is very human, from early age, children who know an answer love to get their hands up first and be called on to speak. The valedictorian is the first in the class. And the most accomplished violinists and cellists in an orchestra are given, "the first chairs." Honor accompanies being first.

Unfortunately, it is also a very human thing to get so focused on coming in first, that we forget who really is first and foremost in life.

"This is what the Lord says ... I am the first and I am the last; apart from me there is no God" (Isa 44:6). "I am the Alpha and the Omega, the First and the Last, the Beginning and the End." (Rev 22:13; 21:6). When anything is ever placed before God in our minds or lives, an awful sin has occurred. The honor due to God, alone, has been stolen from Him and wrongly transferred to another. This is idolatry and we are often guilty of it.

"Listen to me, O Jacob, Israel whom I have called: I am he; I am the first and the last. My own hand laid the foundations of the earth, and my right hand spread out the heavens..." (Isa 48:12-13). He is the Creator and Sustainer of all life. He is first. "In the beginning God created the heavens and the earth." (Gen 1:1). Every human, as His created being, is at his best only when acknowledging God and giving Him the love and honor He deserves. It is foolishness to do otherwise, for whatever momentary gain might seem to come by eclipsing God with someone or something else, such misguided devotion to another ends up in futility. "I am the Lord; that is my name! I will not give my glory to another or my praise to idols" (Isa 42:8).

This God is so great and glorious that whenever a human being sees Him, he humbles himself and falls before Him in a natural, holy and reverent fear. "The fear of the Lord is the beginning of knowledge" (Prov 1:7 – wisdom – 9:10).

Since He is first, put Him first. As Jesus taught, "But seek first his kingdom and his righteousness and all these things will be given you as well" (Matt 6:33). Do not give yourself to an endeavor that opposes Him or His Word. "Ahab asked Jehoshaphat, 'Will you go with me to fight against Ramoth Gilead?'... Jehoshaphat replied...'first seek the counsel of the Lord." (1 Kgs 22:4-5).

And since He is a God of love, love Him first and foremost. "When I saw him. I fell at his feet as though dead. Then he placed his right hand on me and said, 'Do not be afraid. I am the First and the Last. I am the Living One: I was dead and behold I am alive forever and ever! And I hold the keys of death and of Hades,'" (Rev 1:17-18). "We love because he first loved us" (I John 4:19). Run for His glory, not your own. Paul said, "Do you not know that in a race all the runners run, but only one gets the prize? Run in such a way as to get the prize" (1 Cor 9:24). Keep God first and foremost in your life and you will win through the grace of His Son!

Response

I thank you God for showing me _____

_____.

STRATEGY

Follow Jesus today, remembering that, being God, He could tell others what was the absolutely first and most important thing to God, as seen in **Matt 22:34-40** (Read now)

As I follow Jesus today I will remember _____

_____.

OBEDIENCE (I will statement)

The Spirit is convicting or leading me today to do or stop doing: _____

_____

PETITIONS (Following your reciting of The Lord's Prayer)

I pray for these scheduled meetings today:

I pray also for these pressing needs of myself, my family, my church, my disciples my world:

CONFESSION and REPENTANCE

I confess these, my sins, with every intention to never repeat them, but rather to live as Jesus would live, by Your enabling grace and Spirit ...

*Never confess without a faith that looks to the cross of Christ, where the guilt and penalty of all our sins was paid!

WALK (Think about the following hymn)

Jesus- Be the Center (Vineyard)

Jesus, be the centre
Be my source, be my light
Jesus

Jesus, be the centre
Be my hope, be my song
Jesus

Be the fire in my heart
Be the wind in these sails
Be the reason that I live
Jesus, Jesus

Jesus, be my vision
Be my path, be my guide
Jesus

Jesus, be the centre
Be my source, be my light
Jesus

Be my source, be my light
Jesus, Jesus
(Michael Frye, 1999)

Response

Help me Jesus, to _____

_____.

VICTORY

Memorize *Matthew 6:33*

Be prepared for opposition (spiritual warfare) and expect victory in Jesus' name.

Write down the name (s) of those with whom you shared today _____
_____.

____ Check when the day is completed, never beating yourself up if you did not finish; but, just asking Jesus to help you next day!

Day Forty-five

God – The Teacher

ADORATION

Even though we all like to be acknowledged for what we have learned, it is an insult to be called a Know-It-All, for no one truly is that brilliant. Only God knows all. Only God is the true Teacher. As the Psalmist declared, "Does he who teaches man lack knowledge? The Lord knows the thoughts of man; he knows that they are futile" (Ps 94:10b-11).

If we do not like to be called Know-it-Alls, why do we live as if we have so little need of God's instruction? Why do we seek it so little? The truth is, we proudly and selfishly think our thoughts and ways are best. Then God responds in mercy by teaching us the foolishness of our own thoughts, just as He did long ago. "He humbled you, causing you to hunger and then feeding you manna ... to teach you that man does not live on bread alone but on every word that comes from the mouth of the Lord" (Deut 8:3).

He told Moses, "Now go; I will help you speak and will teach you what to say" (Ex 4:12). And later, Moses prayed, "If you are pleased with me, teach me your ways so I may know you and continue to find favor with you. Remember that this nation is your people. The Lord replied, My Presence will go with you, and I will give you rest" (Ex 33:13-14). Even Moses, trained as he was in all the wisdom of Egypt, waited on God like a child, as one who did not know which way to go. And God taught him. Let His Spirit teach you. That is one of His special assignments in your life (See John 14:26; 1 John 2:27).

Mary "sat at the Lord's feet listening to what he said. But Martha was distracted by all the preparations that had to be made. She ... asked, 'Lord, don't you care that my sister has left me to do the work by myself? Tell her to help me!' 'Martha, Martha,' the Lord answered, 'you are worried and upset about many things, but only one thing is needed. Mary has chosen what is better, and it will not be taken away from her." (Luke 10:39-42).

We do not want to sit before the Lord when consumed with our own agenda. We do not want to be taught by His Spirit when we think we know the way to go. How often does pride or worries and cares rob us from time with God. Why do we spend so little time with Jesus? Have we forgotten that He is The Teacher and that His Word is absolute, relevant truth. "You call me 'Teacher' and 'Lord,' and rightly so, for that is what I am. Now that I, your Lord and Teacher, have washed your feet, you also should wash one another's feet." (John 13:13-14).

Maybe we simply do not like what He says. Like, Wash another's feet! Yes, for humbly serving others is best for us all. Let Him have His right as your Teacher. He said, "Nor are you to be called, 'teacher,' for you have one Teacher, the Christ" (Matt 23:10-11). All true disciples reside or abide in His teaching. "If you abide in my word, you are truly my disciples, and you will know the truth, and the truth will set you free" (John 8:31-32-ESV) His teaching frees us! Respond quickly and unreservedly to His invitation. "Take my yoke upon you and learn from me...and you will find rest for your souls" (Matt 11:29). Rest in Him and His teaching today! Let the Spirit be your ever-present Teacher.

Response

I thank you God for showing me _____

_____.

STRATEGY

Follow Jesus today, remembering what He told his disciples about who is the Teacher as seen in **Matt 23:1-12** (Read now)

As I follow Jesus today I will remember _____

_____.

OBEDIENCE (I will statement)

The Spirit is convicting or leading me today to do or stop doing: _____

_____

PETITIONS (Following your reciting of The Lord's Prayer)

I pray for these scheduled meetings today:

I pray also for these pressing needs of myself, my family, my church, my disciples my world:

CONFESSION and REPENTANCE

I confess these, my sins, with every intention to never repeat them, but rather to live as Jesus would live, by Your enabling grace and Spirit …

*Never confess without a faith that looks to the cross of Christ, where the guilt and penalty of all our sins was paid!

WALK (Think about the following hymn)

Teach Me thy Way, O Lord

(1) Teach me Thy way, O Lord, teach me Thy way!
Thy guiding grace afford, teach me Thy way!
Help me to walk aright, more by faith, less by sight;
Lead me with heav'nly light, teach me Thy way!

(2) When I am sad at heart, teach me Thy way!
When earthly joys depart, teach me Thy way!
In hours of loneliness, in times of dire distress,
In failure or success, teach me Thy way!

(3) When doubts and fears arise, teach me Thy way!
When storms o'erspread the skies, teach me Thy way!
Shine through the cloud and rain, through sorrow, toil, and pain;
Make Thou my pathway plain, teach me Thy way!

(4) Long as my life shall last, teach me Thy way!
Where'er my lot be cast, teach me Thy way!
Until the race is run, until the journey's done,
Until the crown is won, teach me Thy way!
(Benjamin M Ramsey, 1849-1923)

Response

Help me Jesus, to _____

_____.

VICTORY

Memorize *John 14:23*

Be prepared for opposition (spiritual warfare) and expect victory in Jesus' name.

Write down the name (s) of those with whom you shared today _____
_____.

____ Check when the day is completed, never beating yourself up if you did not finish; but, just asking Jesus to help you next day!

Day Forty-six

God – The Wise One

ADORATION

The Scriptures declare that the triune God: Father (Rev 7:12), Son (1 Cor 1:30) and Spirit (Isa 11:2), is "wonderful in counsel and magnificent in wisdom" (Isa 28:29). In fact, as with all of God's characteristics, He is infinite or limitless in His wisdom. As Paul declared, "Oh, the depth of the riches of the wisdom and the knowledge of God! How unsearchable his judgments and his ways beyond tracing out!" (Rom. 11:33).

Wisdom involves choosing the best way to accomplish something. Knowledge is knowing facts or reality. Wisdom is acting on those facts in the best possible way. The opposite of wisdom is folly. Many of the Proverbs reveal the distinction between the wise and the foolish. "The fear of the Lord is the beginning of knowledge, but fools despise wisdom and discipline" (Prov. 1:7). So, when God is affirmed to be wise, it is declared that all He is and does--His eternal plan and the execution of that plan--could not be improved on!

We do not often understand and appreciate the wisdom of God's ways because they are just that--God's ways and not ours. The world in its wisdom does not know God or His ways (1 Cor. 1:21). "For my thoughts are not your thoughts, neither are your ways my ways, declares the Lord. As the heavens are higher than the earth, so are my ways higher than your ways and my thoughts than your thoughts" (Isa 5 5:8-9). It is for this reason that we need to seek God for the gift of His wisdom, "For the Lord gives wisdom" (Prov. 2:6). "If any of you lacks wisdom, he should ask of God, who gives generously to all without finding fault, and it will be given to him" (James 1:5). Peace can come only when we trust that the events of this world and our life are governed by "the only wise God" (Rom 16:27).

Since God is all-wise, there is purpose and order in the universe. "But God made the earth by his power; he founded the world by his wisdom" (Jer 10:12). Time will ultimately reveal the wisdom of God's plan through the ages. The way that everything has been carefully selected to achieve His good purposes (Gen 50:20; 1 Pet 1:7). Since He is all-wise, the best strategy in life is to follow Him. As He said, "I am the Lord your God, who teaches you what is best for you" (Isa 48:17). And whenever we do not understand what the wise path is, we need but look to Jesus, "in whom is hidden all the treasures of wisdom and knowledge" (Col 2:3). While we abide in Him, there is no need for worry or fear. He is guiding us and He both knows what He is doing and is always in control. Trust Him!

Response

I thank you God for showing me _____

_____.

STRATEGY

Follow Jesus today, remembering what Paul said about our wisdom coming only through Jesus as seen in **1 Corinthians 1:26-31** (Read now)

As I follow Jesus today I will remember _____

_____.

OBEDIENCE (I will statement)

The Spirit is convicting or leading me today to do or stop doing: _____

_____.

PETITIONS (Following your reciting of The Lord's Prayer)

I pray for these scheduled meetings today:

I pray also for these pressing needs of myself, my family, my church, my disciples my world:

CONFESSION and REPENTANCE

I confess these, my sins, with every intention to never repeat them, but rather to live as Jesus would live, by Your enabling grace and Spirit …

*Never confess without a faith that looks to the cross of Christ, where the guilt and penalty of all our sins was paid!

WALK (Think about the following hymn)

Immortal, Invisible, God Only Wise

(1) Immortal, invisible, God only wise,
In light inaccessible, hid from our eyes,
Most blessed, most glorious, the Ancient of Days,
Almighty, victorious, Thy great name we praise.

(2) Unresting, unhasting, and silent as light,
Nor wanting, nor wasting, Thou rulest in might;
Thy justice, like mountains, high soaring above
Thy clouds, which are fountains of goodness and love.

(3) To all, life Thou givest, to both great and small;
In all life Thou livest, the true life of all;
We blossom and flourish as leaves on the tree,
And wither and perish—but naught changeth Thee.

(4) Great Father of glory, pure Father of light,
Thine angels adore Thee, all veiling their sight;
All praise we would render; oh, help us to see
'Tis only the splendor of light hideth Thee.
(Walter C Smith, 1824-1908)

Response

Help me Jesus, to _____

_____.

VICTORY

Memorize *James 1:5*

Be prepared for opposition (spiritual warfare) and expect victory in Jesus' name.

Write down the name (s) of those with whom you shared today and pray for them! _____

____ Check when the day is completed, never beating yourself up if you did not finish; but, just asking Jesus to help you next day!

Day Forty-Seven

God – The Word

ADORATION

Why is "a man only as good as his word"? When we carefully speak, our words convey the essence of what we are thinking. When we emotionally speak, those words express what we are deeply feeling. So, our words reveal our entire being. We enjoy the unique gift among earthly creatures to ably express ourselves in words. Of course, even words have their limits. Sometimes silence says more about what we are thinking and feeling than would speech. When God revealed Himself as "the Word," all this and much more was meant (See Isa 55:11; Rev 19:13).

"In the beginning was the Word, and the Word was with God, and the Word was God" (John 1: 1). All that God ever wanted to reveal of Himself to humankind, Jesus revealed. God's thoughts, words, passions and actions were perfectly expressed through Jesus, the eternal Word. So, Jesus is for God what words are for us. "The Son is the radiance of God's glory, and the exact representation of his being, sustaining all things by his powerful word" (Heb 1:3). When John later reflected on his relationship with Jesus, he said, "...this we proclaim concerning the Word of life. The life appeared, and we have seen it and testify to it, and we proclaim to you the eternal life which was with the Father and has appeared to us" (1 John 1:1). God wanted to give life, eternal life, to fallen sinners—so Jesus, the Word of God, became and spoke that life. Jesus claimed, "The Spirit gives life; the flesh counts for nothing. The words I have spoken to you are spirit and they are Life" (John 6:63). Is He your life? Is His Word your favorite food?

God's Word reveals God's heart and will. It is medicine for every affliction and light for each step. When we allow it in, intimately touching our secret sins and deepest needs, we invite God, Himself to heal and lead us. "For the word of God is living and active and sharper than any double-edged sword, it penetrates even to dividing soul and spirit, joints and marrow; it judges the thoughts and attitudes of the heart. Nothing in all creation is hidden from God's sight. Everything is uncovered and laid bare before the eyes of him to whom we must give account." (Heb 4:12- 13). Don't be afraid of the Bible—it is the Word of the Word, Jesus. And He is unbelievably good. "The Word became flesh...full of grace and truth" (John 1214). Christ and His Word will set you apart and set you free (John 17:17; 8:31-32). Let Christ bless others through you. "Let the word of Christ dwell in you richly as you teach and admonish one another...." (Col 3:16). Don't just learn the Word, live it! "...you are strong, and the word of God lives in you, and you have overcome the evil one." (1 John 2:15). Listen to and follow Jesus as He followed the word and will of His Father. This is also how earthly fathers want their children to follow them--. literally, knowledgeably, quickly and confidently.

Response

I thank you God for showing me _____

_____.

STRATEGY

Follow Jesus today, remembering what He said about the absolute importance of the fulfillment of God's Word as stated in the Old Testament as seen in **Matt 13:11-17** (Read now)

As I follow Jesus today I will remember _____

_____.

OBEDIENCE (I will statement)

The Spirit is convicting or leading me today to do or stop doing: _____

_____.

PETITIONS (Following your reciting of The Lord's Prayer)

I pray for these scheduled meetings today:

I pray also for these pressing needs of myself, my family, my church, my disciples my world:

CONFESSION and REPENTANCE

I confess these, my sins, with every intention to never repeat them, but rather to live as Jesus would live, by Your enabling grace and Spirit ...

*Never confess without a faith that looks to the cross of Christ, where the guilt and penalty of all our sins was paid!

WALK (Think about the following hymn)

Holy Bible Book Divine

1) Holy Bible, Book divine,
Precious treasure, thou art mine:
Mine to tell me whence I came;
Mine to teach me what I am.

2) Mine to chide me when I rove,
Mine to show a Savior's love;
Mine thou art to guide and guard;
Mine to punish or reward.

3) Mine to comfort in distress,
Suffering in this wilderness;
Mine to show by living faith,
We can triumph over death.

4) Mine to tell of joys to come,
And the rebel sinner's doom:
O thou holy book divine,
Precious treasure thou art mine.
(John Burton, 1773-1822)

Response

Help me Jesus, to _____

_____.

VICTORY

Memorize *John 1:14*

Be prepared for opposition (spiritual warfare) and expect victory in Jesus' name.

Write down the name (s) of those with whom you shared today _____
_____.

____ Check when the day is completed, never beating yourself up if you did not finish; but, just asking Jesus to help you next day!

Day Forty-eight

God – The Life

ADORATION

When speaking of something very serious, we say, "It's a matter of life and death." Since life and death are truly important, it is good for us to know all that we can know about them. If life ultimately is in our hands, then we owe no higher allegiance to any other than to ourselves. But, if someone else is the giver and preserver of our life, then we had better know Him well. God is the center (Gen 1:1), the giver of life. "The Lord formed the man from the dust of the ground and breathed into his nostrils the breath of life, and the man became a living being" (Gen 2:7). And then what? Did He withdraw and let humans search and find the meaning and fullness of life in themselves or in some other part of creation?

Not on your life! God said, "…I have set before you death and life … now choose life … For the Lord is your life" (Deut 30:19-20). The Life-giver must remain central for life to yield its fullest meaning and deepest satisfaction. "You have made known to me the path of life; you will fill me with joy in your presence" (Ps 16:11). Jeremiah rightly concluded, "I know, O Lord, that a man's life is not his own; it is not for man to direct his steps" (Jer 10:23). And David, too "For with you is the fountain of life" (Ps 36:9). We drink from all other wells only to grow thirsty again; but Jesus promised, "whoever drinks of the water I give, will never thirst. Indeed, the water I give will become in him a spring of water welling up to eternal life." Believe and drink!

Jesus claimed, 1 am the…life" (John 14:6). "For as the Father has life in himself, so he has granted the Son to have life in himself" (John 5:26). And, so He boldly asserted, "I have come that they may have life; and have it to the full" (John 10:10). Well, does He really deliver what He promised— life to those who follow Him?

Listen to the answer of those who first followed Him. John said, "In him was life and that life was the light of men" (John 1:4). They had fellowship with him and discovered that "He is the true God and eternal life" (1 John 1:1-4; 5:20). And they were willing to stake their very lives and eternal destiny on His being God, for they had discovered for themselves what David had much earlier said of Him, "your love is better than life" (Ps 63:3). So, to live and die for God is better than to live apart from Him.

Even death is transformed by Jesus, who is "the resurrection and the life" (John 11:25). He turns death from a dark event of horror into a door to eternal joy. So, in learning more from Jesus, you are truly learning how to live and what life is all about as well as how to best prepare for death! In walking with Him by faith, you can have life to the full NOW.

Response

I thank you God for showing me _____

_____.

STRATEGY

Follow Jesus today, realizing how He taught that there was no real life apart from Him as seen in **John 15:1-7** (Read now)

As I follow Jesus today I will remember _____

_____.

OBEDIENCE (I will statement)

The Spirit is convicting or leading me today to do or stop doing: _____

_____.

PETITIONS (Following your reciting of The Lord's Prayer)

I pray for these scheduled meetings today:

I pray also for these pressing needs of myself, my family, my church, my disciples my world:

CONFESSION and REPENTANCE

I confess these, my sins, with every intention to never repeat them, but rather to live as Jesus would live, by Your enabling grace and Spirit …

*Never confess without a faith that looks to the cross of Christ, where the guilt and penalty of all our sins was paid!

WALK (Think about the following hymn)

Look and Live!

1) I've a message from the Lord, hallelujah!
This message unto you I'll give,
'Tis recorded in His word, hallelujah!
It is only that you "look and live."

*"Look and live," my brother, live,
Look to Jesus now, and live;
'Tis recorded in His word, hallelujah!
It is only that you "look and live."*

2) I've a message full of love, hallelujah!
A message, O my friend, for you,
'Tis a message from above, hallelujah!
Jesus said it, and I know 'tis true.

3) Life is offered unto you, hallelujah!
Eternal life thy soul shall have,
If you'll only look to Him, hallelujah!
Look to Jesus who alone can save.

4) I will tell you how I came, hallelujah!
To Jesus when He made me whole—
'Twas believing on His name, hallelujah!
I trusted and He saved my soul.
(William A Ogden, 1841-1897)

Response

Help me Jesus, to _____

_____.

VICTORY

Memorize *Colossians 3:4*

Be prepared for opposition (spiritual warfare) and expect victory in Jesus' name.

Write down the name (s) of those with whom you shared today _____
_____.

____ Check when the day is completed, never beating yourself up if you did not finish; but, just asking Jesus to help you next day!

Day Forty-nine

God – The Enjoyed One

ADORATION

From a very early age, many Reformed Christians are taught the answer to Shorter Catechism Q1 - What is the chief end of man? A. "Man's chief end is to glorify God and to enjoy him forever." The enjoyment of God is a goal of our existence. CS Lewis wrote that we are far too serious, too pressured, too bothered. God wants us to dance. He is not a cosmic Killjoy, but a Delight. We will be surprised to find that JOY is "the business of heaven." "You ...will fill me with joy in your presence, with eternal pleasures at your right hand" (Ps 16:11).

"Splendor and majesty are before him; strength and joy in his dwelling place" (1 Chron 16:27). The Psalms often portray a believer's troubled life. A life that is full of trials. Yet there is a message of joy throughout them. "Shout with joy to God all the earth!" (Ps 66:1). "Come, let us sing for joy to the Lord" (Ps 95:1a). "Surely you have...made him glad about the joy of your presence" (Ps 21:6b).

How can sinners be joyful in the presence of a holy God? The psalmist knew. "Then will I go to the altar of God, to God, my joy and my delight" (Ps 43:4a). The altar provides the way to joy. The victim lain on it pays for sin. His death is our death. And all Old Testament sacrifices offered on the altar foreshadowed the coming of Christ, "the Lamb of God, who takes away the sin of the world" (John 1:29). On the day before He died, Jesus said, "I have told you this so that my joy may be in you and that your joy may be complete" (John 15:11). Later He said, "Until now you have not asked for anything in my name. Ask and you will receive, and your joy will be complete" (John 16:24). You can dance before God in Christ! By living in His name.

God asked Job, "Where were you...while the morning stars sang together, and all the angels shouted for joy?" (Job 38:7). Creation was a time of singing. Sin strangled the song. Salvation restores it to our hearts again. And when Christ returns, joy is not far behind. "They will sing for joy before the Lord, for he comes to judge the earth" (1 Chron 16:33b). Even His judgment, the perfect expression of His justice, will bring relief and rejoicing. The Day when all wrongs are overturned, and all injustice is punished. Then the sighs of all creation will be changed into songs once again.

So now we can say, "Though the fig tree does not bud and there are no grapes on the vine...and no cattle in the stalls, yet I will rejoice in the Lord, I will be joyful in God my Savior." (Hab 3:17-12). Our day is coming! Our worship embraces it now by faith. So, Israel was taught on days of festive worship, "Do not grieve for the joy of the Lord is your strength" (Neh 8:10b). Rejoice in the Lord, come what may, and you will see how strong and true joy is. After being whipped, "Paul and Silas were...singing hymns to God and the other prisoners were listening to them." Following the earthquake, "the jailer...rushed in and fell trembling...and asked, Sirs, what must I do to be saved?" (Acts 16:25-30). An earthquake miraculously opened the door of the prison and joy opened the door of the jailer's heart. Joy is your strength. "Rejoice in the Lord always. I will say it again: Rejoice!" (Phil. 4:4).

Response

I thank you God for showing me _____

_____.

STRATEGY

Follow Jesus today, remembering what He told His disciples about what fills heaven with JOY right now as seen in **Luke 15:1-10** (Read now)

As I follow Jesus today I will remember _____

_____.

OBEDIENCE (I will statement)

The Spirit is convicting or leading me today to do or stop doing:
_____

_____.

PETITIONS (Following your reciting of The Lord's Prayer)

I pray for these scheduled meetings today:

I pray also for these pressing needs of myself, my family, my church, my disciples my world:

CONFESSION and REPENTANCE

I confess these, my sins, with every intention to never repeat them, but rather to live as Jesus would live, by Your enabling grace and Spirit …

*Never confess without a faith that looks to the cross of Christ, where the guilt and penalty of all our sins was paid!

WALK (Think about the following hymn):

Rejoice Ye Pure in Heart

1) Rejoice, O pure in heart,
rejoice, give thanks, and sing;
your festal banner wave on high,
the cross of Christ your King.

Rejoice, rejoice, rejoice, give thanks, and sing!

2) Bright youth and snow-crowned age,
both men and women, raise
on high your free, exulting song,
declare God's wondrous praise.

3) Still lift your standard high,
still chanting as you go,
from youth to age, by night and day,
in gladness and in woe.

4) At last the march shall end;
the wearied ones shall rest,
the pilgrims reach their home at last,
Jerusalem the blest.

5) Praise God, who reigns on high,
the Lord whom we adore:
the Father, Son, and Holy Ghost,
one God forevermore.
(Edward H Plumptre, 1821-1891)

Response

Help me Jesus, to _____

_____.

VICTORY

Memorize *1 Thessalonians 5:16*

Be prepared for opposition (spiritual warfare) and expect victory in Jesus' name.

Write down the name (s) of those with whom you shared today and pray for them_____

_____.

____ Check when the day is completed, never beating yourself up if you did not finish; but, just asking Jesus to help you next day!

Day Fifty

God – The Liberator

ADORATION

We celebrate July the 4th as Independence Day, remembering our national deliverance from an oppressive king. Our Liberty Bell has inscribed on it, "proclaim liberty throughout the land to all its inhabitants" (Lev 25:10). America's Founding Fathers declared liberty as an inalienable human right even though it took time before they applied it to Black slaves. They called God the Author of Liberty. He is that.

"The Lord sets prisoners free" (Ps 146:7). Sin and Satan are the great enslavers (John 8:34; 2 Tim 2:26). Since humanity's Fall into sin, we all struggle against sin's bondage. Even "the creation was subjected to frustration" under which it "groans" until it is "liberated from its bondage to decay" (Rom 8:19-22). Only God can free our world. The great illustration of His liberating power occurred when the children of Israel "groaned in their slavery" (Ex 2:23), were heard by God who sent Moses saying, "I am the Lord and I will bring you out from under the yoke of the Egyptians. I will free you from being slaves to them, and I will redeem you with…mighty acts of judgment. 1 will take you as my own people, and I will be your God" (Ex 6:6-7).

They cried out to God and they were delivered (Ps 8 1:5-7). This is the only pattern successfully followed by all who struggle with any bondage. We may be enslaved by anguish (Ps 25:17) or entrapped by people or passions (Ps 31:10); but when with sincerity and humility we cry out to God, He delivers! "In my anguish I cried to the Lord, and he answered by setting me free" (Ps 118:5; Rom 6:18-22).

When God frees us, He wants us freely and joyfully to extend liberty to others. He told Israel to free their slaves every 7th year and have a great Year of Jubilee every 50th year (Lev 25: 10. "Do not consider it a hardship to set your servant free… and I will bless you in everything you do" (Deut 15: 12-18). God's children show a likeness to their Father and Redeemer when they fight for those oppressed by sin, injustice and poverty. His rule has always been "Freely you have received, freely give" (Matt 10:8b). No one can truly free others except Jesus Christ and His gospel (John 8:32,36) as promised in ages past (Isa 42:7; 49:9; 58:6; 61:1) and fulfilled in His coming (Lk 4: 18-21; Heb 2:15). He makes us happy servants, under a truly pleasant yoke (Matt 11:28-30; Ps 116:16). "Live as free men…as servants of God" (1 Pet 2:16). Spend your days in the joyous freedom Christ lived and died to give you—freely loving & serving Him (Gal 5:1-6). There is no reason for grumpy old men (or women) in His Kingdom!

Response

I thank you God for showing me _____

_____.

STRATEGY

Follow Jesus today, remembering what He declared about Himself as seen in **Luke 4:14-21** (Read now)

As I follow Jesus today I will remember _____

OBEDIENCE (I will statement)

The Spirit is convicting or leading me today to do or stop doing: _____

_____.

PETITIONS (Following your reciting of The Lord's Prayer)

I pray for these scheduled meetings today:

I pray also for these pressing needs of myself, my family, my church, my disciples my world:

CONFESSION and REPENTANCE

I confess these, my sins, with every intention to never repeat them, but rather to live as Jesus would live, by Your enabling grace and Spirit …

*Never confess without a faith that looks to the cross of Christ, where the guilt and penalty of all our sins was paid!

WALK (Think about the following praise song)

Freely, Freely

He said freely freely
You have received
Freely freely give
Go in My name
And because you believe
Others will know that I live

1) God forgave my sin in Jesus' name
I've been born again in Jesus' name
And in Jesus' name I come to you
To share His love as He told me to

2) All pow'r is giv'n in Jesus' name
In earth and heav'n in Jesus' name
And in Jesus' name I come to you
To share His pow'r as He told me to

Response

Help me Jesus, to _____

_____.

VICTORY

Memorize *Romans 6:18*

Be prepared for opposition (spiritual warfare) and expect victory in Jesus' name.

Write down the name (s) of those with whom you shared today _____

_____.

_____ Check when the day is completed, never beating yourself up if you did not finish; but, just asking Jesus to help you next day!

10-Day Period 6

Discipleship and our Understanding the Teaching of Jesus

**Begin by reading Appendix Six – Following Jesus' Teaching concerning the Old Testament Law

In this section, you will have the opportunity to enroll in the School of Jesus. Our ideas of education are so different today from the ideas of the first disciples of Jesus. As noted in Appendix 6, to be a devoted disciple of a rabbi meant to totally understand and endorse those teachings that distinguished him from all other rabbis. Remember that Jesus taught that God's rule, His Kingdom, was to be embraced from the heart. Christ's Law was to be cherished and followed within as well as outwardly. And if His words are truly cherished, they will be noticeably loved. We love Christ's commands simply because we love Him and everything about Him, including His words. Very few Christians seem to hunger and thirst for righteousness today. Few approach Jesus' rules with the same enthusiasm as the Psalmist of old did, "as the deer pants for streams of water, so my soul pants for you, O God" (Ps 42:1). May this period see a notable upgrade in your appreciation and love of God and His Word!

Day Fifty-one

The Glory of God

ADORATION

"For from him and through him and to him are all things. To him be glory forever! Amen!" (Rom 11:36). In this verse, the world's most important fact is followed by its most important duty. The Creator should be put first by His creatures. Only when God is given the center of our life, do we really begin to live. Whenever we view life without a God-is-in-this consciousness, we create a world that does not exist. Like a troubled man who turns to the bottle to escape his problems and pain. Eventually reality hits again with a devastating effect. Trying to make sense of any part of life while ignoring God is as foolish and futile as a man blind from birth trying to convince you that a sunset is neither significant nor beautiful. Yet the culture around us, like the blind man, demands that we not be too religious because it wants to forget God and go on its own merry way. No wonder so many in that world go to bed sick at heart.

To glorify God is to promote and emphasize Him. Most of us spend our days foolishly longing and living for our own glory and advancement, as if we were life's main character. Paul rightly focused on life's one worthy goal when he wrote, "So whether you eat or drink or whatever you do, do it all for the glory of God" (1 Cor 10:31). Why did he speak of such mundane matters as food and drink in the same sentence as God?

Because there is no single moment of our life— no stop at McDonald's or at a drinking fountain— during which God is either absent or unimportant. "In him we live and move and have our being" (Acts 17:28). So, we should be concerned with one basic question at all times: "How can I exalt God at this moment?"

Why should we live for God's glory rather than our own? 1. It answers life's basic question, Why am I here, urging us to live for God rather than for ourselves. 2. It reminds us that any goal excluding GOD will ultimately fail. 3. By it we learn to praise (glorify) God in everything. This anchors us with hope through life's stormy seas, helping us give Him glory rather than give up to hopelessness or give in to pessimism. 4. It points us to Christ, the only One who lived solely for God's glory, for the help we need. God asked, "How long, O men, will you turn my glory into shame? How long will you love delusions and seek false Gods" (Ps 4:2). Wisely resolve, with Jonathan Edwards. "Never to do any manner of thing, whether in soul or body, less or more, than what tends to the glory of God if I can avoid it." (1722).

Response

I thank you God for showing me _____

_____.

STRATEGY

Follow Jesus today, remembering how He glorified His Father as seen in **John 13:31-38** (Read now)

As I follow Jesus today I will remember _____

_____.

OBEDIENCE (I will statement)

The Spirit is convicting or leading me today to do or stop doing: _____

_____.

PETITIONS (Following your reciting of The Lord's Prayer)

I pray for these scheduled meetings today:

I pray also for these pressing needs of myself, my family, my church, my disciples my world:

CONFESSION and REPENTANCE

I confess these, my sins, with every intention to never repeat them, but rather to live as Jesus would live, by Your enabling grace and Spirit ...

*Never confess without a faith that looks to the cross of Christ, where the guilt and penalty of all our sins was paid!

WALK (Think about the following hymn)

Gloria Patri

Glory be to the Father, and to the Son, and to the Holy Ghost;
As it was in the beginning,
Is now, and ever shall be;
World without end. Amen. Amen.
(2nd century Latin hymn)

Response

Help me Jesus, to _____

_____.

VICTORY

Memorize *1 Corinthians 10:31*

Be prepared for opposition (spiritual warfare) and expect victory in Jesus' name.

Write down the name (s) of those with whom you shared today _____

_____.

____ Check when the day is completed, never beating yourself up if you did not finish; but, just asking Jesus to help you next day!

Day Fifty-two

God – The Triune One

ADORATION

"May the grace of the Lord Jesus Christ, and the love of God, and the fellowship of the Holy Spirit be with you all" (2 Cor 13:14). Paul intentionally ended his last Corinthian letter with these words. As such, he presented the truth it contains as the summit of all truth. Gazing from the mountaintop of this text we see some dazzling sights: (1) Who is God; (2) What He is like; (3) What God wants from us all; and, (4) What is good and evil. Here we see God as three-in-one, the Blesser of humans. He is full of grace, love and a longing for fellowship with us all. So, our greatest good (as mortal creatures) is only realized when we commune with Him (our immortal Creator) in the refreshing sunlight of His grace and love. God wants our love. Everything in and around us that keeps us from real closeness to Him is ultimately evil.

The Bible declares, "the Lord is one" (Deut 6:4.). Yet, it also teaches that three Persons equally possess God's character, do the works of God and are rightly worshipped as God. The word "trinity" was chosen to represent the incomprehensible realities of God's Threeness (tri) and oneness (unity). He is 3 in person while being 1 in nature or essence. God is always 3-in-1, ever 3 different persons or 1 same Being. In the Bible, the name that most often stresses oneness or unity is "God." The names Father, Son and Spirit are those which emphasize plurality. So, our God is a perfect plurality in unity.

"Go and make disciples of all nations, baptizing them in the name of the Father and of the Son and of the Holy Spirit" (Matt 28:19). Even with our imperfect grasp of God's Triune existence, we can conclude: (1) As God has enjoyed eternal fellowship within the Trinity, He made us in His image to desire other persons. Our marriages, families, churches and communities only succeed when we live for others. Often ask, "Who matters most to me right now: God, my neighbor or me?" (2) As the Trinity shows perfect unity, so God's children should "make every effort to keep the unity of the Spirit through the bond of peace" (Eph 4:3). We should discard as ungodly all personal preferences, agendas and opinions (not grounded on basic biblical truth) that cause disunity. (3) Just as beautiful art results from many colors and shades, being skillfully combined, so God's kingdom is most beautifully seen where a variety of races, ages, classes and genders live without prejudice (Gal 3:26-27; Eph 2:11-14; Jas 2:1-4; Rev 7:9).

Response

I thank you God for showing me _____

_____.

STRATEGY

Follow Jesus today, seeing how His teaching demands the existence of a triune God as seen in **Matthew 28:16-20** (Read now)

As I follow Jesus today I will remember _____

_____.

OBEDIENCE (I will statement)

The Spirit is convicting or leading me today to do or stop doing: _____

_____.

PETITIONS (Following your reciting of The Lord's Prayer)

I pray for these scheduled meetings today:

I pray also for these pressing needs of myself, my family, my church, my disciples my world:

CONFESSION and REPENTANCE

I confess these, my sins, with every intention to never repeat them, but rather to live as Jesus would live, by Your enabling grace and Spirit ...

*Never confess without a faith that looks to the cross of Christ, where the guilt and penalty of all our sins was paid!

WALK (Think about the following hymn)

Praise Ye the Triune God

1) Praise ye the Father for His loving-kindness,
Tenderly caring for His erring children;
Praise Him, ye angels; praise Him in the heavens;
Praise to the Savior!

2) Praise ye the Savior for His deep compassion,
Graciously caring for His chosen people;
Young men and maidens, ye old men and children,
Praise to the Savior!

3) Praise ye the Spirit, Comforter of Israel,
Sent from the Father and the Son to bless us;
Praise to the Father, Son, and Holy Spirit!
Praise to the triune God!
(Elizabeth R Charles, 1828-1896)

Response

Help me Jesus, to _____

_____.

VICTORY

Memorize *2 Corinthians 13:14*

Be prepared for opposition (spiritual warfare) and expect victory in Jesus' name.

Write down the name (s) of those with whom you shared today _____

_____.

____ Check when the day is completed, never beating yourself up if you did not finish; but, just asking Jesus to help you next day!

Day Fifty-three

God – The Unchanging One

ADORATION

"I the Lord do not change. So, you, O descendants of Jacob, are not destroyed" (Mal. 3:6). The prophet here declares not only an awesome truth but reveals its astounding consequences. Because God does not change, we are not forsaken and destroyed for our sinful fluctuations. God's immutability is a characteristic that we, as creatures, cannot share in. We grow, change and develop for both good and evil. But not He. We marvel with the psalmist: "In the beginning you laid the foundations of the earth, and the heavens are the work of your hands. They will perish, but you remain; they will all wear out like a garment. But you remain the same, and your years will never end." (Ps 102:25-27).

In the essence of His being, in that which makes Him who He is, God remains the same. He "does not change" (James 1:17). He is immutable. He does not love truth at one moment and falsehood at the next. He never delights in evil but only in good. His plan, then, flowing from His nature, cannot be altered. "The Lord foils the plans of the nations; he thwarts the purposes of the peoples, But the plans of the Lord stand firm forever, the purposes of his heart through all generations" (Ps 33:11). His word is eternal, standing firm in the heavens (Ps 119:89) and, unlike man's, His promises will all be fulfilled (Num 23:19). "1 will not violate my covenant or alter what my lips have uttered." (Ps 89:34). He may appear to "change his mind" (from our perspective); but, He has established His rules of engagement with humankind. When the evil remains evil, He brings the judgment they deserve. But when they repent, He promised to relent. "If at any time I announce that a nation or kingdom is to be uprooted, torn down and destroyed, and if that nation I warned repents of its evil, then I will relent and not inflict on it the disaster I had planned." (Jer. 18:7ff).

God's unchanging nature is at the foundation of our hope and peace. Everything around us may falter and crumble; but He will not—and all that He promises to those who trust in Him will surely come to pass. Jesus said, "Heaven and earth will pass away, but my words will never pass away" (Matt 24:35). So, it is wise to follow the Word whatever it now costs. All the love and truth that filled Jesus and thrilled those surrounding Him, will someday fill the earth because He is coming back to reign and "Jesus Christ is the same yesterday, today and forever" (Heb 13:8). All of God's promised gifts, like Himself, are irrevocable (Rom 11:29). He, Himself will be our inheritance, and His life forever our life! Never give in to evil or give up in your trials and sufferings. He and all His promises will win and be realized—fully and completely and eternally.

Response

I thank you God for showing me _____

_____.

STRATEGY

Follow Jesus today, remembering that His words and promises do not change even though long postponed as seen in **Matthew 25:1-13** (Read now)

As I follow Jesus today I will remember _____

_____.

OBEDIENCE (I will statement)

The Spirit is convicting or leading me today to do or stop doing: _____

_____.

PETITIONS (Following your reciting of The Lord's Prayer)

I pray for these scheduled meetings today:

I pray also for these pressing needs of myself, my family, my church, my disciples my world:

CONFESSION and REPENTANCE

I confess these, my sins, with every intention to never repeat them, but rather to live as Jesus would live, by Your enabling grace and Spirit ...

*Never confess without a faith that looks to the cross of Christ, where the guilt and penalty of all our sins was paid!

WALK (Think about the following praise song)

Our God, our Help in Ages Past

1) Our God, our Help in ages past,
our Hope for years to come,
our Shelter from the stormy blast,
and our eternal Home.

2) Under the shadow of Thy throne
Thy saints have dwelt secure;
sufficient is Thine arm alone,
and our defense is sure.

3) Before the hills in order stood
or earth received its frame,
from everlasting Thou art God,
to endless years the same.

4) A thousand ages in Thy sight
are like an ev'ning gone,
short as the watch that ends the night
before the rising sun.

5) Time, like an ever-rolling stream,
bears all its sons away;
they fly forgotten, as a dream
dies at the op'ning day.

6) Our God, our Help in ages past,
our Hope for years to come,
be Thou our Guide while life shall last,
and our eternal Home! (Isaac Watts, 1674-1748)

Response

Help me Jesus, to _____

_____.

VICTORY

Memorize *Malachi 3:6*

Be prepared for opposition (spiritual warfare) and expect victory in Jesus' name.

Write down the name (s) of those with whom you shared today and pray for them. _____

_____.

____ Check when the day is completed, never beating yourself up if you did not finish; but, just asking Jesus to help you next day!

Day Fifty-four

God – The Eternal One

ADORATION

Abraham "called upon the name of the Lord, the Eternal God" (Gen 21:33,), and Paul spoke of "the command of the eternal God" (Rom 16:26). To be eternal is to be infinite in regards to time, without beginning or ending. The Father (John 17:5), the Son (Rev 1:8) and the Spirit (Heb 9:14) are co-eternal. So, "in the beginning," God is depicted as already existing (Gen 1:1; Jn 1:1; 1 Jn 1:1).

Before God made the world, there was no time as we know it. For there to be time, there must be physical objects with space between them, for time is the period that passes when going between two things or events. So, time, to us physical beings, is always connected with matter and space. God is Lord over time. He is not bound by it. Time is His servant. As Moses wrote, "for a thousand years in your sight are like a day that has just gone by" (Ps. 90:4a,). And Peter agreed saying, "with the Lord a day is like a thousand years, and a thousand years like a day' (2 Pet 3:8b). Time is different to God than it is to us. In His essence, He is timeless. He is the eternal I AM (in the present tense- Ex 3:14: John 8:58). In this world God usually works according to time's progressive nature, while retaining perfect control. We should all often remember and constantly say, "my times are in your hands" (Ps 31:15).

Everything about God has an eternal aspect. He is an eternal King (Jer 10:10) with an eternal purpose (Eph 3:11) whose word is 'eternal, standing firm in the heavens' (Ps 119:89). His love for His people is everlasting (Jer 31:3). It is best revealed in His giving us sinners His everlasting righteousness (Ps 119:142: Dan 9:24-25) through Christ's eternal gospel (Rev 14:6: Rom 1:17) giving us eternal life (John 3:16.36) rescuing us from everlasting ruin (Ps 52:5), disgrace (Jer 32:40) and destruction (2 Thes 1:9) in eternal fire (Matt 18:8: Jude 7).

God 'has set eternity in the hearts of men" (Ecc 3:11). So, this world and all its sinful pleasures are far too small to satisfy those who were made to walk with God forever. Let us learn (1) Since time is God's servant, He is in no rush or under any pressure. Keep in step with His Spirit and don't let pressures rob your peace. (2) Since this physical world is not eternal, don't make too much of any one moment or event. Rather live for what is unseen and eternal and rejoice in all God brings into our life now of suffering or trials because they will soon enough change. (3) Since eternal issues surround us, realize the greatness of the gift of eternal life and the awful peril that unbelievers are now in until they repent and follow Jesus.

Response
I thank you God for showing me _____

_____.

STRATEGY

Follow Jesus today, seeing how His teaching demands that we confess and follow Him as the eternal great I AM as seen in **John 8:42-59** (Read now)

As I follow Jesus today I will remember _____

_____.

OBEDIENCE (I will statement)

The Spirit is convicting or leading me today to do or stop doing: _____

_____.

PETITIONS (Following your reciting of The Lord's Prayer)

I pray for these scheduled meetings today:

I pray also for these pressing needs of myself, my family, my church, my disciples my world:

CONFESSION and REPENTANCE

I confess these, my sins, with every intention to never repeat them, but rather to live as Jesus would live, by Your enabling grace and Spirit ...

*Never confess without a faith that looks to the cross of Christ, where the guilt and penalty of all our sins was paid!

WALK (Think about the following praise song)

Great God How Infinite Art Thou!

1) Great God, how infinite art thou!
How poor and weak are we!
Let the whole race of creatures bow,
and pay their praise to thee.

2) Thy throne eternal ages stood,
ere seas or stars were made:
thou art the ever-living God,
were all the nations dead.

3) Eternity, with all its years,
stands present in thy view;
to thee there's nothing old appears;
to thee there's nothing new.

4) Our lives through various scenes are drawn,
and vexed with trifling cares;
while thine eternal thought moves on
thine undisturbed affairs.

5) Great God, how infinite art thou!
How poor and weak are we!
Let the whole race of creatures bow,
and pay their praise to thee.

(Isaac Watts, 1674-1748)

Response

Help me Jesus, to _____

_____.

VICTORY

Memorize *1 Timothy 1:17*

Be prepared for opposition (spiritual warfare) and expect victory in Jesus' name.

Write down the name (s) of those with whom you shared today _____

_____.

____ Check when the day is completed, never beating yourself up if you did not finish; but, just asking Jesus to help you next day!

Day Fifty-five

God – The Sovereign One

ADORATION

    At times, in the Bible, two names are united when referring to God. Emphasis and greatness are goals of such combinations. This is often done in the NIV using the words, "Sovereign Lord." A sovereign is a king. A lord is an owner, the only one who ultimately matters to those under his authority. The basic sense is that God is an Unrivaled, All powerful Owner. An Absolute and Total Master. We belong as solely to Him as an object does to the one who shaped or bought it. Abram was the first to use this combined name in Scripture (Gen 15:2), followed by many others (Moses, Joshua, Gideon, Samson, David and, especially, the prophets).

    God often chooses this as His own title, especially when speaking to His people in times of great trial, distress or discouragement. He reminds them that He is in complete control of both them and the whole world. "This is what the Sovereign Lord says: See, I will beckon the Gentiles...they will bring your sons in their arms...Kings will be your foster fathers, and their queens your nursing mothers...then you will know that I am the Lord" (Isa 49:22-23). Using this name reminds us that He can do the impossible and will always do good to His people.

    Much can be learned from David's use of this name in his famous prayer: "Who am I, O Sovereign Lord, and what is my family, that you have brought me this far? And as if this were not enough in your sight, O Sovereign Lord, you have also spoken about the future of the house of your servant...What more can David say to you? For you know your servant, O Sovereign Lord." (2 Sam 7:18-20). He was absolutely amazed that The Only One That Matters had considered a mere man like him and had graciously given him such promises of love and power.

    In the NT, a special Greek term is similarly used for God in times of great distress (Rev 6:10), trial (Jude 4) and need (Luke 2:29). When the Early Church faced life-threatening danger, they cried out to God as their "Sovereign Lord" (Acts 4:24). And "after they prayed, the place where they were meeting was shaken. And they were all filled with the Holy Spirit and spoke the word of God boldly" (Acts 4:31).

    Do you live like one owned by another? Paul said, "You are not your own; you were bought at a price. Therefore, honor God with your body" (1 Cor 6:19b-20). Jesus warned us that our time, skills, money and health are on loan from God and must be used for His glory (Matt 25). Not to do so joyfully, is to deny that He is a good, Sovereign Lord. To yield unreservedly to Him and His plan, whatever may be happening to us, is one of the greatest witnesses of faith in God that a human can give.

Response

I thank you God for showing me _____

_____.

STRATEGY

Follow Jesus today, seeing how His power extended even over the fiercest of demons as seen in **Mark 5:1-20** (Read now)

As I follow Jesus today I will remember _____

_____.

OBEDIENCE (I will statement)

The Spirit is convicting or leading me today to do or stop doing: _____

_____.

PETITIONS (Following your reciting of The Lord's Prayer)

I pray for these scheduled meetings today:

I pray also for these pressing needs of myself, my family, my church, my disciples my world:

CONFESSION and REPENTANCE

I confess these, my sins, with every intention to never repeat them, but rather to live as Jesus would live, by Your enabling grace and Spirit …

*Never confess without a faith that looks to the cross of Christ, where the guilt and penalty of all our sins was paid!

WALK (Think about the following hymn)

God Moves in a Mysterious Way

1) God moves in a mysterious way
   His wonders to perform;
   He plants His footsteps in the sea
   And rides upon the storm.

2) Deep in unfathomable mines
   Of never failing skill
   He treasures up His bright designs
   And works His sov'reign will.

3) Ye fearful saints, fresh courage take;
   The clouds ye so much dread
   Are big with mercy and shall break
   In blessings on your head.

4) Judge not the Lord by feeble sense,
   But trust Him for His grace;
   Behind a frowning providence
   He hides a smiling face.

5) His purposes will ripen fast,
   Unfolding every hour;
   The bud may have a bitter taste,
   But sweet will be the flow'r.

6. Blind unbelief is sure to err
   And scan His work in vain;
   God is His own interpreter,
   And He will make it plain.
   (William Cowper, 1731-1800)

Response

Help me Jesus, to _____

_____.

VICTORY

Memorize *Daniel 4:25b*

Be prepared for opposition (spiritual warfare) and expect victory in Jesus' name.

Write down the name (s) of those with whom you shared today _____
_____.

____ Check when the day is completed, never beating yourself up if you did not finish; but, just asking Jesus to help you next day!

Day Fifty-six

God is Love

ADORATION

When the Bible declares that "God is love" (1 John 4:8), it teaches that love in its purest, infinite essence fills the Trinity. So, the Father loves (2 Cor 13:14), the Son loves (John 13:34) and the Spirit loves (Rom 15:30). Love to us includes delighting in another, desiring communion with that one and determining to do him/her good. What love is to us, it is also with God, yet infinitely, eternally and unchangeably so! He delights in His people (Ps 149:4), desires their fellowship (Gen 3:8-9; 5:24; Matt 1:23; Rev 21:3) and is pleased when they desire Him and pray to Him (Ps 86:5; Prov 15:8; Lk 11:9-13).

He desires and accomplishes good for all in the world (Ps 104:27-28; 145:15-16); but especially to those who love Him (Rom 8:28; Jer 29:11; Ps 119:71,75). Those who have eyes to see it, recognize that God's love is ever before us (Ps 26:3), filling the whole earth (Ps 119:64).

God's love is like a perfectly cut diamond with many beautiful facets. Look at it as it relates to those in a pitiful or desperate condition and it is called *mercy*. View it extended to the undeserving and it is called *grace*. For those who are in need, it is termed *kindness*. To the forsaken who have been treated roughly, it is described as *tenderness*. God's love to the brokenhearted is His *compassion*. And even to those who recklessly run away from God and rush towards ruin, God's love is expressed as *patience*.

God's love is the theme of themes. Bible writers searched for countless ways to describe its beauty and wonder. It is like the love of a father (Prov 3:1 1-12), a mother (Isa 66:13), of a groom for his bride (Isa 62:5) and a husband for his wife (Eph 5:25), and even as a mother hen for her chicks (Lk 13:34). It is God's desire that we would meditate on His love (Ps 48:9), sing about it (Ps 59:16; 101:1), never concealing it (Ps 40:10), but rejoice in it (Ps 3 1:7) and proclaim it (Ps 92:2). Christians should be charmed and transformed by His love.

"What a man desires is unfailing love" (Prov 19:22). Sadly, many try to satisfy their craving to be loved and to love on unworthy objects, becoming "lovers of themselves, lovers of money...lovers of pleasure rather than lovers of God" (2 Tim 3:1-4). Only an unfailing God can meet our desire and love us with an unfailing love! Let us pursue God as those who love Him! May we love to pray to Him, to obey Him, to wait on Him. As God's #1 commandment and that which fulfills all our being, let us seek His enabling grace to follow Jesus in living a life of selfless, joyful love.

Response

I thank you God for showing me _____

_____.

STRATEGY

Follow Jesus today, seeing how His teaching demands a life of love as seen in **Luke 10:25-37** (Read now)

As I follow Jesus today I will remember _____

_____.

OBEDIENCE (I will statement)

The Spirit is convicting or leading me today to do or stop doing: _____

_____.

PETITIONS (Following your reciting of <u>The Lord's Prayer</u>)

I pray for these scheduled meetings today:

I pray also for these pressing needs of myself, my family, my church, my disciples my world:

CONFESSION and REPENTANCE

I confess these, my sins, with every intention to never repeat them, but rather to live as Jesus would live, by Your enabling grace and Spirit …

*Never confess without a faith that looks to the cross of Christ, where the guilt and penalty of all our sins was paid!

WALK (Think about the following praise song)

The Love of God

1) The love of God is greater far
Than tongue or pen can ever tell.
It goes beyond the highest star
And reaches to the lowest hell.
The guilty pair, bowed down with care,
God gave His Son to win;
His erring child He reconciled
And pardoned from his sin.

O love of God, how rich and pure!
How measureless and strong!
It shall forevermore endure—
The saints' and angels' song.

2) When hoary time shall pass away,
And earthly thrones and kingdoms fall;
When men who here refuse to pray,
On rocks and hills and mountains call;
God's love, so sure, shall still endure,
All measureless and strong;
Redeeming grace to Adam's race—
The saints' and angels' song.

3) Could we with ink the ocean fill,
And were the skies of parchment made;
Were every stalk on earth a quill,
And every man a scribe by trade;
To write the love of God above
Would drain the ocean dry;
Nor could the scroll contain the whole,
Though stretched from sky to sky.
(Frederick M Lehman, 1868-1953)

Response

Help me Jesus, to _____

_____.

VICTORY

Memorize *John 3:16*

Be prepared for opposition (spiritual warfare) and expect victory in Jesus' name.

Write down the name (s) of those with whom you shared today and pray for them. _____

_____.

____ Check when the day is completed, never beating yourself up if you did not finish; but, just asking Jesus to help you next day!

Day Fifty-seven

God – The Jealous One

ADORATION

    We are made in God's image. The whole range of natural human emotions reveal, in some way, our Creator. However, whenever God's divine nature is compared with ours, we must remove from our minds any thought of our limitation and imperfection. We are broken and fallen. He is unimaginably glorious and beautiful--without defect. His anger, displeasure and judgment are as sinless and awesome as are His love and patience. Those attributes of His that can be mirrored in us are so much greater and purer than what exists in us, that though they are similar, it is just barely so.

    This is true of jealousy, which I have chosen to follow His love. We may be jealous of those whom we love. Humans can have "godly jealousy" (2 Cor 11:2), though often our jealousy is mixed with ungodly rage, hatred and violence (Prov 6:32-35; Rom 13:13; 1 Cor 3:3; 12:20; Gal 5:20).

    To be jealous is to be "watchful in guarding" or to "demand exclusive loyalty" or to be "resentfully suspicious of a rival" according to Webster's New World Dictionary. Since God is perfect, if He is jealous of something, then THAT thing should be loved, honored and preserved, for it is good.

    First to be mentioned in relationship with His jealousy is His worship. He commanded the children of Israel, "You shall not make for yourself an idol...you shall not bow down to them or worship them, for I, the Lord your God am a jealous God..." (Ex 20:4-5). Moses reminded them, "Do not worship any other god, for the Lord, whose name is Jealous, is a jealous God" (Ex 34:14). Idolatry occurs when we place anything or anyone in priority before God. He deserves to be first. His Law or His covenant made with Israel was to be obeyed, "for the Lord your God is a consuming fire, a jealous God" (Deut 4:24; see Josh 24:19).

    When the nations oppose the ways of the Lord, God's wrath eventually falls on them because He must be jealous of His own glory. "The Lord is a jealous and avenging God; the Lord takes vengeance and is filled with wrath. The Lord takes vengeance on his foes and maintains his wrath against his enemies" (Nahum 1:2). But He does this only after being "slow to anger" (Nahum 1:3a). Eventually the whole world must be destroyed for its opposition of the Lord and His holy ways, "The whole world will be consumed by the fire of my jealous anger (Zeph 3:8).

When His people rebel against His holy nature, embracing sin, God jealously chastens them, showing that the preservation of His own glory is greater than ourselves. God is first, and we are second. "Judah did evil in the eyes of the Lord. By the sins they committed they stirred up his jealous anger...." (1 Kings 14:22). The NT also reminds its readers not to refuse Jesus, but to "worship God acceptably with reverence and awe for our God is a consuming fire" (Heb 11:29). Paul warned the sinning Corinthians, "Are we trying to arouse the Lord's jealousy? Are we stronger than he?' (1 Cor 10:22). Even though we are imperfect, God is also jealous of the life and care of His people. "This is what the Lord Almighty says: I am very jealous for Zion; lam burning with jealousy for her" (Zech 2:2; Joel 2:18). He truly loves us and resents our being mistreated, rejected and persecuted. His future judgment against those who reject Him and oppose His people will prove just how infinitely jealous our great God is!

Response

I thank you God for showing me _____

_____.

STRATEGY

Follow Jesus today, seeing how jealous He was for the disciples whom He so loved, even when they were forsaking Him, as seen in **John 18:1-14** (Read now)

As I follow Jesus today I will remember _____

_____.

OBEDIENCE (I will statement)

The Spirit is convicting or leading me today to do or stop doing: _____

_____.

PETITIONS (Following your reciting of The Lord's Prayer)

I pray for these scheduled meetings today:

I pray also for these pressing needs of myself, my family, my church, my disciples my world:

CONFESSION and REPENTANCE

I confess these, my sins, with every intention to never repeat them, but rather to live as Jesus would live, by Your enabling grace and Spirit …

*Never confess without a faith that looks to the cross of Christ, where the guilt and penalty of all our sins was paid!

WALK (Think about the following praise song)

O Come and Mourn with Me Awhile

1) O come and mourn with me awhile,
O come ye to the Savior's side
O come, together let us mourn,
Jesus our Lord is crucified.

2) Seven times He spake seven words of love;
And all three hours His silence cried
For mercy on the souls of men;
Jesus our Lord is crucified.

*O love of God! O sin of man!
In this dread act Your strength is tried;
And victory remains with love;
Jesus our Lord is crucified!*

3) O break, O break, hard heart of mine!
Thy weak self-love and guilty pride
His Pilate and His Judas were:
Jesus our Lord is crucified.

4) A broken heart, a fount of tears,
Ask, and they will not be denied;
A broken heart love's cradle is:
Jesus our Lord is crucified. (Repeat chorus)
(Frederick W Faber, 1814-1863)

Response

Help me Jesus, to _____

VICTORY

Memorize *Zechariah 1:14*

Be prepared for opposition (spiritual warfare) and expect victory in Jesus' name.

Write down the name (s) of those with whom you shared today _____
_____.

____ Check when the day is completed, never beating yourself up if you did not finish; but, just asking Jesus to help you next day!

Day Fifty-eight

God – The Pure One

ADORATION

When we think of something that is pure, we think of it being 100%. No mixture. No impurities. The real deal. Give me 6 oz. of fresh squeezed orange juice over a 16 oz. glass of made from concentrate juice any day.

God is the only pure One. "Your eyes are too pure to look on evil; you cannot tolerate wrong" (Hab 1:13). Evil hurts the eyes of God because He is accustomed to purity. He is especially pleased when He sees simple honesty, real repentance and sheer brokenness. When the act is set aside, and our hearts stop pretending, realizing it's no use, then God enters with blessing. "To the pure you show yourself pure" (Ps 18:26a).

Everything in us is defiled, impure — imperfect. We struggle with that because we hate the duplicity. No one likes a fake. We all want to be what God wants us to be—His image bearer. We long to be like Him, so we cry out with David, "Create in me a pure heart, O God," (Ps 51:1 a). Our hearts agree with the aged Apostle John who spoke for every Christian when he said, "Everyone who has this hope in him purifies himself, just as he is pure" (1 John 3:3).

It is here, though, that we balk. The process of purifying is not pleasant. Usually it is slow and searing. It involves heating up and stripping away. A burning process over time. "He will sit as a refiner and purifier of silver; he will purify the Levites and refine them like gold and silver. Then the Lord will have men who will bring offerings in righteousness" (Mal 3:3). Or as Paul would put it, "Jesus Christ, who gave himself for us to redeem us from all wickedness and to purify for himself a people that are his very own, eager to do what is good" (Titus 2:14). That could scare us if we did not add God's grace to the formula of purification. He shortens the process for us by demanding a long and hard burning of His Son.

We would not have to be purified if we were pure. Spiritually, we are corrupt and need cleansing. A deep and thorough cleansing. When Jesus died, the heat was put on Him. He went through the blast furnace for us, on the cross, so we can go through the purifying process with unusual speed. We do not have to wait a long time. In fact, if we believe that His death paid the price for our purification, we can be cleansed and progressed immediately. Speaking of the Gentiles, Peter said, "He made no distinction between us and them, for he purified their hearts by faith" (Acts 15:9). John explains the way that faith purifies when he said, "If we confess our sins, he is faithful and just an will forgive us our sins and purify us from all unrighteousness" (1 John 1:9). Faith in Jesus combined with a true, honest, humble repentance purifies the heart and pleases our pure God.

Jesus declared, "Blessed are the pure in heart, for they shall see God' (Matt 5:8). May we ever be open and honest before the Father, never worrying that our honest confession will bring His wrath. It can't, for His justice has been satisfied by the cross. He saves sinners, so be transparent about your weakness. God's grace has made Christ our total purity.

Response

I thank you God for showing me _____

STRATEGY

Follow Jesus today, seeing how His life was sinless and His enemies could not impugn it as seen in **John 8:42-47** (Read now)

As I follow Jesus today I will remember _____

OBEDIENCE (I will statement)

The Spirit is convicting or leading me today to do or stop doing: _____
_____.

PETITIONS (Following your reciting of The Lord's Prayer)

I pray for these scheduled meetings today:

I pray also for these pressing needs of myself, my family, my church, my disciples my world:

CONFESSION and REPENTANCE

I confess these, my sins, with every intention to never repeat them, but rather to live as Jesus would live, by Your enabling grace and Spirit …

*Never confess without a faith that looks to the cross of Christ, where the guilt and penalty of all our sins was paid!

WALK (Think about the following praise song)

Holy God, We Praise Your Name

1) Holy God, we praise Thy name;
Lord of all, we bow before Thee!
All on earth Thy scepter claim,
All in Heaven above adore Thee;
Infinite Thy vast domain,
Everlasting is Thy reign.

2) Hark! the loud celestial hymn
Angel choirs above are raising,
Cherubim and seraphim,
In unceasing chorus praising;
Fill the heavens with sweet accord:
Holy, holy, holy, Lord.

3) Lo! the apostolic train
Join the sacred name to hallow;
Prophets swell the loud refrain,
And the white robed martyrs follow;
And from morn to set of sun,
Through the Church the song goes on.

4) Holy Father, Holy Son,
Holy Spirit, Three we name Thee;
While in essence only One,
Undivided God we claim Thee;
And adoring bend the knee,
While we own the mystery.

5) Thou art King of glory, Christ:
Son of God, yet born of Mary;
For us sinners sacrificed,
And to death a tributary:
First to break the bars of death,
Thou has opened Heaven to faith.

6) From Thy high celestial home,
Judge of all, again returning,
We believe that Thou shalt come
In the dreaded doomsday morning;
When Thy voice shall shake the earth,
And the startled dead come forth.

7) Therefore do we pray Thee, Lord:
Help Thy servants whom, redeeming
By Thy precious blood out-poured,
Thou hast saved from Satan's scheming.
Give to them eternal rest
In the glory of the blest.

8) Spare Thy people, Lord, we pray,
By a thousand snares surrounded:
Keep us without sin today,
Never let us be confounded.
Lo, I put my trust in Thee;
Never, Lord, abandon me.
(Ignace Franz, 1828-1896; translated by Clarence Walworth, 1853)

Response

Help me Jesus, to _____

_____.

VICTORY

Memorize *1 John 1:9*

Be prepared for opposition (spiritual warfare) and expect victory in Jesus' name.

Write down the name (s) of those with whom you shared today _____

_____.

_____ Check when the day is completed, never beating yourself up if you did not finish; but, just asking Jesus to help you next day!

Day Fifty-nine

God – The Righteous One

ADORATION

God is perfect, or as Ezra declared, "O Lord, God of Israel, you are righteous!" (Ezra 10:15). But ever since Adam's fall, every one of us have had a righteousness problem. "All have sinned and fall short of the glory of God" (Rom 3:23). That deficiency bars us from heaven—the perfect abode of a righteous God. We are imperfect or unrighteous and, therefore, in ourselves can be rightful heirs of only an imperfect abode.

God, knowing our dilemma, and wanting our eternal fellowship, promised to solve our problem of moral imperfection by sending the Messiah to provide sinners with His righteousness. "The days are coming when I will raise up to David a righteous Branch, a King. In His days Judah will be saved...This is the name by which he will be called: The Lord our Righteousness" (Jer 23:6). He spoke to the Messiah, "I the Lord have called you in righteousness; I will take hold of you by the hand...1 will make you a light for the Gentiles.... (Isa 42:6).

When Christ came, He perfectly obeyed the Law of God. He was righteous. Those who trust in Him for salvation are given the gift of His righteousness. Paul said, "But now a righteousness from God apart from the Law, has been made known, to which the Law and the Prophets testify. This righteousness from God comes through faith in Jesus Christ to all who believe." (Rom 3:21-22). Perfection comes through faith not through effort. Therefore, the Law failed and could not save anyone. Its path was too hard for us sinners. Paul said, "Moses describes in this way the righteousness that is by the law: 'The man who does these things will live by them.' But the righteousness that is by faith says. if you confess with your mouth, 'Jesus is Lord,' and believe in your heart that God raised him from the dead, you will be saved" (Rom 10:5-10).

Since righteousness is a gift, our relationship with God is not based on our works. Our peace is the product of faith in Christ. In what He did for us. Many Christians today follow the old error of the Galatians: "After beginning with the Spirit, are you now trying to attain your goal by human effort?" (Gal 3:5). This approach can only frustrate us and create guilt because none of our works can be perfect. God wants us to have JOY, but guilt kills joy. The gospel of God's grace forever frees us from guilt. It also unleashes within us a great desire to obey Christ, to follow Him, to walk in the Spirit, to be holy. And all this we can do with the humble honesty that constantly exalts Christ rather than ourselves. For "all our righteous acts are like filthy rags" (Is 64:6). So, God did not lessen His standard for entering heaven. He raised us up in Christ, who enables us to enter where only the righteous may go!

Response

I thank you God for showing me _____

_____.

STRATEGY

Follow Jesus today, seeing how His teaching demands a righteousness that only He can give as a gift as seen in **Matthew 19:16-26** (Read now)

As I follow Jesus today I will remember _____

OBEDIENCE (I will statement)

The Spirit is convicting or leading me today to do or stop doing: _____

_____.

PETITIONS (Following your reciting of The Lord's Prayer)

I pray for these scheduled meetings today:

I pray also for these pressing needs of myself, my family, my church, my disciples my world:

CONFESSION and REPENTANCE

I confess these, my sins, with every intention to never repeat them, but rather to live as Jesus would live, by Your enabling grace and Spirit …
*Never confess without a faith that looks to the cross of Christ, where the guilt and penalty of all our sins was paid!

WALK (Think about the following praise song)

My Hope is in the Lord

1) My hope is in the Lord
Who gave Him-self for me
And paid the price
Of all my sin at Cal-va-ry.

For me He died;
For me He lives,
And everlasting life
And light He free-ly gives.

2) No merit of my own
His anger to suppress
My only hope is found
In Jesus' righteousness

3) And now for me He stands
Before the Father's throne
He shows His wounded hands
And names me as His own

4) His grace has planned it all
'Tis mine but to believe
And recognize His work of love
And Christ receive
(Norman J Clayton, 1903-1992)

Response

Help me Jesus, to _____

_____.

VICTORY

Memorize *Romans 3:10*

Be prepared for opposition (spiritual warfare) and expect victory in Jesus' name.

Write down the name (s) of those with whom you shared today _____
_____.

____ Check when the day is completed, never beating yourself up if you did not finish; but, just asking Jesus to help you next day!

Day Sixty

God – The Worshipped One

ADORATION

What is worship? It is when a person humbles himself and appropriately declares another One to be totally glorious and infinitely greater than he, himself, is and all other creatures are. Worship is the sincerest and fullest adoration of one's Supreme Being. Worship is the great goal for which a Creator would create a rational creature. It is the ultimate moment of the most ultimate truth. So, worship is truly beautiful when it is directed to the one true and living God. Otherwise it is a horrendous deception and sham, for it is exalting an imposter and deceiving and degrading oneself. There is no other sin so great as false worship. It demands of a true God His opposition and displeasure, for it is the greatest wrong imaginable. Exalting and adoring another in the place of the Lord! "All this I will give you, he said, if you will bow down and worship me. Jesus said to him, Away from me, Satan! For it is written, Worship the Lord your God, and serve him only" (Matt 4:9-10).

"I am the Lord your God, who brought you out of Egypt, out of the land of slavery. You shall have no other gods before me. You shall not make for yourself an idol. You shall not bow down to them or worship them for 1 the Lord your God am a jealous God, punishing the children for the sin of the fathers to the third and fourth generation of those who hate me, but showing love to a thousand generations of those who love me and keep my commandments" (Ex 20:2-6).

The God of the Bible "desires" to be worshiped by His created beings. How? "God is spirit, and his worshipers must worship in spirit and in truth" (John 4:22-24). From the heart, with sincerity. With all of one's heart. With joy and gladness! "Worship the Lord with gladness; come before him with joyful songs." (Ps 100:2). Not in a compromising manner, but in a holy and suitable way. "Bring an offering and come before him; worship the Lord in the splendor of his holiness." (1 Chron 16:29). "They worshiped the Lord, but they also served their own gods in accordance with the customs of the nations from which they had been brought." (2 Kgs 17:33). Worship God His way.

Worship must be with true humility, as it recognizes the infinite difference between our great God and us lowly and finite beings. "Come let us bow down in worship, let us kneel before the Lord our Maker" (Ps 95:6).

This is always man at his best—because it is really our condition. We sometimes get delirious with pride when comparing ourselves to others; but, we are truly nothing in comparison to Almighty God. Such reflection demands one response. "Offer your bodies as living sacrifices, holy and pleasing to God—this is your spiritual act of worship" (Rom 12:1). Those who worship MUST serve the One they are worshiping. So, we worship and serve the God of the Bible: Father, Son and Holy Spirit. Equally and eternally God over us, before us, around us and ahead of us. The good God who incredibly reconciled us to Himself by the blood of His Eternal Son! And gave us the name of His Son Jesus to be exalted by our lips every moment in devout worship! No other name! No other Mediator. He is our Way to God and is our God, too.

Response

I thank you God for showing me _____

_____.

STRATEGY

Follow Jesus today, seeing how He, as God, received worship while on earth as seen in **Matthew 28:16-18** (Read now)

As I follow Jesus today I will remember _____

_____.

OBEDIENCE (I will statement)

The Spirit is convicting or leading me today to do or stop doing: _____

_____.

PETITIONS (Following your reciting of <u>The Lord's Prayer</u>)

I pray for these scheduled meetings today:

I pray also for these pressing needs of myself, my family, my church, my disciples my world:

CONFESSION and REPENTANCE

I confess these, my sins, with every intention to never repeat them, but rather to live as Jesus would live, by Your enabling grace and Spirit ...

*Never confess without a faith that looks to the cross of Christ, where the guilt and penalty of all our sins was paid!

WALK (Think about the following praise song)

O Worship the King

1) O worship the King, all glorious above,
O gratefully sing His power and His love;
Our Shield and Defender, the Ancient of Days,
Pavilioned in splendor, and girded with praise.

2) O tell of His might, O sing of His grace,
Whose robe is the light, whose canopy space,
His chariots of wrath the deep thunderclouds form,
And dark is His path on the wings of the storm.

3) The earth with its store of wonders untold,
Almighty, Thy power hath founded of old;
Established it fast by a changeless decree,
And round it hath cast, like a mantle, the sea.

4) Thy bountiful care, what tongue can recite?
It breathes in the air, it shines in the light;
It streams from the hills, it descends to the plain,
And sweetly distills in the dew and the rain.

5) Frail children of dust, and feeble as frail,
In Thee do we trust, nor find Thee to fail;
Thy mercies how tender, how firm to the end,
Our Maker, Defender, Redeemer, and Friend.

6) O measureless might! Ineffable love!
While angels delight to worship Thee above,
The humbler creation, though feeble their lays,
With true adoration shall all sing Thy praise.
(Robert Grant, 1778-1838)

Response

Help me Jesus, to _____

_____.

VICTORY

Memorize *John 4:24*

Be prepared for opposition (spiritual warfare) and expect victory in Jesus' name.

Write down the name (s) of those with whom you shared today _____

_____.

____ Check when the day is completed, never beating yourself up if you did not finish; but, just asking Jesus to help you next day!

10-Day Period 7

Discipleship and our Imitating the Life of Jesus

**Begin by reading Appendix Seven - Following Jesus' Way of Life

Christianity was never meant to be mainly a list of doctrines one believes while regularly going to church. The Christian Faith is captured most simply in following Jesus. Walking with God throughout the day and, thus, throughout life. We must know Him to follow Him. And, then, just like the earliest disciples, we can show others the Way. The main aspect of true Christian leadership is—follower-ship. We cannot lead others where we have not been. And we truly go nowhere without following Jesus. Every believer is to become a leader of others, that is, a disciple maker.[33] We learn from Him and imitate His life, by the power of the Spirit, as we disciple others.

Living as a disciple will create quite a testimony. People are always looking at and assessing the lives of others. When a disciple meets a person along the paths of life, that person is brought into the presence of Jesus! The One who is always within us and guiding us forward. A simple sentence "in His Name" might influence another forever! What is your daily testimony? "They overcame him (Satan) by the blood of the Lamb and by the word of their testimony" (Rev. 12:11). As you "follow in his steps" (1 Pet 2:21), you will powerfully influence others. What was said long ago by the famous poet, Edgar Guest, still holds true today,

> "I'd rather see a sermon than hear one any day;
> I'd rather one should walk with me than merely tell the way.
> The eye is a better pupil, more willing than the ear;
> Fine counsel is confusing, but example is always clear...."

---

[33] See Matt. 4:19; 5:14-16; 28:18-20; John 20:21; Acts 1:8; Rom. 15:14; Heb. 5:11-14

Day Sixty-one

God – The Great One

ADORATION

When we think of greatness, we often think in terms of bigger or better. "A great meal" or "a great football game" represent better than usual things. When we ascribe greatness to God, we speak of His special nature and works. He is greater than anyone. "Great is the Lord and most worthy of praise; his greatness no one can fathom" (Ps 145:3). His greatness is sometimes depicted by the word "infinite." To be infinite is to be without limitation. Only God is infinite. All His creation is finite.

Everywhere, the Scriptures reveal God's greatness. "How awesome is the Lord Most High, the great king over all the earth!" (Ps 47:2). His rule is not limited to a certain nation or time, like human rulers. "His dominion is an eternal dominion; his kingdom endures from generation to generation ... He does as he pleases with the powers of heaven and the peoples of the earth" (Dan 4:34b).

What is true of His sovereignty is true of every aspect of His being. He is great beyond words—infinitely great. So, the Bible speaks of His great majesty (Ex 15:7), great wrath (Deut 29:28) and mercy (2 Sam 24:14), great faithfulness (Lam 3:23), purposes (Jer 32:19), and His incomparably great power (Eph 1:19). But, His Word especially declares His great LOVE! "How great is the love the Father has lavished on us, that we should be called children of God! And that is what we are! (1 John 3:1a).

In Jesus' love, we have the defining moment of love in human history. "This is how we know what love is: Jesus Christ laid down his life for us" (1 John 3:16a). Something great happens when a Christian is consumed by the love of God. David said, "Whosoever is wise let him heed these things and consider the great love of the Lord" (Ps 107:43). We can do nothing wiser than be filled with the wonder of God's love for us and the world. Nothing will help us more to live as we should, to worship and witness as we should—than to consider the great love of the Lord.

Satan often attempts to appear greater than God to us—more understanding, more relevant, more powerful. So, the people of Samaria regarded Simon the sorcerer as, "The Great Power" (Acts 8:10). They then learned the power of the name of Jesus, that Name which is above every name. And Satan's lies were exposed. "The one who is in you is greater than the one who is in the world" (1 John 4:4). We should never live like anything the world offers is greater than what God delivers! A great God deserves great worship and service. So, everywhere "praise the greatness of our God!" (Deut 32:3). And be joyful.

Response

I thank you God for showing me _____

_____.

STRATEGY

Follow Jesus today, seeing how He redefined greatness as seen in **Matt 20:20-28** (Read now)

As I follow Jesus today I will remember _____

_____.

OBEDIENCE (I will statement)

The Spirit is convicting or leading me today to do or stop doing: _____

_____.

PETITIONS (Following your reciting of The Lord's Prayer)

I pray for these scheduled meetings today:

I pray also for these pressing needs of myself, my family, my church, my disciples my world:

CONFESSION and REPENTANCE

I confess these, my sins, with every intention to never repeat them, but rather to live as Jesus would live, by Your enabling grace and Spirit …

*Never confess without a faith that looks to the cross of Christ, where the guilt and penalty of all our sins was paid!

WALK (Think about the following praise song)

Great God of Wonders!

1) Great God of wonders! all thy ways
are matchless, godlike and divine;
but the fair glories of thy grace
more godlike and unrivaled shine,
more godlike and unrivaled shine.

Who is a pard'ning God like thee?
Or who has grace so rich and free?
Or who has grace so rich and free?

2) In wonder lost, with trembling joy
we take the pardon of our God;
pardon for crimes of deepest dye,
a pardon bought with Jesus' blood,
a pardon bought with Jesus' blood.

3) O may this strange, this matchless grace,
this God-like miracle of love,
fill the whole earth with grateful praise,
and all th'angelic choirs above,
and all th'angelic choirs above.
(Samuel Davies, 1723-1761)

Response

Help me, Jesus, to _____

_____.

VICTORY

Memorize *1 John 3:1*

Be prepared for opposition (spiritual warfare) and expect victory in Jesus' name.

Write down the name (s) of those with whom you shared today _____

_____.

____ Check when the day is completed, never beating yourself up if you did not finish; but, just asking Jesus to help you next day!

Day Sixty-two

God – The Choosing One

ADORATION

God's nature is immeasurably greater than ours. He is infinite, eternal and unchanging. We are finite, limited and changing. He is God the Creator and we are human creatures. As Isaiah said, "Yet, O Lord, you are our Father. We are the clay, you are the potter; we are all the work of your hand" (Isa 64:8). It is a humbling thing to be likened to clay and to let God alone be God. To acknowledge that He is the only One in ultimate control. Why is it so important to believe this?

When Adam sinned, he brought sin and death to both himself and to all his descendants (Rom 5:12,19). As a result, all who are naturally born, have a nature that sins. Here is the verdict: "The Lord looks down from heaven ... to see if there are any who understand, any who seek God. All have turned aside, they have become corrupt; there is no one who does good, not even one" (Ps 14:2-3). It is as Paul concluded, "All have sinned and fall short of the glory of God" (Rom 3:23). The dilemma that our sin created was that we all became lost, incapable of saving ourselves. Praise God that He did not allow us to go our desired way towards sin and eternal death! He had decided to show His love, making a divine choice.

He chose to reveal His way of salvation to Abraham (Gen 12:1-3) and to use the Hebrew nation to bring it about. "The Lord your God has chosen you out of all the peoples of the earth to be his people, his treasured possession" (Deut 7:6b). When Jesus was revealed as the Savior of the world, He also chose a small group of men saying, "You did not choose me, but I chose you" (John 15:16a). In fact, He declared, "No one can come to me unless the Father who sent me draws him" (John 6:44a). Further Jesus declared, "No one knows the Father except the Son and those to whom the Son chooses to reveal him" (Lk 10:22).

Sometimes this divine choosing is called "election" and the chosen are called "God's elect." There are elect angels (1 Tim 5:21), who will gather the elect humans together at the end of this age (Mk 13:27; Matt 24:22). Peter wrote to the elect (1 Pet 1:11) and Paul endured great sufferings for the sake of God's elect (2 Tim 2:10). God's election is also called predestination (Rom 8:29; 11:2; 1 Pet 1:2). The Bible clearly teaches that God knows everything, ruling and reigning over all creation. His sovereign plan is followed, yet in such a way that we all are responsible for our choices.

The NT teaches that "believers were chosen before the foundation of the world" (2 Tim 1:9; 2 Thes 2:13) in Christ (Eph 1:4) to adoption (Eph 1:5) and to good works (2:10). The source of election is God's grace, not our human choice or will (John 1:13; Eph 1:4-5; Rom 9:11; 11:5). "We love because he first loved us" (1 John 4:19).

It would have been amazing grace for even one so unworthy as we to be saved! Yet millions believe, taken from every tribe, tongue and nation. God orders the Church to share the gospel with everyone. All who reject it do so because they do not want to repent and submit to Christ. All who accept the good news do so by His grace alone, not because they are better than the others. Praise God for the gift of saving faith!

Response

I thank you God for showing me _____

_____.

STRATEGY

Follow Jesus today, seeing how He often spoke of salvation as seen in **Luke 13:22-30** (Read now)

As I follow Jesus today I will remember _____

_____.

OBEDIENCE (I will statement)

The Spirit is convicting or leading me today to do or stop doing: _____

_____.

PETITIONS (Following your reciting of The Lord's Prayer)

I pray for these scheduled meetings today:

I pray also for these pressing needs of myself, my family, my church, my disciples my world:

CONFESSION and REPENTANCE

I confess these, my sins, with every intention to never repeat them, but rather to live as Jesus would live, by Your enabling grace and Spirit ...

*Never confess without a faith that looks to the cross of Christ, where the guilt and penalty of all our sins was paid!

WALK (Think about the following praise song)

Tis Not that I did Choose Thee

1) 'Tis not that I did choose Thee,
For Lord, that could not be;
This heart would still refuse Thee,
Hadst Thou not chosen me.
Thou from the sin that stained me
Hast cleansed and set me free;
Of old Thou hast ordained me,
That I should live to Thee.

2) 'Twas sov'reign mercy called me
And taught my op'ning mind;
The world had else enthralled me,
To heav'nly glories blind.
My heart owns none before Thee,
Hast cleansed and set me free;
For Thy rich grace I thirst;
This knowing, if I love Thee,
Thou must have loved me first.
(Joshua Conder 1789-1855)

Response

Help me, Jesus, to _____

_____.

VICTORY

Memorize *John 6:44-45*

Be prepared for opposition (spiritual warfare) and expect victory in Jesus' name.

Write down the name (s) of those with whom you shared today _____
_____.

_____ Check when the day is completed, never beating yourself up if you did not finish; but, just asking Jesus to help you next day!

Day Sixty-three

God – The True One

ADORATION

Truth is the opposite of falsehood and error. What is true is real. It can be relied on and will not disappoint legitimate expectations. Lies are like dreams, without a lasting foundation. Error will ultimately disappoint those relying on it, Paul was right when he affirmed, "For we can do nothing against the truth, but only for the truth" (2 Cor 13:2). Truth will out. It will have its day and win. How can we be so sure of this?

One reason is that a God of truth reigns over heaven and earth. He, alone, is "the God of truth" (Isa. 65:16). "... The Lord is the true God. he is the living God" (Jer 10:10). He tells the truth and supports the truth. "for the word of the Lord is right and true" (Ps 33:4; 119:160): ...every good promise of the Lord your God has come true" (Josh 23:1 5). Even when He allows the truth of His existence and love to be trampled upon and nearly lost. He remains unchangeably devoted to it and will, in His perfect time. exalt and establish it. "For a long time, Israel was without the true God" (2 Chron 15:3). God said, "Go up and down the streets of Jerusalem ... search through her squares. If you can find but one person who deals honestly and seeks the truth, I will forgive this city... The prophets prophesy lies...and my people love it this way. But what will you do in the end?" (Jer 5:1, 31). Even when all around looks bleak, and error is advancing. "Let God be true and every man a liar" (Rom 3:4a). He, alone, does not deceive and can be trusted—forever. You will surely win if you trust Him.

When Christ came, He was "the true light" (John 1:9). "the true vine" (John 15:1) in contrast to the cunning and convincing counterfeits of Satan. John declared. "The Word became flesh and made his dwelling among us. We have seen his glory, the glory of the One and Only. Who came from the Father, full of grace and truth" (John 1:14). He was so filled by truth, unlike any other, that He was called its revealer. Only Jesus perfectly, always and in everything revealed the truth of God. "For the law was given through Moses: grace and truth came through Jesus Christ" (John 1:17). He constantly began His words with, "I tell you the truth" (Matt 5:18. etc.). Do we live as though we utterly believe Him?

Jesus is "the truth" (John 14:6). the common thread running through all that endures. "Surely you desire truth in the inner parts" (Ps 51:6a). So, let us, "Buy the truth and do not sell it" (Prov 23:23a), resisting the strong pull to "suppress" and "exchange the truth of God for a lie" (Rom 1:18.25). "If you hold to my teaching. you are really my disciples. Then you will know the truth, and the truth will set you free" (John 8:31-2). You will end up where everyone wants to go only if you know and follow Christ as "the truth."

Response

I thank you God for showing me _____

_____.

STRATEGY

Follow Jesus today, remembering His claim to be the truth as seen in **John 18:28-40** (Read now)

As I follow Jesus today I will remember _____

_____.

OBEDIENCE (I will statement)

The Spirit is convicting or leading me today to do or stop doing: _____

_____.

PETITIONS (Following your reciting of The Lord's Prayer)

I pray for these scheduled meetings today:

I pray also for these pressing needs of myself, my family, my church, my disciples my world:

CONFESSION and REPENTANCE

I confess these, my sins, with every intention to never repeat them, but rather to live as Jesus would live, by Your enabling grace and Spirit …

*Never confess without a faith that looks to the cross of Christ, where the guilt and penalty of all our sins was paid!

WALK (Think about the following praise song)

We Come, O Christ, to You

1) We come, O Christ, to you, true Son of God and man,
By whom all things consist, in whom all life began:
In you alone we live and move and have our being in your love.

2) You are the Way to God, your blood our ransom paid;
In you we face our Judge and Maker unafraid.
Before the throne absolved we stand, your love has met your law's demand.

3) You are the living Truth! All wisdom dwells in you,
The Source of every skill, the one eternal TRUE!
O great I AM! In you we rest, sure answer to our every quest.

4) You only are true Life, to know you is to live
The more abundant life that earth can never give:
O risen Lord! We live in you, in us each day your life renews!

5) We worship you, Lord Christ, our Savior and our King,
To you our youth and strength adoringly we bring,
So, fill our hearts, that all may view your life in us, and turn to you.
(E Margaret Clarkson, 1957)

Response

Help me, Jesus, to _____

_____.

VICTORY

Memorize *John 14:6*

Be prepared for opposition (spiritual warfare) and expect victory in Jesus' name.

Write down the name (s) of those with whom you shared today _____
_____.

____ Check when the day is completed, never beating yourself up if you did not finish; but, just asking Jesus to help you next day!

Day Sixty-four

God – The Anointing One

ADORATION

  In every culture, special people are treated differently than others. Presidents are sworn into office, but cashiers just show up and begin their jobs without any fanfare. Mickie Mantle's foul ball, when caught by a fan, was treated differently than the one I hit when playing Little League.

  God touches and uses some differently than others. In the OT times, He wanted prophets (1 Kgs 19:16), priests (Ex. 28:40-41) and kings (2 Kgs 9:3) to be anointed with oil before assuming their positions of authority. The oil represented His blessing coming on them to assist them in fulfilling their very important duties. The positions of prophet, priest and king were more consequential for Israel's wellbeing than that of farmer, shepherd or soldier—so they were specially and solemnly set apart by anointing. Prophets were needed to teach the people God's ways. Priests, to intercede between them as sinners and their holy God. And kings were anointed to rule over and defend the weak. It was a grave sin to oppose or harm those whom God had anointed. "Do not touch my anointed ones; do my prophets no harm" (1 Chron 16:22; Ps 105:15). When Saul, his arch enemy, was killed, and the event reported to David, he was not overjoyed, but asked, "Why were you not afraid to lift your hand to destroy the Lord's anointed?" (2 Sam 1:16).

  All those anointed ones helped only temporarily and imperfectly. But they were foretastes of a Coming One, who would be perfectly anointed to save sinners forever! That is why the predicted One was called the Messiah, which means—The Anointed One. Many OT passages of the Messiah were ascribed to Jesus in the NT (like Ps 45:7 with Heb 1:9 and Lk 4:18a with Is. 61:1). Just like His prophetic predecessors, the perfectly Anointed One was also hated and opposed. "The kings of the earth take their stand and the rulers gather together against the Lord and against His Anointed One" (Ps 2:2; Acts 4:26), Jesus is the only Messiah from God.

  Unless God helps us, we are doomed. Sometimes He strengthens us, Himself, without use of others. "You anoint my head with oil; my cup overflows" (Ps 23:5b). But often He uses imperfect Christians to do His work. Every Christian is anointed by God to be a blessing to others in this world. "...You have an anointing from the Holy One, and all of you know the truth" (1 John 2:20, 27). We are, in following Christ, little prophets, priests and kings. "He made us to be a kingdom and priests, to serve His God and Father" (Rev 1:6; 5:10). "You are a chosen people, a royal priesthood, a holy nation, a people belonging to God...Live such good lives among the pagans that ... they may see your good deeds and glorify God..." (1 Pet 2:9,12). "Do not repay evil with evil or insult with insult, but with blessing, because to this you were called...." (1 Pet 3:9). We are anointed by the Holy Spirit so that the blessings of Christ may flow through us to all those on earth. "He anointed us, set his seal of ownership on us, and put his Spirit in our hearts as a deposit, guaranteeing what is to come" (2 Cor 1:21-22). You have been anointed by God. Be a blessing!

Response

I thank you God for showing me _____

_____.

STRATEGY

Follow Jesus today, seeing how He claimed to be the Anointed One of God as seen in **Luke 4:14-30** (Read now)

As I follow Jesus today I will remember _____

_____.

OBEDIENCE (I will statement)

The Spirit is convicting or leading me today to do or stop doing: _____

_____.

PETITIONS (Following your reciting of <u>The Lord's Prayer</u>)

I pray for these scheduled meetings today:

I pray also for these pressing needs of myself, my family, my church, my disciples my world:

CONFESSION and REPENTANCE

I confess these, my sins, with every intention to never repeat them, but rather to live as Jesus would live, by Your enabling grace and Spirit ...

*Never confess without a faith that looks to the cross of Christ, where the guilt and penalty of all our sins was paid!

WALK (Think about the following praise song)

Come, Holy Spirit

1) Come, Holy Spirit, heav'nly Dove,
with all Thy quickening powers;
kindle a flame of sacred love
in these cold hearts of ours.

2) O raise our thoughts from things below,
from vanities and toys,
then shall we with fresh courage to
to reach eternal joys.

3) Awake our souls to joyful songs;
let pure devotion rise,
till praise employs our thankful tongues,
and doubt forever dies.

4) Come, Holy Spirit, heav'nly Dove,
with all Thy quickening powers;
come, shed abroad a Savior's love,
and that shall kindle ours.
(Isaac Watts, 1674-1748)

Response

Help me, Jesus, to _____

_____.

VICTORY

Memorize *1 John 2:27*

Be prepared for opposition (spiritual warfare) and expect victory in Jesus' name.

Write down the name (s) of those with whom you shared today _____
_____.

____ Check when the day is completed, never beating yourself up if you did not finish; but, just asking Jesus to help you next day!

Day Sixty-five

God – The Giver

ADORATION

  Generosity is not usually the shining characteristic of those who are wealthy. And let's remember that we are wealthy—compared to most others living on God's earth. Just because we do not use our capital wisely, pressuring ourselves with overspending, doesn't make us poor. It simply reveals that we are unwise in our use of finances. We often work so hard to get "financially secure" (wealth) that we rarely notice how often the price we pay is becoming stingy, tightfisted--deaf and blind to the needs of others. Having worked so long for our own ends, once they are achieved, we lack the capacity, the ability, to give away freely, lavishly and happily (See Luke 21:1-4). Realizing this tendency of our human nature, Paul felt compelled to tell Timothy to "Command those who are rich ...not to be arrogant or put their hope in wealth" but "to do good, to be rich in good deeds, and to be generous and wilting to share" (1 Tim 6: 17-18).Paul had urged the Corinthians to "excel in this grace of giving" reminding them of the way Christ had given, "that though he was rich, yet for your sakes he became poor, so that you through his poverty might become rich" (2 Cor 9:7,9). Children of God are born again by God and reveal their birth-link with God by reflecting His likeness. And God is an amazing Giver. "Every good and perfect gift is from above, coming down from the Father" (James 1: 17a). None of the good things we have enjoyed in this life have their source elsewhere than the generous heart of God. Thank Him often for all those things you enjoy!

  The Bible reveals a God who loves to give gifts, even to those who do not deserve them. "The eyes of all look to you, and you give them their food at the proper time. You open your hand and satisfy the desire of every living thing" (Ps 145:15-16). "He causes his sun to rise on the evil and the good and sends rain on the righteous and the unrighteous" (Matt 5:45b). It is His nature to give. And Jesus revealed that aspect of God when on earth. "This is how we know what love is: Jesus Christ laid down his life for us. And we ought to lay down our lives for our brothers" (1 John 3:16). Paul reminded elders that Jesus taught it is more blessed to give than to receive" (Acts 20:35).

  We have so much more to give than merely money. We have time, skills, smiles, warm embraces, truth, sympathy, tears, encouragement, prayers, cookies, umbrellas, advice, the Gospel—the list is endless. In Christ, we are so truly wealthy! "He who did not spare his own Son, but gave him up for us all—how will he not also, along with him, graciously give us all things?" (Rom 8:32). The resurrection of Jesus Christ is portrayed as leading to His ascension, His taking captives and his giving gifts to men (Eph 4:8; Ps 68:18). And the greatest gift He has given, 'the promised gift of the Father" is the Holy Spirit (Acts 1:4; 2:33) and through Him—eternal life. Those who are born again of the Spirit enter a relationship of sonship with the Father that encourages us to enjoy all the incredible gifts of God's grace as often as we desire—through prayer. (Matt 7:7-11; John 15:7, 16; 16:23). Don't live like orphans any longer! Freely you have received. Freely — give (Matt 10:8), remembering that God loves a cheerful giver (2 Cor 9:7).

Response

I thank you God for showing me _____

_____.

STRATEGY

Follow Jesus today, seeing how Paul commands husbands to give themselves in love to their wives as Christ gave Himself for the Church as seen in **Ephesians 5:25-33** (Read now)

As I follow Jesus today I will remember _____

_____.

OBEDIENCE (I will statement)

The Spirit is convicting or leading me today to do or stop doing: _____

_____.

PETITIONS (Following your reciting of The Lord's Prayer)

I pray for these scheduled meetings today:

I pray also for these pressing needs of myself, my family, my church, my disciples my world:

CONFESSION and REPENTANCE

I confess these, my sins, with every intention to never repeat them, but rather to live as Jesus would live, by Your enabling grace and Spirit ...

*Never confess without a faith that looks to the cross of Christ, where the guilt and penalty of all our sins was paid!

WALK (Think about the following praise song)

Give of Your Best to the Master

1) Give of your best to the Master;
Give of the strength of your youth;
Throw your soul's fresh, glowing ardor
Into the battle for truth.
Jesus has set the example,
Dauntless was He, young and brave;
Give Him your loyal devotion;
Give Him the best that you have.

Give of your best to the Master;
Give of the strength of your youth;
Clad in salvation's full armor,
Join in the battle for truth.

2) Give of your best to the Master;
Give Him first place in your heart;
Give Him first place in your service;
Consecrate every part.
Give, and to you will be given;
God His Beloved Son gave;
Gratefully seeking to serve Him,
Give Him the best that you have.

3) Give of your best to the Master;
Naught else is worthy His love;
He gave Himself for your ransom,
Gave up His glory above.
Laid down His life without murmur,
You from sin's ruin to save;
Give Him your heart's adoration;
Give Him the best that you have.
(Howard B Grose, 1851-1939)

Response

Help me, Jesus, to _____

_____.

VICTORY

Memorize *2 Corinthians 9:7*

Be prepared for opposition (spiritual warfare) and expect victory in Jesus' name.

Write down the name (s) of those with whom you shared today _____

_____.

_____ Check when the day is completed, never beating yourself up if you did not finish; but, just asking Jesus to help you next day!

Day Sixty-six

God – The Tester

ADORATION

Life is full of tests. When we pass a test, we celebrate because we have proven some progress or achievement. Since tests often create stress in us, there must be a good reason for them. They aren't fun; but they are important. Tests happen when it has become necessary for someone to prove something. So, passing or failing a test proves something about us.

God tests us. Sometimes severely, like Job. "But he knows the way I take; when he has tested me, I will come forth as gold" (Job 23:10). Or Abraham, who was told to "offer Isaac as a sacrifice when God tested him" (Heb 11:17). Or like the people of Israel, "For you, O God, tested us; you refined us like silver. You brought us into prison and laid burdens on our backs" (Ps 66:10-11). So, what is the purpose of the testing of the Lord? Do we really need it?

David understood life's trials and wrote, "I know, my God, that you test the heart and are pleased with integrity" (1 Chron 29:1 7a). The heart is a tricky thing. It is hard to read. Hard to uncover. God knows what tests will uncover the true state of our hearts. "Test me, O God, and try me, examine my heart and my mind; for your love is ever before me, and I walk continually in your truth" (Ps 26:2-3). God tests our hearts to reveal to us whether we really love Him and His truth (See 2 Thess 2:5-12; Deut. 13:1-5). We need such testing because we can fool ourselves into thinking our hearts love God when they really don't.

We were created for God. We were made to love and serve Him. In other words--we were made to glorify God. And that is another reason He tests us. "See, I have refined you. I have tested you in the furnace of affliction, for my own sake, for my own sake I do this. How can I let myself be defamed? I will not yield my glory to another" (Isa 48:10-11). It would seem wrong for a loving Creator to leave His creation self-deceived when administering a test could help them see the truth about themselves and their Creator. So, God is very kind and good to purify our hearts and help us focus on him rather than on ourselves. And to go onwards to our own destruction. What test is best to achieve this?

The greatest Test for sinners is Jesus. He reveals everything about us, coming near and interacting with us. He goes where no one else dares to go, yet in love. So, we open our hearts to Him and His light, even though we know it will expose our sin. "So, this is what the Sovereign Lord says: See I lay a stone in Zion, a tested stone, a precious cornerstone for a sure foundation; the one who trusts will never be dismayed" (Isa 28:16). This stone is Jesus. Peter told the Jewish leaders that they had rejected this Stone which God made the very capstone (Acts 4:11). And he wrote that "to you who believe, this stone is precious. But to those who do not believe, he is a stone that causes men to stumble and a rock that makes them fall" (1 Pet 2:7-8; Isa 8:14). We welcome the test of Jesus. "Blessed is the man who perseveres under trial, because when he has stood the test, he will receive the crown of life that God has promised to those who love him" (James 1:12). To continue in love to Jesus is to pass the test.

Response

I thank you God for showing me _____

STRATEGY

Follow Jesus today, seeing how He endured the severe tests of Satan, allowed by His Father, as seen in **Luke 4:1-13** (Read now)

As I follow Jesus today I will remember _____

_____.

OBEDIENCE (I will statement)

The Spirit is convicting or leading me today to do or stop doing: _____

_____.

PETITIONS (Following your reciting of <u>The Lord's Prayer</u>)

I pray for these scheduled meetings today:

I pray also for these pressing needs of myself, my family, my church, my disciples my world:

CONFESSION and REPENTANCE

I confess these, my sins, with every intention to never repeat them, but rather to live as Jesus would live, by Your enabling grace and Spirit ...

*Never confess without a faith that looks to the cross of Christ, where the guilt and penalty of all our sins was paid!

WALK (Think about the following praise song)

It is Well with my Soul

1) When peace, like a river, attendeth my way,
When sorrows like sea billows roll;
Whatever my lot, Thou has taught me to say,
It is well, it is well, with my soul.

*It is well, with my soul,
It is well, with my soul,
It is well, it is well, with my soul.*

2) Though Satan should buffet, though trials should come,
Let this blest assurance control,
That Christ has regarded my helpless estate,
And hath shed His own blood for my soul.

3) My sin, oh the bliss of this glorious thought
My sin, not in part but the whole,
Is nailed to the cross, and I bear it no more,
Praise the Lord, praise the Lord, O my soul!

4) For me, be it Christ, be it Christ hence to live:
If Jordan above me shall roll,
No pang shall be mine, for in death as in life
Thou wilt whisper Thy peace to my soul.

5) But, Lord, 'tis for Thee, for Thy coming we wait,
The sky, not the grave, is our goal;
Oh trump of the angel! Oh, voice of the Lord!
Blessed hope, blessed rest of my soul!

(6) And Lord, haste the day when my faith shall be sight,
The clouds be rolled back as a scroll;
The trump shall resound, and the Lord shall descend,
Even so, it is well with my soul.
(Horatio G Spafford, 1828-1888)

Response

Help me, Jesus, to _____

_____.

VICTORY

Memorize: *James 1:2-3*

Be prepared for opposition (spiritual warfare) and expect victory in Jesus' name.

Write down the name (s) of those with whom you shared today and pray for them. _____

_____.

_____ Check when the day is completed, never beating yourself up if you did not finish; but, just asking Jesus to help you next day!

Day Sixty-seven

God – The Hated One

ADORATION

True hatred represents one of the deepest negative feelings of which we humans are capable. Some synonyms of "to hate" are "to loathe" and "to despise." Whenever possible, we will either remove what we hate or quickly leave its presence. So, what or whom do you hate? Certain tastes and smells repel you. Do you think you repel others? You should!

It might surprise you to consider how deeply some people hate the Lord. In the Ten Commandments, the Lord mentions, "those who hate me" (Ex 20:5b; see 2 Chron 19:2). The prophet Isaiah spoke of the Coming Messiah, saying, "He was despised and rejected by men, a man of sorrows, and familiar with suffering. Like one from whom men hide their faces he was despised, and we esteemed him not" (Isa 53:3).

Those who hate the Lord, hate His Word. "But to the wicked God says ... you hate my instruction and cast my words behind you" (Ps 50; 16-17). They hate His Wisdom, which says, "I love those who love me, and those who seek me find me. For whoever finds me finds life and receives favor from the Lord. But whoever fails to find me harms himself; all who hate me love death" (Prov 8:17, 35-36). They hate His light. "This is the verdict: Light has come into the world, but men loved darkness rather than light because their deeds were evil. Everyone who does evil hates the light and will not come into the light for fear that his deeds will be exposed" (John 3:19-20). That explains why He is so hated. They love their sin and their darkness. They cannot smell the stink of death around them. They are blind to see that their way leads off a cliff to destruction. It is He and we who look and smell like death to them (2 Cor 2:15-16).

Many people hate Christ, the Light and Wisdom of God. Jesus felt this. In a parable He spoke of His relationship with others and said, "But his subjects hated him and sent a delegation after him to say, 'We don't want this man to be our king'" (Luke 19:14). He reminded His disciples, "If the world hates you, keep in mind that it hated me first" (John 15:18).

In fact, Jesus knew just how hard it would be for us on this earth because of humans' innate hatred of God. It is such a shocking thing that the apostle John wrote, "Do not be surprised, my brothers, if the world hates you" (1 John 3:13). We have been sent into the world with a message of love. The Law of Christ commands us that when struck, we turn the other cheek.

When cursed, we are to bless. When compelled to go one mile, we should gladly go two (Matt 5). We are to forgive and to die in this service of those who hate our God and us. This is shocking. But it was all predicted. "... But now they have seen these miracles, and yet they have hated both me and my Father. But this is to fulfill what is written in their Law: they hated me without reason" (John 15:24-25). It just doesn't make sense. But this hatred is very real and very hard. Jesus said, "All men will hate you because of me, but he who stands firm to the end will be saved" (Matt 10:22). May your faith focus on HIM and may you love HIM more than anyone or anything—even more than your own life itself.

Response

I thank you God for showing me _____

_____.

STRATEGY

Follow Jesus today, seeing how He taught His disciples to forgive their hateful enemies as He did as seen in **Matthew 5:43-48** (Read now)

As I follow Jesus today I will remember _____

_____.

OBEDIENCE (I will statement)

The Spirit is convicting or leading me today to do or stop doing: _____

_____.

PETITIONS (Following your reciting of The Lord's Prayer)

I pray for these scheduled meetings today:

I pray also for these pressing needs of myself, my family, my church, my disciples my world:

CONFESSION and REPENTANCE

I confess these, my sins, with every intention to never repeat them, but rather to live as Jesus would live, by Your enabling grace and Spirit ...

*Never confess without a faith that looks to the cross of Christ, where the guilt and penalty of all our sins was paid!

WALK (Think about the following praise song)

Stricken, Smitten and Afflicted

1) Stricken, smitten, and afflicted,
See Him dying on the tree!
'Tis the Christ by man rejected;
Yes, my soul, 'tis He, 'tis He!
'Tis the long-expected prophet,
David's Son, yet David's Lord;
Proofs I see sufficient of it:
'Tis a true and faithful Word.

2) Tell me, ye who hear Him groaning,
Was there ever grief like His?
Friends through fear His cause disowning,
Foes insulting his distress:
Many hands were raised to wound Him,
None would interpose to save;
But the deepest stroke that pierced Him
Was the stroke that Justice gave.

3) Ye who think of sin but lightly,
Nor suppose the evil great,
Here may view its nature rightly,
Here its guilt may estimate.
Mark the Sacrifice appointed!
See Who bears the awful load!
'Tis the Word, the Lord's Anointed,
Son of Man, and Son of God.

4) Here we have a firm foundation,
Here the refuge of the lost.
Christ the Rock of our salvation,

> Christ the Name of which we boast.
> Lamb of God for sinners wounded!
> Sacrifice to cancel guilt!
> None shall ever be confounded
> Who on Him their hope has built.
> (Thomas Kelly, 1769-1855)

Response

Help me, Jesus, to _____

_____.

VICTORY

Memorize *Psalm 139:21*

Be prepared for opposition (spiritual warfare) and expect victory in Jesus' name.

Write down the name (s) of those with whom you shared today _____

_____.

_____ Check when the day is completed, never beating yourself up if you did not finish; but, just asking Jesus to help you next day!

Day Sixty-eight

God – The Orderly One

ADORATION

"God is not a God of disorder but of peace" (1 Cor 14:33). Webster defines "order" as "the sequence or arrangement of things or events; a fixed or definite plan; system; a state of peace and serenity." At Easter, we marvel at God's plan that gave us peace. The plan was implied in such verses as: "The Son of Man goes just as it is written about him. But woe to that man who betrays the Son of Man" (Mk 14:2 1). "You will all fall away, Jesus told them, for it is written, I will strike the shepherd, and the sheep will be scattered" (Mk 14:27). "Put your sword back in its place ... Do you not think I cannot call my Father, and he will at once put at my disposal more than 12 legions of angels? But how then would the Scriptures be fulfilled that say it must happen this way?" (Matt 26:52-54). "This man was handed over ... by God's set purpose and foreknowledge; and you, with the help of wicked men, put him to death by nailing him to the cross. But God raised him from the dead" (Acts 2:23-24).

What is true of the events surrounding Easter, according to the Bible, is true of every event, everywhere, at all times! God has a plan. God is in ultimate control and His order cannot be thwarted. Joseph's brothers selling him into slavery was by divine plan (Gen 50:20). The random shooting of an arrow (I Kgs 22:34), the feeding of birds and growth of flowers (Matt 6:26,30), the words spoken at any moment (Prov 16:1), the configuration of dice when they are thrown (16:33)—in fact, all things (Rom 8:28) reveal the outworking of the plan of God (Amos 3:7; Eph 1:11).

The plan of God must occur because no one, anywhere at any time is greater than God. "There is no wisdom, no insight, no plan that can succeed against the Lord" (Prov 21:30). Infinite wisdom and power have established God's orderly plan. He, alone, truly reigns. Yet, as we have seen, in such a way that all are personally responsible for all that they do. And in such a way that God cannot be accused of being the causative force behind sin and evil. God is good and, so, His plan is good, even when we just cannot see it. "It is God who works in you both to will and to do his good purpose" (Phil 2:13).

Satan is the author of confusion and chaos; but Jesus is the Prince of peace and order. He is a wise Man with a clear plan. We follow Him when we trust and wait on God—in peace. May we, as God's children, show purpose and planning in our lives, rather than laziness or disorderliness. Order, even in small things, can impact our faith in Christ, as Paul shows, "I delight to see how orderly you are and how firm your faith in Christ is" (Col. 2:5). When your life takes a crazy, out-of-control turn, slow down, pray and follow Jesus!

Response

I thank you God for showing me _____

_____.

STRATEGY

Follow Jesus today, seeing how He trusted God's purpose and timing and taught His disciples to do the same as seen in **Acts 1:1-9** (Read now)

As I follow Jesus today I will remember _____

_____.

OBEDIENCE (I will statement)

The Spirit is convicting or leading me today to do or stop doing: _____

_____.

PETITIONS (Following your reciting of The Lord's Prayer)

I pray for these scheduled meetings today:

I pray also for these pressing needs of myself, my family, my church, my disciples my world:

CONFESSION and REPENTANCE

I confess these, my sins, with every intention to never repeat them, but rather to live as Jesus would live, by Your enabling grace and Spirit ...

*Never confess without a faith that looks to the cross of Christ, where the guilt and penalty of all our sins was paid!

WALK (Think about the following hymn)

All Things Bright and Beautiful

Refrain:
All things bright and beautiful,
All creatures great and small,
All things wise and wonderful:
The Lord God made them all.

1) Each little flow'r that opens,
Each little bird that sings,
He made their glowing colors,
He made their tiny wings.

2) The purple-headed mountains,
The river running by,
The sunset and the morning
That brightens up the sky.

3) The cold wind in the winter,
The pleasant summer sun,
The ripe fruits in the garden,
He made them everyone.

4) The tall trees in the greenwood,
The meadows where we play,
The rushes by the water,
To gather every day.

5) He gave us eyes to see them,
And lips that we might tell
How great is God Almighty,
Who has made all things well.
(Cecil F Alexander, 1818-1895)

Response

Help me, Jesus, to _____

_____.

VICTORY

Memorize *Romans 8:28*

Be prepared for opposition (spiritual warfare) and expect victory in Jesus' name.

Write down the name (s) of those with whom you shared today _____
_____.

____ Check when the day is completed, never beating yourself up if you did not finish; but, just asking Jesus to help you next day!

Day Sixty-nine

God – The Servant

ADORATION

    Nature seems to teach that those who are less serve those who are greater. The younger and weaker give way to the older and stronger. Privates are subordinate to their ranking officers. But why is this? Is it because those who are more powerful always deserve greater respect and regard? It was this norm of human rule and domination that Jesus overturned. "Not so with you. Instead, whoever wants to become great among you must be your servant. For even the Son of Man did not come to be served but to serve, and to give his life as a ransom for many" (Mark: 10:43, 45). And to make the point even more precisely on the night that He inaugurated the New Covenant, He laid aside His garments and performed the menial task of a house slave in washing the feet of his disciples. A job so demeaning in Peter's mind, that he heartily resisted it. At the close of the event, Jesus said, "You call me Teacher and Lord, and rightly so, for that is what I am. Now that I, your Lord and Teacher have washed your feet, you also should wash one another's feet" (John 13:13-14).

    Jesus came as the Son of Man, the perfect and full man, the true Adam, to live for all and to show all mankind how to live. Life for the best human was joyful service. The Coming Messiah would say, "I desire to do your will, O my God; your law is within my heart" (Ps 40:8; Matt 26:39). The Father proclaims of Him, "Here is my servant, whom I uphold, my chosen one in whom I delight" (Isa 42:1; Matt 12:18). God in human flesh is the quintessential servant of the Lord. "By his knowledge my righteous servant will justify many, and he will bear their iniquities" (Isa 53:11).

    The servanthood of God, the Son, to the Father and to all mankind became the center of His disciples' new identity. They followed their Master/Servant into a life of service to all. They had no problem glorifying Jesus in prayer as a servant, saying, "Stretch out your hand to heal. through the name of your holy servant Jesus" (Acts 4:30). Service was their honor. The greatest among them, the Apostles, routinely identified themselves as slaves of Christ and His church (Rom 1:1; James 1:1; 2Pet 1:12; Jude 1:1; Rev 1:1). "For we do not preach ourselves, but Jesus Christ as Lord, and ourselves as your servants for Jesus' sake" (2 Cor 4:5). And they called on all to follow Christ as they had learned to follow him. "Your attitude should be the same as that of Christ Jesus...Who, being in very nature God...made himself nothing, taking the very nature of a servant" (Phil 2:5-7). When will the Church in our land repent of its master mentality and begin anew to follow Christ in selfless service? Maybe when we hear and respond to Paul's command, "You...were called to be free. But do not use your freedom to indulge the sinful nature; rather, serve one another in love" (Gal 5:13). Maybe when YOU begin to humbly and sacrificially help others, to do whatever is needed, even wash your brothers' feet with joy in the name of Jesus. And when you let him wash yours!

Response

I thank you God for showing me _____

_____.

STRATEGY

Follow Jesus today, seeing how He, emphasized serving others as seen in **Matt 6:19-24** (Read now)

As I follow Jesus today I will remember _____

_____.

OBEDIENCE (I will statement)

The Spirit is convicting or leading me today to do or stop doing: _____

_____.

PETITIONS (Following your reciting of The Lord's Prayer)

I pray for these scheduled meetings today:

I pray also for these pressing needs of myself, my family, my church, my disciples my world:

CONFESSION and REPENTANCE

I confess these, my sins, with every intention to never repeat them, but rather to live as Jesus would live, by Your enabling grace and Spirit ...

*Never confess without a faith that looks to the cross of Christ, where the guilt and penalty of all our sins was paid!

WALK (Think about the following praise song)

Let All Mortal Flesh Keep Silence

1) Let all mortal flesh keep silence,
and with fear and trembling stand;
ponder nothing earthly minded,
for with blessing in His hand
Christ our God to earth descendeth,
our full homage to demand.

2) King of kings, yet born of Mary,
as of old on earth He stood,
Lord of lords, in human vesture -
in the body and the blood.
He will give to all the faithful
His own self for heavenly food.

3) Rank on rank the host of heaven
spreads its vanguard on the way,
as the Light of light descendeth
from the realms of endless day,
that the pow'rs of hell may vanish
as the darkness clears away.

4) At His feet the six-winged seraph,
cherubim, with sleepless eye,
veil their faces to the Presence,
as with ceaseless voice they cry,
"Alleluia, alleluia!
Alleluia, Lord most high!"
(From the 4th century Greek Liturgy of St James, translated by Gerard Moultrie, 1864)

Response

Help me, Jesus, to _____

_____.

VICTORY

Memorize *Matthew 20:28*

Be prepared for opposition (spiritual warfare) and expect victory in Jesus' name.

Write down the name (s) of those with whom you shared today _____

_____.

_____ Check when the day is completed, never beating yourself up if you did not finish; but, just asking Jesus to help you next day!

Day Seventy

God – The Savior

ADORATION

To save is to rescue from danger or harm. So, where there is neither harm nor danger, there is no need to save. But the Bible is full of God's works of salvation in behalf of his needy people. "You save the humble but bring low those whose eyes are haughty (Ps 18:27). Throughout the OT, God is represented as the One who "hears their cry and saves them" (Ps 145:19b). He is zealous to save those who realize their need and desperately seek his help. "The Lord your God is with you, he is mighty to save. He will take great delight in you, he will quiet you with his love, he will rejoice over you with singing" (Zeph 3:17).

The Lord declares, "there is no God apart from me, a righteous God and a Savior; there is none but me. Turn to me and be saved, all you end of the earth; for I am God, and there is no other" (Is 45:21-22). Why does the earth not turn to him for salvation? Our pride leads us to conclude that we can either save ourselves or we can discover another god who will deliver us. "Some trust in chariots and some in horses, but we trust in the name of the Lord our God" (Ps 20:7). "Ignorant are those... who pray to gods that cannot save" (Is 45:20b).

The name Jesus is the Greek name for Joshua which means, "The Lord saves." The angel told Joseph, "you are to give him the name Jesus, because he will save his people from their sins" (Matt 1:21). "The Father has sent his Son to be the Savior of the world (I John 4: 14b). Jesus said, 'For the Son of Man came to seek and to save what was lost" (Lk 19:10). But to Israel's spiritual leaders, who rejected him, he said, "You diligently study the Scriptures because you think that by them you possess eternal life. These are the Scriptures that testify about me, yet you refuse to come to me to have life" (John 5:39-40). To others, though, grace was given to believe and be saved by the Spirit (Eph 2:5,8; Tit 3:5).

Since God alone can save us, let us humbly trust him for every great or small need. Let us see it as foolish and futile whenever we lean on another for deliverance. They might help us temporarily, but only Jesus "is able to save completely those who come to God through him, because he always lives to intercede for them" (Heb 7:25). Since God is faithful, let us wait patiently for his salvation. "To him who can keep you from falling ...to the only God our Savior be glory, majesty, power and authority, through Jesus Christ our Lord, before all ages, now and forevermore! Amen" (Jude 24-25).

Response

I thank you God for showing me _____

_____.

STRATEGY

Follow Jesus today, and His mission to save as seen in **Matt 1:18-21** (Read now)

As I follow Jesus today I will remember _____

OBEDIENCE (I will statement)

The Spirit is convicting or leading me today to do or stop doing: _____

_____

PETITIONS (Following your reciting of <u>The Lord's Prayer</u>)

I pray for these scheduled meetings today:

I pray also for these pressing needs of myself, my family, my church, my disciples my world:

CONFESSION and REPENTANCE

I confess these, my sins, with every intention to never repeat them, but rather to live as Jesus would live, by Your enabling grace and Spirit …

*Never confess without a faith that looks to the cross of Christ, where the guilt and penalty of all our sins was paid!

WALK (Think about the following praise song)

Man of Sorrows! What a Name

1) "Man of Sorrows," what a name
For the Son of God who came
Ruined sinners to reclaim!
Hallelujah! what a Savior!

2) Bearing shame and scoffing rude,
In my place condemned He stood;
Sealed my pardon with His blood;
Hallelujah! what a Savior!

3) Guilty, vile, and helpless, we,
Spotless Lamb of God was He;
Full redemption—can it be?
Hallelujah! what a Savior!

4) Lifted up was He to die,
"It is finished!" was His cry;
Now in heaven exalted high;
Hallelujah! what a Savior!

5) When He comes, our glorious King,
To His kingdom us to bring,
Then anew this song we'll sing
Hallelujah! what a Savior!!
(Philip P Bliss, 1838-1876)

Response

Help me, Jesus, to _____

_____.

VICTORY

Memorize John _3:17_

Be prepared for opposition (spiritual warfare) and expect victory in Jesus' name.

Write down the name (s) of those with whom you shared today _____

_____.

____ Check when the day is completed, never beating yourself up if you did not finish; but, just asking Jesus to help you next day!

10-Day Period 8

Discipleship and our Duplicating in the Kingdom of Jesus

**Begin by reading Appendix Eight – Truly Witnessing like NT Disciples

The remaining month or 30 days with Jesus focuses on our privilege of representing His cause in the world. Because of the law of self-preservation, we will not endanger ourselves unnecessarily. But, the Bible clearly portrays the followers of Jesus as living in a hostile world and commissioned on a perilous task—to save sinners from their sin and its judgment. We go on this mission "like sheep during wolves" (Lk 10:3; Matt 10:1). And so, He tells us to be careful and even crafty. It is imperative that we follow His commands concerning "going" so that we do not recklessly imperil our lives. Luke 10:1ff was given to help keep us relatively safe from the wolves who desire to destroy us. Many are following that biblical strategy and powerfully making disciples in very dangerous places.

Jesus has given us two chief ways to reach and redeem the world: (1) preach the Gospel, and (2) make disciples. We must do both empowered by the love of God's Spirit! We reproduce, spiritually, in these two ways. Preaching the Gospel represents what we say. Making disciples stands for what we do. Our goal is to make disciples of a receptive person (person of peace) who becomes increasingly ready to surrender to Jesus by repentance and faith.

Historically, one of the chief markers determining when children pass into adulthood is when they go through puberty. That is, when they become physically able to produce or bear children. The Bible, in many places, speaks of a believer's maturity or fruitfulness occurring when he/she begins to reproduce spiritually.[34] Let us all "go on to maturity" (Heb 6:1).

---

[34] See my Fruitful or Unfruitful: *Why it really matters* for a short and very challenging handling of this subject

Day Seventy-one

God – The Owner of All

ADORATION

It appears you cannot be a respectable and successful American these days without understanding how to make a lot of money—and succeeding at it! Of course, this means you must look rich. You must spend it because you got it. Let the money flow like water. "No, no—I'll take care of it. We can afford it. No problem." And if it is really a problem, you must not show it. Just live like you've got it—even if you don't. Just keep dreaming that if you invest "wisely," then someday, after years of toil, you will be able to live it up. Retire in comfort. That is, if you live that long; if you don't have a heart attack, stroke or cancer; if the stock market doesn't crash; if terrorists give up trying to destroy us; if you hold on to your job; if no money-draining problem arises; if you've got plenty of insurance, and if.... Now that's a plan to brag about!

When one looks at the way GOD lived while on earth, this selfish American Dream seems like a very strange way of life. Americans really think they are rich and Jesus was poor by comparing our standard of living to His. Like the Laodiceans, many today "say, 'I am rich; I have acquired wealth and do not need a thing." But, Jesus said, "You do not realize you are wretched, pitiful, poor, blind and naked" (Rev 3:17). We might equate life with "liberty and the pursuit of happiness." But God equates it with following Christ as His slaves, dying to self, taking up our cross (trials) and giving away possessions we most cherish. The bottom line is NOT how much profit we make. The bottom line is-- God owns it all!

"The earth is the Lord's, and everything in it, the world and all who live in it" (Ps 24:1). "Although the whole earth is mine, you will be for me a kingdom of priests and a holy nation" (Ex 19:5b-6a; 1 Pet 2:9). "For the Israelites belong to me as servants. They are my servants, whom I brought out of Egypt. I am the Lord your God" (Lev 25:55). "Who has a claim against me that I must pay? Everything under heaven belongs to me" (Job 41:11). "The nobles of the nations assemble as the people of the God of Abraham, for the kings of the earth belong to God; he is greatly exalted" (Ps 47:9). "If I were hungry I would not tell you, for the world is mine and all that is in it" (Ps 50:12). "In his hand are the depths of the earth, and the mountain peaks belong to him. The sea is his, for he made it...." (Ps 95:4-5a).

"Last night an angel of the God whose I am and whom I serve...." (Acts 28:23). "Paul, a [slave] of Christ Jesus...And you also are among those who are called to belong to Jesus Christ" (Rom 1:1, 6). "He anointed us, set his seal of ownership on us" (2 Cor 1:21b).

God owns everything. To Him we must give an account of how we have used His gifts of life, time, family, intelligence, ingenuity, money and possessions. Who owns you? Freedom of speech, indeed! The ungodly and many Christians today say, "we own our lips—who is our master" (Ps 12:4b). The true disciple of Christ declares, "For none of us lives to himself alone ... if we live, we live to the Lord; and if we die, we die to the Lord. So, whether we live or die, we belong to the Lord" (Rom 14:7-8). Are you a proud owner or are you humbly owned by Christ?

Response

I thank you God for showing me _____

_____.

STRATEGY

Follow Jesus today, seeing how He claimed to own everything—even our lives—as seen in **Luke 17:7-10** (Read now)

As I follow Jesus today I will remember _____

_____.

OBEDIENCE (I will statement)

The Spirit is convicting or leading me today to do or stop doing: _____

_____.

PETITIONS (Following your reciting of The Lord's Prayer)

I pray for these scheduled meetings today:

I pray also for these pressing needs of myself, my family, my church, my disciples my world:

CONFESSION and REPENTANCE

I confess these, my sins, with every intention to never repeat them, but rather to live as Jesus would live, by Your enabling grace and Spirit …

*Never confess without a faith that looks to the cross of Christ, where the guilt and penalty of all our sins was paid!

WALK (Think about the following praise song)

Jesus, Master Whose I Am

1) Jesus, Master, whose I am,
Purchased Thine alone to be
By Thy blood, O spotless Lamb
Shed so willingly for me,
Let my heart be all Thine own,
Let me live for Thee alone.

2) Other lords have long held sway;
Now Thy Name alone to bear,
Thy dear voice alone obey,
Is my daily, hourly prayer;
Whom have I in heaven but Thee?
Nothing else my joy can be.

3) Jesus, Master, whom I serve,
Though so feebly and so ill,
Strengthen hand and heart and nerve
All Thy bidding to fulfill;
Open Thou mine eyes to see
All the work Thou hast for me.

4) Lord, Thou needest not, I know,
Service such as I can bring,
Yet I long to prove and show
Full allegiance to my King.
Jesus, let me always be
In Thy service glad and free.

> (5) Jesus, Master, I am Thine;
> Keep me faithful, keep me near;
> Let Thy presence in me shine
> All my homeward way to cheer,
> Jesus, at Thy feet I fall,
> O be Thou my all in all.
> (Frances R Havergal, 1836-1879)

Response

Help me, Jesus, to _____

_____.

VICTORY

Memorize *1 Corinthians 6:19-20*

Be prepared for opposition (spiritual warfare) and expect victory in Jesus' name.

Write down the name (s) of those with whom you shared today _____

_____.

____ Check when the day is completed, never beating yourself up if you did not finish; but, just asking Jesus to help you next day!

Day Seventy-two

God – The Worthy One

ADORATION

Worth describes value. Everyone loves to get a deal, paying little for something of worth. When we say, "It just isn't worth it," we are saying that something is simply not worth the cost. We tend to think too much in terms of physical value. Gold is worth more than copper. But a rich man is not really worth more than a poor man. Both are made in God's image and all humans "are worth more than many sparrows" (Matt 10:31). A healthy child is not worth more than one born with Downs Syndrome.

To be deemed "worthy" is to be valued by someone. It is not to be forgotten by them. It is to be pursued, loved and cherished. We sacrifice for that which we esteem valuable. We save up for a new refrigerator or car, not buying lesser things to get the more valuable. How worthy is God to you? How valuable is His truth, His honor, His Son, His gospel? In a culture idolizing objects, we must re-assess our values. "Great is the Lord and most worthy of praise; his greatness no one can fathom (Ps 145:3). Those in heaven who know more and are better than we, declare, "You are worthy, O Lord our God, to receive glory and honor and power, for you created all things, and by your will they were created and have their being" (Rev 4:11; 5:12). Since He is worthy, they give him praise. We do not give him praise whenever we forget Him and begin to value something or someone else more than God. "Does a maiden forget her jewelry, a bride her wedding ornaments? Yet my people have forgotten me, days without number" (Jer. 2:32). We are all tempted to "exchange the truth of God for a lie" and "(do) not think it worthwhile to retain the knowledge of God..." (Rom 1:25, 28). We value that which is of little worth and forsake "the pearl of great price" (Mart. 13:45). Whereas, "The apostles left rejoicing because they had been counted worthy of suffering disgrace for the Name" (Acts 5:41). Is Jesus worth that much to you?

John the Baptist said, "He is the one who comes after me, the thongs of whose sandals I am not worthy to untie" (John 1:27). Judas did not value His worth and complained when Mary poured costly perfume on Jesus. He asked, "Why wasn't this perfume sold and the money given to the poor? It was worth a year's wages." (John 12:4). Knowing His own worth, Jesus replied, "You will always have the poor among you, but you will not always have me" (John 12:8). What is He worth to you? How loosely do you hold to His commands and how tightly to the praise and pleasures of this passing world? Paul had the right value system and declared, "I consider my life worth nothing to me, if only I may...complete the task the Lord Jesus has given me—the task of testifying to the gospel of God's grace" (Acts 20:24). "Conduct yourselves in a manner worthy of the gospel of Christ" (Phil 1:27).

Response

I thank you God for showing me _____

_____.

STRATEGY

Follow Jesus today, whom all worship—or proclaim Him to be worthy—whose praise will forever fill heaven and earth as seen in **Rev 5:1-14** (Read now)

As I follow Jesus today I will remember _____

_____.

OBEDIENCE (I will statement)

The Spirit is convicting or leading me today to do or stop doing: _____

_____.

PETITIONS (Following your reciting of The Lord's Prayer)

I pray for these scheduled meetings today:

I pray also for these pressing needs of myself, my family, my church, my disciples my world:

CONFESSION and REPENTANCE

I confess these, my sins, with every intention to never repeat them, but rather to live as Jesus would live, by Your enabling grace and Spirit …
*Never confess without a faith that looks to the cross of Christ, where the guilt and penalty of all our sins was paid!

WALK (Think about the following praise song)

I've Found the Pearl of Greatest Price!

1) I've found the pearl of greatest price,
My heart doth sing for joy:
And sing I must, a Christ is mine;
Christ shall my song employ.

2) Christ is my Prophet, Priest and King,
A Prophet full of light,
My great High Priest before the throne,
My King of heav'nly might.

3) For He indeed is Lord of lords,
And He the King of kings;
He is the Sun of righteousness,
With healing in His wings

4) Christ is my Peace; He died for me,
For me He gave His blood;
And as my wondrous Sacrifice,
Offered Himself to God.

5) Christ Jesus is my All in all,
My Comfort and my Love,
My Life below, and He shall be
My Joy and Crown above.
(John Mason, 1645-1694)

Response

Help me, Jesus, to _____

VICTORY

Memorize *1 Peter 1:6-7*

Be prepared for opposition (spiritual warfare) and expect victory in Jesus' name.

Write down the name (s) of those with whom you shared today _____.

____ Check when the day is completed, never beating yourself up if you did not finish; but, just asking Jesus to help you next day!

Day Seventy-three

God – The Pattern

ADORATION

When something is perfect, a pattern or model is made of it. This helps preserve its perfection and reproduce its superior beauty or usefulness. Since God is perfect, there is no possible improvement to Him. When God created man he said, "Let us make man in our image, in our likeness, and let them rule..." (Gen 1:26). So, there are ways in which we are like God. "With our tongue we praise our Lord and Father, and with it we curse men, who have been made in God's likeness" (James 3:9). The reason humans are cursed is that the image of God in us has been largely lost due to our sin. This loss of perfection has led to the loss of heaven. Can the image be renewed? Can we be saved?

Yes, through Jesus. "The Son is the radiance of God's glory and the exact representation of his being" (Heb 1:3a). "He is the image of the invisible God, the firstborn over all creation" (Col 1:15). "No one has ever seen God, but God the One and Only, who is at the Father's side, has made him known" (John 1:18). Faith in Christ gives us life and restores the image! But only gradually - "For God ... made his light shine in our hearts to give us the light of the knowledge of the glory of God in the face of Christ. But we have this treasure in jars of clay to show that this all surpassing power is from God and not from us" (2 Cor 4:6- 7). "...You have taken off your old self with its practices and have put on the new self, which is being renewed in knowledge in the image of its Creator" (Col 3:9b-10). This is the great work of the Spirit within us. "And we...are being transformed into his likeness with ever-increasing glory, which comes from the Lord, who is the Spirit" (2 Cor 3:18).

The goal of Christian life and ministry is to follow Christ. To be like Christ. To lead others to Christ, the perfect Image. "Follow my example, as I follow the example of Christ" (1 Cor 11:1). "You became imitators of us and of the Lord; despite severe suffering...and so you became a model to all the believers (1 Thes 1:6-7).

Since Jesus is the perfection of God in human nature, follow Him! Refuse all counterfeits, however many may follow them. "In the name of the Lord Jesus Christ, we command you, brothers, to keep away from every brother who., does not live according to the teaching you received from us. For you, yourselves know how you ought to follow our example" (2 Thes

3:6-7a). A pattern has been made. A model exists for us all to follow. Realize that your happiness and satisfaction in this world depend on the degree that you bear His image. What you and others need NOW is what you will experience in heaven - "And I, in righteousness will see your face; when I awake, I will be satisfied with seeing your likeness" (Ps 17:15).

So, ask the Spirit to remove whatever is unlike Christ in you and to make you an encouragement and example to others, by His grace. In this way, you will become a disciple worthy of emulation; worthy of being given the privilege of making other disciples. This is what God has planned for you. "For those God foreknew he also predestined to be conformed to the likeness of his Son, that he might be the firstborn among many brothers" (Rom 8:29). Truly, what the world needs is Jesus to be seen in and through you today.

Response

I thank you God for showing me _____

_____.

STRATEGY

Follow Jesus today, whose Father spoke from heaven twice and reminded His disciples to listen and pattern their lives after Him as seen in **Matt 17:1-9** (Read now)

As I follow Jesus today I will remember _____

_____.

OBEDIENCE (I will statement)

The Spirit is convicting or leading me today to do or stop doing: _____

_____.

PETITIONS (Following your reciting of The Lord's Prayer)

I pray for these scheduled meetings today:

I pray also for these pressing needs of myself, my family, my church, my disciples my world:

CONFESSION and REPENTANCE

I confess these, my sins, with every intention to never repeat them, but rather to live as Jesus would live, by Your enabling grace and Spirit …

*Never confess without a faith that looks to the cross of Christ, where the guilt and penalty of all our sins was paid!

WALK (Think about the following hymn)

More Like the Master

1) More like the Master I would ever be,
More of His meekness, more humility;
More zeal to labor, more courage to be true,
More consecration for work He bids me do.

*Take Thou my heart, I would be Thine alone;
Take Thou my heart and make it all Thine own.
Purge me from sin, O Lord, I now implore,
Wash me and keep me Thine forevermore.*

2) More like the Master is my daily prayer;
More strength to carry crosses I must bear;
More earnest effort to bring His kingdom in;
More of His Spirit, the wanderer to win.

3) More like the Master I would live and grow;
More of His love to others I would show;
More self-denial, like His in Galilee,
More like the Master I long to ever be.
(Charles Gabriel, 1856-1932)

Response

Help me, Jesus, to _____

_____.

VICTORY

Memorize *1 Peter 2:21*
Be prepared for opposition (spiritual warfare) and expect victory in Jesus' name.

Write down the name (s) of those with whom you shared today_____
_____.

_____ Check when the day is completed, never beating yourself up if you did not finish; but, just asking Jesus to help you next day!

Day Seventy-four

God – The Witness

ADORATION

A witness is one who knows. One who has seen. But usually this word is used in legal settings. When a case is being prosecuted or when something very important needs verification. A notary is a professional witness whose seal verifies authenticity. When God calls Himself a Witness, He is saying more than He knows everything. He is reminding us that He will act on that knowledge. He will not remain silent when it is His time to testify. The truth really is known and will be honored—ultimately—by God, Himself.

When judgment was coming on God's beloved people, He said, "For they have done outrageous things in Israel...1 knows it and am a witness to it," (Jer 29:23; Mic 1:2). He knows all about us. He knows what we truly love. And that really matters because, at the perfect time, He acts to vindicate truth. "A truthful witness saves lives, but a false witness is deceitful" (Prov 14:25). Sometimes people refuse to speak up for the truth. Often, we sin by silence. But God cannot condone evil and will not endure wrong forever. He will surely take the stand as Witness and Judge. It is Jesus who is "the Amen, the faithful and true witness, the ruler of God's creation" (Rev 3:14).

Job believed in Him as his Messiah and said, "Even now my witness is in heaven; my advocate is on high. My intercessor is my friend...on behalf of a man he pleads with God as a man pleads for his friend" (Job 16:19-21). And it is our only hope, too. "My dear children, I write this to you so that you will not sin. But if anybody does sin, we have one who speaks to the Father in our defense—Jesus Christ the Righteous One" (1 John 2:1). Our salvation includes the gift of Jesus' perfect obedience of God's Law (righteousness). So, Paul could boldly declare that no one can "bring any charge against those whom God has chosen" (Rom 8:33). God has justified us. He has legally, as Judge, pardoned us since we have trusted in Christ alone as our Savior. We have been freed from sin's penalty by faith in our sin-bearing Lord!

As children of God, we are to be like God. Witnesses of truth and life! We "have put on the new self, which is being renewed ... in the image of its Creator" (Col. 3:10). "You are my witnesses, declares the Lord" (Isa 43:10). We are to testify in God's behalf. We are to tell what He has said. Jesus said, "But you will receive power when the Holy Spirit comes on you, and you will be my witnesses" (Acts 1:8). Christ's Word and work, His gospel, is our speech. The world is condemned and awaits eternal judgment (John 3:18-19). But Christ has died to remove our judgment. Can you remain silent? Get strength through the Spirit to boldly point others to "Jesus Christ who is the faithful witness...the ruler of the kings of the earth" (Rev 1:5). And on judgment day, He will acknowledge you as His.

Response

I thank you God for showing me _____

_____.

STRATEGY

Follow Jesus today, who spoke as a bold witness against false teachers and others who opposed and denied Him as seen in **John 5:24-47** (Read now)

As I follow Jesus today I will remember _____

_____.

OBEDIENCE (I will statement)

The Spirit is convicting or leading me today to do or stop doing: _____

_____.

PETITIONS (Following your reciting of The Lord's Prayer)

I pray for these scheduled meetings today:

I pray also for these pressing needs of myself, my family, my church, my disciples my world:

CONFESSION and REPENTANCE

I confess these, my sins, with every intention to never repeat them, but rather to live as Jesus would live, by Your enabling grace and Spirit …

*Never confess without a faith that looks to the cross of Christ, where the guilt and penalty of all our sins was paid!

WALK (Think about the following hymn)

O for a Thousand Tongues to Sing

1) O for a thousand tongues to sing
my great Redeemer's praise,
the glories of my God and King,
the triumphs of his grace!

2) My gracious Master and my God,
assist me to proclaim,
to spread thro' all the earth abroad
the honors of your name.

3) Jesus! the name that charms our fears,
that bids our sorrows cease,
'tis music in the sinner's ears,
'tis life and health and peace.

4) He breaks the power of cancelled sin,
he sets the prisoner free;
his blood can make the foulest clean;
his blood availed for me.

5) To God all glory, praise, and love
be now and ever given
by saints below and saints above,
the Church in earth and heaven.

11) With me, your chief, ye then shall know,
Shall feel your sins forgiven;
Anticipate your heaven below,
And own that love is heaven.
(Charles Wesley, 1707-1788)

Response

Help me, Jesus, to _____

_____.

VICTORY

Memorize *Acts 1:8*

Be prepared for opposition (spiritual warfare) and expect victory in Jesus' name.

Write down the name (s) of those with whom you shared today _____
_____.

____ Check when the day is completed, never beating yourself up if you did not finish; but, just asking Jesus to help you next day!

Day Seventy-five

God – The Pleader

ADORATION

Over and over again, the Scriptures reveal God as one who "longs to be gracious" to us, as a God who truly loves the world. He is one who seeks, who pleads with His insane, straying people: "Come now, let us reason together" (Isa. 1:1 8a).

At Adam's great Fall into sin, we read, "But the Lord God called to the man, Where are you?" (Gen 1:9). And when John lays down his quill, ending God's inspired revelation to the world, it is with these words: "The Spirit and the bride say, Come! And let him who hears say, Come! Whoever is thirsty, let him come; and whoever wishes, let him take of the free gift of the water of life." (Rev 22:17). Read these expressions of His great heart and be moved by His patient love for you and for all the world.

"Come, all you who are thirsty, come to the waters; and you who have no money, come buy and eat! Come buy wine and milk without money and without cost. Why spend your money on what is not bread, and your labor on what does not satisfy? Listen, listen to me, and eat what is good, and your soul will delight in the richest of fare" (Isa. 55:1-2).

"This is what the Lord says: What fault did your fathers find in me, that they have strayed far from me? They followed worthless idols and became worthless themselves." (Jer. 2:5). "Say to them, as surely as I live, declares the Sovereign Lord, I take no pleasure in the death of the wicked, but rather that they turn from their ways and live. Turn! Turn from your evil ways! Why will you die, O house of Israel?" (Eze. 33:11).

Being God, this yearning heart filled Jesus, too. "Come to me, all you who are weary and burdened, and I will give you rest. Take my yoke upon you and learn from me, for I am gentle and humble in heart, and you will find rest for your souls. For my yoke is easy and my burden is light." (Matt 11:28-30). He cried, "O Jerusalem, Jerusalem, you who kill the prophets and stone those sent to you, how often I have longed to gather your children together, as a hen gathers her chicks under her wings, but you were not willing!" (Lk 13:34)

How should we respond to such a God? He patiently leads us all to repentance (Rom. 2:4) with words like, "How long, O men, will you turn my glory into shame? How long will you love delusions and seek false gods?" (Ps. 4:2). What shall we do? PRAY for grace and TURN from sin. We must respond. Faith like a mustard seed will produce an amazing harvest in you. He has always been willing. Are you?

Response

I thank you God for showing me _____

_____.

STRATEGY

Follow Jesus today, who interceded for others even when they were running from Him, as seen in **Luke 22:24-34** (Read now)

As I follow Jesus today I will remember _____

_____.

OBEDIENCE (I will statement)

The Spirit is convicting or leading me today to do or stop doing: _____

_____.

PETITIONS (Following your reciting of The Lord's Prayer)

I pray for these scheduled meetings today:

I pray also for these pressing needs of myself, my family, my church, my disciples my world:

CONFESSION and REPENTANCE

I confess these, my sins, with every intention to never repeat them, but rather to live as Jesus would live, by Your enabling grace and Spirit …

*Never confess without a faith that looks to the cross of Christ, where the guilt and penalty of all our sins was paid!

WALK (Think about the following gospel song)

Jesus Calls Us

1) Jesus calls us o'er the tumult
of our life's wild, restless sea;
day by day his sweet voice soundeth,
saying, "Christian, follow me!"

2) As of old the apostles heard it
by the Galilean lake,
turned from home and toil and kindred,
leaving all for Jesus' sake.

3) Jesus calls us from the worship
of the vain world's golden store,
from each idol that would keep us,
saying, "Christian, love me more!"

4) In our joys and in our sorrows,
days of toil and hours of ease,
still he calls, in cares and pleasures,
"Christian, love me more than these!"

5) Jesus calls us! By thy mercies,
Savior, may we hear thy call,
give our hearts to thine obedience,
serve and love thee best of all.
(Cecil F Alexander, 1818-1895)

Response

Help me, Jesus, to _____

_____.

VICTORY

Memorize *Matthew 11:28*

Be prepared for opposition (spiritual warfare) and expect victory in Jesus' name.

Write down the name (s) of those with whom you shared today and pray for them. _____

_____.

____ Check when the day is completed, never beating yourself up if you did not finish; but, just asking Jesus to help you next day!

Day Seventy-six

God – The Patient One

ADORATION

When things go "our way" there is no need for patience. Patience implies struggle, waiting through a trial, being stretched. And patience is GOOD. It is of God. "And he passed in front of Moses proclaiming, The Lord, the Lord, the compassionate and gracious God, slow to anger, abounding in love and faithfulness" (Ex 34:6). God is infinitely patient. "Christ Jesus came into the world to save sinners—of whom I am the worst. But for that very reason I was shown mercy so that in me, the worst of sinners, Christ Jesus might display his unlimited patience as an example for those who would believe..." (1 Tim 1:16). And those who wait on Him, through deep struggles and dark paths, are thereby made better, more like Him. "The fruit of the Spirit is ... patience" (Gal 5:22).

Now we pass over a very sacred threshold and onto very holy ground. It is here we can better understand, according to the Bible, why God allowed evil. His plan includes evil without making Him its Author or removing our responsibility. Without evil there would be no trials—and hence—no understanding or need of either patience or salvation. We could not know of God's patience without evil. Similarly, we would not know grace if there was not sin—for grace is God's love to the undeserving—and it is sin that makes us undeserving. Paul dared to make this assertion to the Romans and wrote, "What if God, choosing to show his wrath and make his power known, bore with great patience the objects of his wrath—prepared for destruction? What if he did this to make the riches of his glory known to the objects of his mercy, whom he prepared in advance for glory." (Rom 9:22-23).

Never forget that our greatest good, as creatures, is to know and adore the nature of our Creator. He wants us to love Him and to walk with Him. And we cannot love One we do not know. One reason He allowed evil was that we might see His patience and grace—and love Him for them! "...God waited patiently in the days of Noah while the ark was being built" (1 Pet 3:20). "Or do you show contempt for the riches of his kindness, tolerance and patience. Not realizing that God's kindness leads you to repentance" (Rom 2:4). "Bear in mind that our Lord's patience means salvation" (2 Pet 3:15).

So, to be patient is to be godly. To be like Jesus. "I, John your brother and companion in the suffering and kingdom and patient endurance that are ours in Jesus..." (Rev 1:9). Hang in there. This is only a passing moment. Soon enough our eternal joy will come! "Since you have kept my command to wait patiently, I will also keep you...." (Rev 3:10). May the presence of Christ encourage you to be like Abraham of old, "who after waiting patiently received what was promised" (Heb 6:15). The best is yet to come—for those who endure to the end!

Response

I thank you God for showing me _____

_____.

STRATEGY

Follow Jesus today, seeing how He knew He must patiently endure pains and death, and reminding us that we must do the same as seen in **Matt 16:21-28** (Read now)

As I follow Jesus today I will remember _____

_____.

OBEDIENCE (I will statement)

The Spirit is convicting or leading me today to do or stop doing: _____

_____.

PETITIONS (Following your reciting of The Lord's Prayer)

I pray for these scheduled meetings today:

I pray also for these pressing needs of myself, my family, my church, my disciples my world:

CONFESSION and REPENTANCE

I confess these, my sins, with every intention to never repeat them, but rather to live as Jesus would live, by Your enabling grace and Spirit ...

*Never confess without a faith that looks to the cross of Christ, where the guilt and penalty of all our sins was paid!

WALK (Think about the following hymn)

When I Survey

1) When I survey the wondrous cross
on which the Prince of glory died,
my richest gain I count but loss,
and pour contempt on all my pride.

2) Forbid it, Lord, that I should boast
save in the death of Christ, my God!
All the vain things that charm me most,
I sacrifice them through his blood.

3) See, from his head, his hands, his feet,
sorrow and love flow mingled down.
Did e'er such love and sorrow meet,
or thorns compose so rich a crown?

4) Were the whole realm of nature mine,
that were a present far too small.
Love so amazing, so divine,
demands my soul, my life, my all.
(Isaac Watts, 1674-1748)

Response

Help me, Jesus, to _____

_____.

VICTORY

Memorize *1 Corinthians 13:4*

Be prepared for opposition (spiritual warfare) and expect victory in Jesus' name.

Write down the name (s) of those with whom you shared today _____
_____.

_____ Check when the day is completed, never beating yourself up if you did not finish; but, just asking Jesus to help you next day!

Day Seventy-seven

God – The Redeemer

ADORATION

Because He is God, He will win. The evil one may seem to have blanketed this world with evil; but, God will suddenly, powerfully and personally rescue His children and creation. His plan is called redemption throughout Scripture. And to redeem is "to buy back; to get back, recover as by paying a fee" (Webster's New World Dictionary). This world will not be lost. God will not scrap it and start again. He will liberate it from its enslavements and renew it all over again. He will not be defeated!

The ancient believer, Job, amazingly grasped this when he declared, "I know that my Redeemer lives, and that in the end he will stand upon the earth. And after my skin has been destroyed, yet in my flesh I will see God; I myself will see him with my own eyes—I, and not another. How my heart yearns within me!" (Job 19:25-27). The Psalmist agreed, "No man can redeem the life of another or give to God a ransom for him—the ransom for a life is costly, no payment is ever enough—that he should live on forever and not see decay...But God will redeem my life from the grave, he will surely take me to himself" (Ps 49:7-9, 15). "...and with him is full redemption" (Ps 130:7b). God promises, "I will ransom them from the power of the grave; I will redeem them from death. Where, O death, are your plagues? Where...is your destruction?" (Hos. 14:14a).

But, oh how great was the price to be paid! "For you know it was not with perishable things such as silver and gold that you were redeemed from the empty way of life handed down to you from your forefathers, but with the precious blood of Christ, a lamb without blemish or defect" (I Pet 1:18-19; see Eph 1:7). "...He entered the Most Holy Place once for all, by his own blood, having obtained eternal redemption" (Heb 9:12). Jesus is the Redeemer. "Christ redeemed us from the curse of the law by becoming a curse for us" (Gal 3:13a). "God sent forth his Son...to redeem those under law, that we might receive the full rights of sons. Because you are sons, God sent the Spirit of his Son into our hearts" (Gal 4:4-5a).

We should treasure the gift of the Holy Spirit whom the Father and Son have given to us as "...a deposit guaranteeing our inheritance until the redemption of those who are God's possession (Eph 1:14). So, we are warned, "And do not grieve the Holy Spirit of God, with whom you were sealed for the day of redemption" (Eph 4:30). Live in the Spirit and resist sin because "Jesus Christ...gave himself for us to redeem us from all wickedness" (Titus 2:14a).

When will the day of redemption take place? Jesus said, "At that time they will see the Son of Man coming in a cloud with power and great glory. When these things begin to take place... lift your heads, because your redemption is drawing near" (Lk 21:27-28). And then He will renew the world and resurrect our mortal bodies! "We know that the whole creation has been groaning ... not only so, but we ourselves, who have the firstfruits of the Spirit, groan inwardly as we \wait eagerly for our adoption as sons, the redemption of our bodies" (Rom 8:22-23). Come Lord Jesus!

Response

I thank you God for showing me _____

_____.

STRATEGY

Follow Jesus today, seeing how He began the work of redemption which is now spreading over the globe as seen in **Matt 8:5-13** (Read now)

As I follow Jesus today I will remember _____

_____.

OBEDIENCE (I will statement)

The Spirit is convicting or leading me today to do or stop doing: _____

_____.

PETITIONS (Following your reciting of The Lord's Prayer)

I pray for these scheduled meetings today:

I pray also for these pressing needs of myself, my family, my church, my disciples my world:

CONFESSION and REPENTANCE

I confess these, my sins, with every intention to never repeat them, but rather to live as Jesus would live, by Your enabling grace and Spirit ...

*Never confess without a faith that looks to the cross of Christ, where the guilt and penalty of all our sins was paid!

WALK (Think about the following praise song)

Redemption Ground

1) Come sing, my soul, and praise the Lord,
Who hath redeemed thee by His blood;
Delivered thee from chains that bound,
And brought thee to redemption ground.

Redemption ground, the ground of peace!
Redemption ground, O wondrous grace!
Here let our praise to God abound!
Who saves us on redemption ground.

2) Once from my God I wandered far,
And with His holy will made war;
But now my songs to God abound;
I'm standing on redemption ground.

3) O joyous hour! when God to me
A vision gave of Calvary;
My bonds were loosed—my soul unbound;
I sang upon redemption ground.

4) No words of merit now I plead,
But Jesus take for all my need;
No righteousness in me is found,
Except upon redemption ground.

5) Come, weary soul, and here find rest;
Accept redemption, and be blest;
The Christ who died, by God is crowned
To pardon on redemption ground.
(Daniel Whittle, 1840-1901)

Response

Help me, Jesus, to _____

_____.

VICTORY

Memorize *Colossians 1:13-14*

Be prepared for opposition (spiritual warfare) and expect victory in Jesus' name.

Write down the name (s) of those with whom you shared today _____

_____.

_____ Check when the day is completed, never beating yourself up if you did not finish; but, just asking Jesus to help you next day!

Day Seventy-eight

God – The Joyful One

ADORATION

Of all the pictures painted of God, very few portray Him as One who is rejoicing. Happy. Delighted. Yet, He is. In the core of His being. It is not He who made a mess of the earth! It is we who have. He beheld His original creation and "God saw all that he had made, and it was very good" (Gen 1:28a). And though history's long centuries sometimes seemed largely like years and eras of sadness, God's mercy broke through creating happiness once again. Bringing new seasons, new births and new hopes. Never forget, we are moving forward to when He will invite His faithful disciples, "Come and share your master's happiness!" (Matt 25:21,23).

"Splendor and majesty are before him; strength and joy in his dwelling place" (1 Chron 16:27). The Psalms portray a believer's troubled life. A life that is full of trials. Yet there is a message of joy throughout them. "Shout with joy to God all the earth!" (Ps 66:1). "Come, let us sing for joy to the Lord" (Ps 95:1 a). "Surely you have … made him glad about the joy of your presence" (Ps 21:6b). How can sinners be joyful in the presence of a holy God? The psalmist knew. "Then will I go to the altar of God, to God, my joy and my delight" (Ps 43:4a). The altar provides the way to joy. The victim lain on it pays for sin. His death is our death. And all Old Testament sacrifices offered on the altar foreshadowed the coming of Christ, "the Lamb of God, who takes away the sin of the world" (John 1:29). On the day before He died, Jesus said, "I have told you this so that my joy may be in you and that your joy may be complete" (John 15:11). Later He said, "Until now you have not asked for anything in my name. Ask and you will receive, and your joy will be complete" (John 16:24). You can dance before God in Christ! In His name.

God asked Job, "Where were you... while the morning stars sang together, and all the angels shouted for joy?" (Job 38:7). Creation was a time of singing. Sin strangled the song. Salvation restores it to our hearts again. And when Christ returns, joy is not far behind. "They will sing for joy before the Lord, for he comes to judge the earth" (1 Chron 16:33b). Even His judgment, the perfect expression of His justice, will bring relief and rejoicing. When all wrongs are overturned, and all injustice is punished. Then the sighs of all creation will be changed into songs once again.

So now we can say, "Though the fig tree does not bud and there are no grapes on the vine ... and no cattle in the stalls, yet I will rejoice in the Lord, I will be joyful in God my Savior." (Hab 3:17-18). Our day is coming! Our worship embraces it now by faith. So, Israel was taught on days of festive worship, "Do not grieve for the joy of the Lord is your strength" (Neh 8:10b). Rejoice in the Lord, come what may, and you will see how strong true joy is. After being whipped, "Paul and Silas were ... singing hymns to God and the other prisoners were listening to them." Following the earthquake, "the jailer ... rushed in and fell trembling ... and asked, Sirs, what must I do to be saved?" (Acts 16:25-3 0). An earthquake miraculously opened the door of the prison and joy opened the door of the jailer's heart. Joy is your strength. "Rejoice in the Lord always. I will say it again: Rejoice!" (Phil. 4:4).

Response

I thank you God for showing me _____

_____.

STRATEGY

Follow Jesus today, seeing how He emphasized joy to His disciples as seen in **Luke 15:1-10** (Read now)

As I follow Jesus today I will remember _____

_____.

OBEDIENCE (I will statement)

The Spirit is convicting or leading me today to do or stop doing: _____

_____.

PETITIONS (Following your reciting of The Lord's Prayer)

I pray for these scheduled meetings today:

I pray also for these pressing needs of myself, my family, my church, my disciples my world:

CONFESSION and REPENTANCE

I confess these, my sins, with every intention to never repeat them, but rather to live as Jesus would live, by Your enabling grace and Spirit …

*Never confess without a faith that looks to the cross of Christ, where the guilt and penalty of all our sins was paid!

WALK (Think about the following praise song)

Joyful, Joyful We Adore Thee

1) Joyful, joyful, we adore Thee, God of glory, Lord of love;
Hearts unfold like flowers before Thee, opening to the sun above.
Melt the clouds of sin and sadness; drive the dark of doubt away;
Giver of immortal gladness, fill us with the light of day!

2) All Thy works with joy surround Thee, earth and heaven reflect Thy rays,
Stars and angels sing around Thee, center of unbroken praise.
Field and forest, vale and mountain, flowery meadow, flashing sea,
Singing bird and flowing fountain call us to rejoice in Thee.

3) Thou art giving and forgiving, ever blessing, ever blessed,
Wellspring of the joy of living, ocean depth of happy rest!
Thou our Father, Christ our Brother, all who live in love are Thine;
Teach us how to love each other, lift us to the joy divine.

(4) Mortals, join the happy chorus, which the morning stars began;
Father love is reigning o'er us, brother love binds man to man.
Ever singing, march we onward, victors in the midst of strife,
Joyful music leads us Sunward in the triumph song of life.
(Henry van Dyke, 1852-1933)

Response

Help me, Jesus, to _____

_____.

VICTORY

Memorize *Psalm 16:11*

Be prepared for opposition (spiritual warfare) and expect victory in Jesus' name.

Write down the name (s) of those with whom you shared today _____
_____.

____ Check when the day is completed, never beating yourself up if you did not finish; but, just asking Jesus to help you next day!

Day Seventy-nine

God – The Delighting One

ADORATION

I have heard various people say, "I love him, but I do not like him." That confuses me. It is like saying, "I love you, but I dislike you." Can you really love someone whom you only detest? I don't think so. I think love includes liking. "I love you," that does not mean that I like or approve of all you are or do. But if I truly love you, I must like something about you, whoever you are. We must remember that we all are in fact much more than merely what we do. You are a human made in the image of a lovely God. Hence, you are, at least in some part, lovely. You are fashioned after a loveable Creator. Therefore, you are in ways loveable. Not completely. Not perfectly. But, even after a great fall, you remain an image bearer whom I not only can but should love.

If I do not love someone, I have departed from Christ. And I have started down the road of hatred. That is why Jesus commanded, "Love your enemies ... that you may be sons of your Father in heaven. He causes his sun to rise on the evil and the good ... If you love those who love you, what reward will you get? Are not even the tax collectors doing that?" (Matt 5:44-46). We have so much to learn about true love. And we can only learn of it by going to the God who is love.

One element of love is delighting in another. We take delight in those we love. We see something delightful that we cherish about them. Believe it or not--God loves us in this way! David rejoiced, "He brought me out into a spacious place; he rescued me because he delighted in me" (2 Sam 22:20; Ps 18:19). When He created the world, He saw that all He had made "was very good" Gen 1:31). God, in His wisdom, surveys His creation, and He is "filled with delight day after day, rejoicing always in his presence, rejoicing in his whole world and delighting in mankind" (Prov 8:30-31).

Though God loves the world, He has a special love for His people and takes a greater delight in them. "For the Lord your God is with you, he is mighty to save. He will take great delight in you, he will quiet you with his love, he will rejoice over you with singing" (Zeph 3:17). "His pleasure is not in the strength of the horse, nor his delight in the legs of a man; the Lord delights in those who fear him, who put their hope in his unfailing love" (147: 10-1 1). "For the Lord takes delight in his people; he crowns the humble with salvation" (Ps 149:4). So great is His delight in us that the day is coming when "No longer will they call you Deserted or name your land Desolate. But you will be called Hephzibah, and your land Beulah; for the Lord will take delight in you, and your land will be married" (Isa 62:4).

As followers of Christ, we are to be people of love. People who truly like others. Who smile and delight in our neighbors. Are you pleased when you see another human being? Or could you simply do without them. Ask God to fill you with delight in Him and in others. Then smile.

Response

I thank you God for showing me _____

_____.

STRATEGY

Follow Jesus today, seeing how He loved even the unlovely, as seen in **Luke 7:36-50** (Read now)

As I follow Jesus today I will remember _____

_____.

OBEDIENCE (I will statement)

The Spirit is convicting or leading me today to do or stop doing: _____

_____.

PETITIONS (Following your reciting of The Lord's Prayer)

I pray for these scheduled meetings today:

I pray also for these pressing needs of myself, my family, my church, my disciples my world:

CONFESSION and REPENTANCE

I confess these, my sins, with every intention to never repeat them, but rather to live as Jesus would live, by Your enabling grace and Spirit …

*Never confess without a faith that looks to the cross of Christ, where the guilt and penalty of all our sins was paid!

WALK (Think about the following praise song)

God Sees the Little Sparrow Fall

1) God sees the little sparrow fall,
it meets his tender view;
if God so loves the little birds,
I know he loves me too.

*He loves me too, he loves me too,
I know loves me too;
because he loves the little things,
I know loves me too.*

2) He paints the lily of the field,
perfumes each lily bell;
if he so loves the little flow'rs,
I know he loves me well. [Refrain]

3) God made the little birds and flow'rs,
and all things large and small;
he'll not forget his little ones,
I know he loves them all.
(Maria Straub, 1838-1898)

Response

Help me, Jesus, to _____

_____.

VICTORY

Memorize *Psalm 37:4*

Be prepared for opposition (spiritual warfare) and expect victory in Jesus' name.

Write down the name (s) of those with whom you shared today _____

_____.

_____ Check when the day is completed, never beating yourself up if you did not finish; but, just asking Jesus to help you next day!

Day Eighty

God – The Victorious One

ADORATION

We do not have to be very astute to conclude that God will ultimately win. King Nebuchadnezzar, when humbled, declared, "No one can hold back his hand" (Dan 4:34b). Since God is all powerful and ever active, He cannot be defeated. That is not to say, He never is slandered, resisted, despised or rejected. Many a believer has struggled with the fact that some proudly and brashly challenge Him all their lives, living long and dying rich. All this shows is that God is not like us. We see winning differently. Victory to God is not merely or mainly the quick crushing of all enemies; but the patient and persevering accomplishment of His perfect and loving plan. God wins by being God. And no one in the end really wins unless he follows the Lord to victory. "The horse is made ready for the day of battle, but victory rests with the Lord" (Prov 21:31).

With victory comes joy. "O Lord, the king rejoices in your strength. How great is his joy in the victories you give!" (Ps 21:1). "Shouts of joy and victory resound in the tents of the righteous" (Ps 118:15a). But what happens to joy when the enemy reappears and defeats us? Whether it be Philistine opponents or a cancerous growth deep in our body? Can there be joy in defeat? Only when our definition of victory changes, becoming more like God's, will we be able to join Paul and say, "in all our troubles my joy knows no bounds" (2 Cor 7:4b).

Was Jesus a loser or a winner? I am not asking if He finally won in the end. I am asking you, was His choice of poverty, humility, non-political alignment, children, women, Galileans and sinners —wise? Was His choosing to be an outsider and an underdog a winning strategy all along? Did He really win in letting go of glory, choosing to serve rather than to be in control? To die to what was rightly His rather than to demand His rights and reign with eye-popping parades and due distinction? Until we see Jesus' life as a winning life, we will never choose to follow Him. Until it really sinks in that it is "more blessed to give than to receive" (Acts 20:35b), and that we can "overcome evil with good" (Rom 12:21b) — will we keep blindly walking down the self-serving path of defeat wondering why lasting joy eludes us.

Jesus came to live the winning life that Adam had deserted. "This is the victory that has overcome the world, even our faith. Who is it that overcomes the world? Only he who believes that Jesus is the Son of God."

(1 John 5:4-5). "Thanks be to God who gives us the victory through our Lord Jesus Christ" (1 Cor 15:57). You are a winner if you are in Christ!

Response

I thank you God for showing me _____

_____.

STRATEGY

Follow Jesus today, seeing the victory He celebrated over sin and death as seen in **John 21:19-31** (Read now)

As I follow Jesus today I will remember _____

_____.

OBEDIENCE (I will statement)

The Spirit is convicting or leading me today to do or stop doing: _____

_____.

PETITIONS (Following your reciting of The Lord's Prayer)

I pray for these scheduled meetings today:

I pray also for these pressing needs of myself, my family, my church, my disciples my world:

CONFESSION and REPENTANCE

I confess these, my sins, with every intention to never repeat them, but rather to live as Jesus would live, by Your enabling grace and Spirit …

*Never confess without a faith that looks to the cross of Christ, where the guilt and penalty of all our sins was paid!

WALK (Think about the following gospel song)

Victory in Jesus

1) I heard an old, old story how a Savior came from glory,
How He gave His life on Calvary to save a wretch like me;
I heard about His groaning, of His precious blood's atoning,
Then I repented of my sins and won the victory.

O victory in Jesus, my Savior, forever.
He sought me and bought me with His redeeming blood;
He loved me ere I knew Him, and all my love is due Him,
He plunged me to victory beneath the cleansing flood.

2) I heard about His healing, of His cleansing power revealing.
How He made the lame to walk again and caused the blind to see;
And then I cried, "Dear Jesus, come and heal my broken spirit,"
And somehow Jesus came and brought to me the victory.

3) I heard about a mansion He has built for me in glory.
And I heard about the streets of gold beyond the crystal sea;
About the angels singing and the old redemption story,
And some sweet day I'll sing up there the song of victory.
(Eugene M Bartlett, 1885-1941)

Response

Help me, Jesus, to _____

_____.

VICTORY

Memorize *1 John 5:4b*

Be prepared for opposition (spiritual warfare) and expect victory in Jesus' name.

Write down the name (s) of those with whom you shared today _____

_____.

_____ Check when the day is completed, never beating yourself up if you did not finish; but, just asking Jesus to help you next day!

335

10-Day Period 9

Discipleship and our Praying in Jesus' name.

**Begin by reading Appendix Nine – Why Most Christians Prayers are not Answered

One of my disciplers was an African leader (former Muslim) who trained us concerning prayer. He began by saying, "You will never see a DMM (Disciple Making Movement) until you learn how to pray." How to "give your attention to prayer" (Acts 6:4a) or how to "devote yourselves to prayer" (Col. 4:2). Examining global DMMs, David Watson affirmed that this was true when he wrote, "We have found many common elements among the different groups, but the only element that was present in every team was a high commitment to prayer."[35] Jesus commanded His 72 disciples to go only AFTER they had sufficiently prayed (Luke 10:1-3). He even told them what to pray! Our next ten days is devoted to helping you to establish the practice of constant prayer in your lives. How else can you walk with God but through prayer? Prayer, truly, is the breath and life of discipleship.

Learning how to "practice the presence of God"[36] means that you must be absolutely convinced that He is with you. And you cannot be convinced of that without utterly changing the way that you live. You cannot just "believe" without acting on that belief. Being convinced that "I am with you always" (Jesus) is an essential conviction if your life or behavior is going to truly be in "fellowship with the Father and with his Son, Jesus Christ" (1 John 1:3). So, over the next 10 days, ask the Spirit to help you to begin "praying without ceasing" so that nothing that arises in your daily life comes between you and Jesus.

---

[35] D Watson & P Watson, Contagious Disciple-making, 79
[36] See Brother Lawrence's very helpful booklet, The Practice of the Presence of God

Day Eighty-one

God – The Powerful One

ADORATION

"Great is our Lord and mighty in power" (Ps 147:5a). Just how great or powerful is God? Jeremiah answers, "Nothing is too hard for you" (Jer. 32:17). And Jesus adds, "With God all things are possible" (Matt 19:26). He alone is "the Almighty" (Rev. 1:8). Theologians call this His omnipotence. Moses praises God's power as displayed in Israel's triumph over Pharaoh, saying, "Your right hand, O Lord, was majestic in power. Your right hand, O Lord, shattered the enemy" (Ex. 15:6). So, God is more powerful than the most powerful king. And more powerful than the "powers of the dark world" (fallen spirits - Eph 6:12; Col. 1:16; 2:15) whom Christ has displaced and defeated. So powerful is God that all heaven joins in ascribing power, in its ultimate sense, to Him alone, "Hallelujah! Salvation and glory and power belong to our God" (Rev 19:1). He is infinite or without limit in the degree of His power. What a mighty God we serve!

It is in this area where humans are so often deceived. We think of ourselves as powerful because of our dominance over other creatures and our advancements in this world. But, in ourselves we have little actual power if we understand by that term the concept of force. We have the power to move our voluntary muscles, to focus our attention on some object and to change that focus. Beyond this very narrow area of direct influence, we rely on other objects to help us accomplish our objectives. We can lift and move very little by our own power. We ourselves cannot greatly affect others apart from the use of some instrument of persuasion. Read Job 38-41 for a humbling comparison between the power of God and that of humans. In fact, in many areas we are powerless. As Paul said, "You see, at just the right time, when we were still powerless, Christ died for the ungodly" (Rom. 5:6).

Let's remember, however, that God is not only infinite power. He is also infinite wisdom and goodness. Understanding this, we can see how there are some things God can't do. An infinitely good God cannot lie (Heb 6:18) or change (Mal 3:6). So, it is only God's nature that can limit what God can do. He cannot deny himself (2 Tim 2:13). Remember that His power is ever attached to His love, truth, justice and holiness. God does not have the power to be malevolent, unfair or unholy. Paul rightly said, "we cannot do anything against the truth, but only for the truth" (2 Cor 13:8), because God's truth is ultimately all-powerful.

Considering God's infinite power and our great weakness, we can draw some very helpful conclusions. Since God is all-powerful, His will shall be accomplished. How foolish, then, is all opposition to Him. His promises will come to pass. How shortsighted is all our doubt! Even though Sarah was well past child-bearing age, Abraham "did not waver through unbelief regarding the promise of God but was strengthened in his faith and gave glory to God being fully persuaded that God had power to do what he had promised" (Rom 4:20-21). Though the world despised and destroyed Him, Jesus rose from the dead and now reigns. And though it still denies and disregards Him, Jesus will be universally honored. Since God is all powerful, only those who trust in Him will be safe (Ps 118:5-9). Take your stand with Him. And as you follow Jesus, expect Him "to do immeasurably more than all we ask or imagine according to his power that is at work within us" (Eph 3:20)!

Response

I thank you God for showing me _____

_____.

STRATEGY

Follow Jesus today, whose unlimited power was often displayed as seen in **Mark 2:1-12** (Read now)

As I follow Jesus today I will remember _____

_____.

OBEDIENCE (I will statement)

The Spirit is convicting or leading me today to do or stop doing: _____

_____.

PETITIONS (Following your reciting of The Lord's Prayer)

I pray for these scheduled meetings today:

I pray also for these pressing needs of myself, my family, my church, my disciples my world:

CONFESSION and REPENTANCE

I confess these, my sins, with every intention to never repeat them, but rather to live as Jesus would live, by Your enabling grace and Spirit ...

*Never confess without a faith that looks to the cross of Christ, where the guilt and penalty of all our sins was paid!

WALK (Think about the following hymn)

Pentecostal Power

1) Lord, as of old at Pentecost
Thou didst Thy power display,
With cleansing purifying flame,
Descend on us today.

Lord, send the old-time power, the Pentecostal power!
Thy floodgates of blessing on us throw open wide!
Lord send the old-time power. the Pentecostal power.
That sinners be converted, and Thy name glorified!

2) For mighty works for Thee, prepare
And strengthen every heart;
Come, take possession of Thine own
And nevermore depart. [Chorus]

3) All self-consume, all sin destroys!
With earnest zeal endue
Each waiting heart to work for Thee;
O Lord, our faith renews! [Chorus]

4) Speak, Lord! before Thy throne we wait,
Thy promise we believe,
And will not let Thee go until
The blessing we receive. [Chorus]
(Charles Gabriel, 1856-1932)

Response

Help me, Jesus, to _____

_____ .

VICTORY

Memorize *2 Timothy 1:7*

Be prepared for opposition (spiritual warfare) and expect victory in Jesus' name.
Write down the name (s) of those with whom you shared today _____
_____.

____ Check when the day is completed, never beating yourself up if you did not finish; but, just asking Jesus to help you next day!

Day Eighty-two

God – The Hearer of Prayer

ADORATION

I know of people who are nearly deaf, but you would not know it. They do not strain to hear what you are saying. They just smile. Why? Because they are unusually holy? No, it's at times because they no longer want to hear others. They are quite happy staying within themselves. Absorbed in their own world. But for one who loves others, the loss of hearing is a severe trial, for the voices and noises of those beloved are the cause of such joy and delight.

God is called, "O you who hear prayer" (Ps 65:2a). What does he really think of our prayers? Is He amused, insulted or angered? "The Lord detests the sacrifice (outward worship) of the wicked, but the prayer of the upright pleases him" (Prov 15:8). God loves to hear you pray. Christ gives you such invitations as these: "Ask and it will be given; seek and you will find; knock and the door will be opened to you. For everyone who asks receives, he who seeks finds; and to him who knocks, the door is opened" (Matt 7:7-8)."Again I tell you that if two of you on earth will agree about anything you ask for, it will be done for you by my Father in heaven. For where two or three come together in my name, there am I with them" (Matt 18:19-20). "If you believe, you will receive whatever you ask for prayer" (Matt 21:22).

It grieves God when we think that He is uninterested in us, ambivalent to our prayers. "Surely the arm of the Lord is not too short to save, nor his ear too dull to hear. But your iniquities have separated you from God; your sins have hidden his face from you, so that he will not hear" (Is 59:1-2). As His disciples, if we rightly deal with our sins through faith and repentance, the lines of communication are open wide and fruitful prayer results. "If my people...will humble themselves, and pray and seek my face, and turn from their wicked ways, then will I hear from heaven and will forgive their sin and will heal their land" (2 Chron 7:14). In that future age when sin no longer dulls our love, we will see just how willing God is to answer prayer. "Before they call I will answer; while they are still speaking I will hear" (Is 66:24). Jesus, never hindered by sin, "looked up and said, Father, I thank you that you have heard me. I knew that you always hear me, but I said this for the benefit of the people standing here, that they may believe that you sent me" (John 11:41-42).

May God help us honestly walk with Him confessing our sins, so that we might have a living fellowship with Him now (1 John 1:5-9) and declare, "This is the confidence we have in approaching God: that if we ask anything according to his will, he hears us. And if we know that he hears us—whatever we ask—we know that we have what we ask of him" (1 John 5:14-15). May our hearts ever be filled with joy as we declare to all, "I love the Lord for he heard my voice; he heard my cry for mercy. Because he turned his ear to me, I will call on him as long as I live" (Ps 116:1-2).

Response

I thank you God for showing me _____

_____.

STRATEGY

Follow Jesus today, who lived a life of prayer as seen in **Mark 1:35-39** (Read now)

As I follow Jesus today I will remember _____

_____.

OBEDIENCE (I will statement)

The Spirit is convicting or leading me today to do or stop doing: _____

_____.

PETITIONS (Following your reciting of The Lord's Prayer)

I pray for these scheduled meetings today:

I pray also for these pressing needs of myself, my family, my church, my disciples my world:

CONFESSION and REPENTANCE

I confess these, my sins, with every intention to never repeat them, but rather to live as Jesus would live, by Your enabling grace and Spirit ...

*Never confess without a faith that looks to the cross of Christ, where the guilt and penalty of all our sins was paid!

WALK (Think about the following hymn)

What a Friend we have in Jesus

1) What a Friend we have in Jesus, all our sins and griefs to bear!
What a privilege to carry everything to God in prayer!
O what peace we often forfeit, O what needless pain we bear,
All because we do not carry everything to God in prayer.

2) Have we trials and temptations? Is there trouble anywhere?
We should never be discouraged; take it to the Lord in prayer.
Can we find a friend so faithful who will all our sorrows share?
Jesus knows our every weakness; take it to the Lord in prayer.

3) Are we weak and heavy laden, cumbered with a load of care?
Precious Savior, still our refuge, take it to the Lord in prayer.
Do your friends despise, forsake you? Take it to the Lord in prayer!
In His arms He'll take and shield you; you will find a solace there.

4) Blessed Savior, thou hast promised Thou wilt all our burdens bear
May we ever, Lord, be bringing all to Thee in earnest prayer.
Soon in glory bright unclouded there will be no need for prayer
Rapture, praise and endless worship will be our sweet portion there.
(Joseph Scriven, 1819-1886)

Response

Help me, Jesus, to _____

_____.

VICTORY

Memorize *John 15:7*

Be prepared for opposition (spiritual warfare) and expect victory in Jesus' name.

Write down the name (s) of those with whom you shared today _____
_____.

____ Check when the day is completed, never beating yourself up if you did not finish; but, just asking Jesus to help you next day!

Day Eighty-three

God – The Uniter

ADORATION

God is one. "Hear, O Israel: The Lord our God, the Lord is one" (Deut 6:4). He is also triune: Father, Son and Holy Spirit, "I and the Father are one" (John 10:30). One in nature, three in persons. Never in discord, disunity or dysfunction. And so, should the children of God strive to be, for this is what He wants for us. "I pray also for those who will believe in me through their message, that all of them may be one, Father, just as you are in me and I am in you. May they also be one in us so that the world may believe that you have sent me. I have given them the glory that you gave me, that they may be one as we are one: I in them and you in me. May they be brought to complete unity to let the world know that you sent me and have loved them even as you have loved me" (John 17:20b-23). We can better understand why the Psalmist wrote, "How good and pleasant it is when brothers live together in unity" (Ps. 133:1).

Satan divides, scatters, destroys. God unites, gathers and quickens. Jesus said, "He who is not with me is against me, and he who does not gather with me, scatters" (Matt 12:30). The Good Shepherd seeks lost sheep and brings them home. Satan seeks to devour. God has warned that He will scatter His people in judgment, if that is what it takes. But, He prefers mercy. "For he does not willingly bring affliction or grief to the children of men" (Lam 3:33). God will ultimately restore and re-unite His people. "Hear the word of the Lord, O nations ... He who scattered Israel will gather them and will watch over his flock like a shepherd" (Jer 31:10; Isa 11:12).

One of the great, prevailing sins among Christians today is that of unnecessary disunity. Paul urged, "Make every effort to keep the unity of the Spirit through the bond of peace. There is one Spirit—just as you were called to one hope ...-one Lord, one faith, one baptism; one God who is over all and through all and in all" (Eph 4:3-6). Unity in diversity. "...God has combined the members of the body ... so that there should be no division in the body, but that its parts should have equal concern for each other" (1 Cor 12:24-25).

So, it is no small thing to divide the church! "I urge you, brothers, to watch out for those who cause divisions and put obstacles in your way that are contrary to the teaching you have learned. Keep away from them" (Rom 16:17). Even when church discipline demands a division, it is to achieve a later reconciliation and deeper unity. Be a peacemaker, where your love leads you to unity (Col 3:14), and "May the God who gives endurance and encouragement give you a spirit of unity among yourselves as you follow Christ Jesus, so that with one heart and mouth you may glorify the God and father of our Lord Jesus Christ" (Rom 15:5-6).

Response

I thank you God for showing me _____

_____.

STRATEGY

Follow Jesus today, who emphasized peace and unity among disciples, but understood that His call would divide people as seen in **Matt 10:32-39** (Read now)

As I follow Jesus today I will remember _____

_____.

OBEDIENCE (I will statement)

The Spirit is convicting or leading me today to do or stop doing: _____

_____.

PETITIONS (Following your reciting of The Lord's Prayer)

I pray for these scheduled meetings today:

I pray also for these pressing needs of myself, my family, my church, my disciples my world:

CONFESSION and REPENTANCE

I confess these, my sins, with every intention to never repeat them, but rather to live as Jesus would live, by Your enabling grace and Spirit ...

*Never confess without a faith that looks to the cross of Christ, where the guilt and penalty of all our sins was paid!

WALK (Think about the following hymn)

The Church's One Foundation

1) The church's one Foundation
is Jesus Christ her Lord;
she is His new creation,
by water and the Word;
from heav'n He came and sought her
to be His holy bride;
with His own blood He bought her,
and for her life He died.

2) Elect from ev'ry nation,
yet one o'er all the earth,
her charter of salvation,
one Lord, one faith, one birth;
one holy Name she blesses,
partakes one holy food,
and to one hope she presses,
with ev'ry grace endued.

3) Tho' with a scornful wonder,
men see her sore oppressed,
by schisms rent asunder,
by heresies distressed,
yet saints their watch are keeping,
their cry goes up, "How long?"
And soon the night of weeping
shall be the morn of song.

4) The church shall never perish!
Her dear Lord, to defend,
to guide, sustain, and cherish,
is with her to the end;
tho' there be those that hate her

    and false sons in her pale,
    against the foe or traitor
    she ever shall prevail.

   5) 'Mid toil and tribulation,
    and tumult of her war,
   she waits the consummation
    of peace for evermore;
   till with the vision glorious
    her longing eyes are blest,
  and the great church victorious
   shall be the church at rest.

  6) Yet she on earth hath union
   with God the Three in One,
  and mystic sweet communion
   with those whose rest is won.
    O happy ones and holy!
   Lord, give us grace that we,
   like them, the meek and lowly,
   on high may dwell with Thee.
    (Samuel J Stone, 1839-1900)

Response

Help me, Jesus, to _____

_____.

VICTORY

Memorize *John 17:20-21*

Be prepared for opposition (spiritual warfare) and expect victory in Jesus' name.

Write down the name (s) of those with whom you shared today _____

_____.

_____ Check when the day is completed, never beating yourself up if you did not finish; but, just asking Jesus to help you next day!

Day Eighty-four

God – The Listener

ADORATION

Often, we are not very good listeners. Why this is so and what this reveals have really surprised and stopped me dead in my tracks. I hope they grab you, too, for much of the Bible was written with this theme in mind. Throughout history, humans have been trying to get God to listen to them on their terms. When they needed Him. And Scripture records how God has been listening to us and patiently saying that all will go well if we just listen to Him.

"Then the man and his wife heard the sound of the Lord God as he was walking in the garden ... and they hid from the Lord God.... But the Lord God called to the man, 'Where are you?'" (Gen 3:8-9). Sin had stolen their hearts, telling them lies that they had listened to and believed. God and sin are still calling. To which are you listening?

What does God hear? Because He is omnipresent, He hears it all! He hears our complaints as we "groan" and "grumble" and rebel (Ex. 6:5; 16:7-8), as Moses said, The Lord heard you when you wailed, 'If only we had meat to eat. We were better off in Egypt!'" (Num 11:18). "Miriam and Aaron began to talk against Moses because of the Cushite wife ... And the Lord heard this" (Num 12). He taught those leaders not to seek more than what He had given to them. Read the whole story and listen, because discontentment reigns today.

Our patient God bears with our deafness and slowly brings us to the place of wisdom. The place where we humbly cry out to Him and listen to what He says. "You hear, O Lord, the desire of the afflicted; you encourage them, and you listen to their cry" (Ps 10:17). When stained with sin and filled with the stench of our own rebellion, He listens to us when we come repenting. "I have listened attentively, but they did not say what is right. No one repents of his wickedness saying, 'What have I done?'" (Jer 8:6). The Psalmist knew "If I have cherished sin in my heart, the Lord would not have listened; but God has surely listened and heard my voice in prayer" (Psa 66:18-19). So, do not think you should wait until your situation improves, for, "The Lord hears the needy and does not despise his captive people" (Psa 69:33). Come and be set free!

Jesus lived a life of listening (Luke 2:46). Everything He heard, God heard, for He is God. He loved sinners and was drawn to them. This endeared Him to His Father, the great Listener, who always heard His Son (John 11:41) because Jesus always sought the Father enthusiastically. So, should we. "Then you will seek me and find me when you seek me with all your heart" (Jer 29:12-13). "The Lord is far from the wicked, but he hears the prayer of the righteous" (Prov 15:29). You are righteous before Him by your faith in Jesus. So, go to the father in His Name and be heard today!

Response

I thank you God for showing me _____

_____.

STRATEGY

Follow Jesus today, whose love led Him to listen as no one else ever had as seen in **Mark 10:46-52** (Read now)

As I follow Jesus today I will remember _____

_____.

OBEDIENCE (I will statement)

The Spirit is convicting or leading me today to do or stop doing: _____

_____.

PETITIONS (Following your reciting of The Lord's Prayer)

I pray for these scheduled meetings today:

I pray also for these pressing needs of myself, my family, my church, my disciples my world:

CONFESSION and REPENTANCE

I confess these, my sins, with every intention to never repeat them, but rather to live as Jesus would live, by Your enabling grace and Spirit ...

*Never confess without a faith that looks to the cross of Christ, where the guilt and penalty of all our sins was paid!

WALK (Think about the following hymn)

Hark, the Voice of Jesus Calling

1) Hark, the voice of Jesus calling,
"Who will go and work today?
Fields are white and harvests waiting,
Who will bear the sheaves away?"
Loud and long the master calls you;
Rich reward he offers free.
Who will answer, gladly saying,
"Here am I. Send me, send me"?

2) If you cannot speak like angels,
If you cannot preach like Paul,
You can tell the love of Jesus;
You can say he died for all.
If you cannot rouse the wicked
With the judgment's dread alarms,
You can lead the little children
To the Savior's waiting arms.

3) If you cannot be a watchman,
Standing high on Zion's wall,
Pointing out the path to heaven,
Offering life and peace to all,
With your prayers and with your bounties
You can do what God demands;
You can be life faithful Aaron,
Holding up the prophet's hands.

4) Let none hear you idly saying,
"There is nothing I can do,"
While the multitudes are dying
And the master calls for you.
Take the task he gives you gladly;
Let his work your pleasure be.
Answer quickly when he calls you,
"Here am I. Send me, send me!"
(Daniel March 1816-1909)

Response

Help me, Jesus, to _____

_____.

VICTORY

Memorize *Psalm 34:15*

Be prepared for opposition (spiritual warfare) and expect victory in Jesus' name.

Write down the name (s) of those with whom you shared today _____

_____.

_____ Check when the day is completed, never beating yourself up if you did not finish; but, just asking Jesus to help you next day!

Day Eighty-five

God – The Helper

ADORATION

There is nothing like a desperate cry for help. It stops us, focuses us and consumes us. We must respond—if we can. Often there seems to be little we can do. But, since we are not alone, there is always much we can do! We know where help may be found. "I will life up my eyes to the hills—where does my help come from? My help comes from the Lord, the Maker of heaven and earth" (Ps 121:1-2). Our Helper is always near.

Only the weak need help. The strong can carry the load and are quite happy to do so as it reveals their strength. Weakness opens the door for assistance. God opposes the proud but gives grace to the humble, the needy (James 4:6). Have you ever said, "In my distress I called to the Lord; I cried to my God for help ... my cry came before him, into his ears (Ps 18:6)? Of course, you have. And the same testimony has been yours as has been His people throughout all ages.

With Moses you have cried, "there is no one like the God of Jeshurun, who rides on the heavens to help you and on the clouds in his majesty. The eternal God is your refuge, and underneath are the everlasting arms" (Deut 33:26-27). With Samuel you have acted, "Then Samuel took a stone ... he named it Ebenezer, saying 'Thus far the Lord has helped us'" (1 Sam 7:12). With the sons of Korah you have affirmed, "God is our refuge and strength—an ever-present help in trouble" (Ps 46:1). With Mary you have praised, "He has filled the hungry with good things ... He has helped his servant Israel, remembering to be merciful" (Lk 1:53-54). And with Paul you have heard God say, "My grace is sufficient for you, for my power is made perfected in weakness," and have responded, "Therefore, I will boast more gladly about my weakness, so that Christ's power may rest on me ... For when I am weak, then am I strong" (2 Cor 12:9-10).

Everyone in the world needs help. It is yours, through Christ, to give it. Seek out the needy. Ask questions that show you sincerely want to help whomever you meet. Do not let feelings of fear grip you, fears of your inadequacy, your lack of knowledge or your own imperfections. You are not the helper—God is!

Always remember— "The Lord is my helper, I will not be afraid. What can man do to me?" (Heb 13:6; Ps 118:6-7). We do not serve a God who is slow or reluctant to help. "...You, O God, do see trouble and grief;

you consider it to take it in hand ... you are the helper of the fatherless" (Ps 10:14). It is He who always says to you and others, "So do not fear, for I am with you; do not be dismayed, for I am your God. I will strengthen you and help you; I will uphold you with my righteous right hand" (Is 41:10). Receive God's help through Christ and let it flow through you to those in need around you. This will greatly glorify Him.

Response

I thank you God for showing me _____

_____.

STRATEGY

Follow Jesus today, whose desire and ability to help others was amazing as seen in **Mark 1:40-45)** (Read now)

As I follow Jesus today I will remember _____

OBEDIENCE (I will statement)

The Spirit is convicting or leading me today to do or stop doing: _____

_____.

PETITIONS (Following your reciting of The Lord's Prayer)

I pray for these scheduled meetings today:

I pray also for these pressing needs of myself, my family, my church, my disciples my world:

CONFESSION and REPENTANCE

I confess these, my sins, with every intention to never repeat them, but rather to live as Jesus would live, by Your enabling grace and Spirit ...

*Never confess without a faith that looks to the cross of Christ, where the guilt and penalty of all our sins was paid!

WALK (Think about the following hymn)

Help Me O Lord

1) Help me, O Lord, the God of my salvation;
I have no hope, no refuge but in Thee;
Help me to make this perfect consecration,
In life or death Thine evermore to be.

2) Help me, O Lord, to keep my pledge unbroken;
Guard Thou my ways, my thoughts, my tongue, my heart;
Help me to trust the word which Thou hast spoken,
That from Thy paths my feet may ne'er depart.

3) Help me, O Lord, when sore temptations press me;
O lift the clouds that hide Thee from my sight;
Help me, O Lord, when anxious cares distress me,
To look beyond, where all is calm and bright.

4) Help me, O Lord, my strength is only weakness;
Thine, Thine the power by which alone I live;
Help me each day, to bear the cross with meekness,
Till Thou at last the promised crown shalt give.
(Fanny Crosby, 1820-1915)

Response

Help me, Jesus, to _____

_____.

VICTORY

Memorize *Isaiah 41:10*

Be prepared for opposition (spiritual warfare) and expect victory in Jesus' name.

Write down the name (s) of those with whom you shared today _____
_____.

_____ Check when the day is completed, never beating yourself up if you did not finish; but, just asking Jesus to help you next day!

Day Eighty-six

God – The Mother-like

ADORATION

We have seen how the Scriptures use so many good things in creation to point to our good God. So, it should not surprise us that He likens Himself to one of the most beautiful and beneficial of all people on earth—to our mothers! Wanting His children to know that He will not abandon them, God said, "As a mother comforts her child, so will I comfort you" (Isa 66:13a). How often in life is it only the mother who holds out hope for the prodigal son or daughter? Therefore, Hallmark cards discovered that male prisoners long to send Mother's Day cards, but that there is almost no market among them for Father's Day cards!

The longing heart of a loving God cried out in Jesus, "O Jerusalem, Jerusalem ... how often I have longed to gather your children together, as a hen gathers her chicks under her wings, but you were not willing. Look, your house is left to you desolate" (Matt 23:37-38). Few representations in the whole of Scripture tug more at the heart than Christ's lamentation. Roosters are not well known for gathering chicks under their wings. But hens are.

Certainly, it would be unbiblical to address God as, "our Mother who art in heaven," when Jesus commanded His disciples to pray to Him as "Our Father." We want to call God what He has told us to call Him. However, challenging it may be to our egalitarian culture, through the Bible we learn that there are some aspects of the Being of God that are best represented by certain masculine characteristics. Every role that a man is created and commanded to play, God plays perfectly and forever. He is infinitely better and greater than the best man. This could be one reason that Jesus so loved to refer to Himself as the "Son of man." He is the only true man, the quintessential man.

But we make too much of God's "maleness" if we exclude from His nature those glorious attributes that make females, mothers and motherhood so beautiful and good. Patience, gentleness, amazing grace, inner strength and ravishing beauty are often ascribed to women. We must also remember, too, that it is God who gives birth to us spiritually in our new birth (John 1:12-13; 3:3-5). In all these and every other way, God is better than the best woman and mother. "Though my father and my mother forsake me, the Lord will receive me" (Ps 27:10).

God created both male and female in His image. "So, God created man in his own image, in the image of God he created him; male and female, he created them. God blessed them and said to them, 'Be fruitful, fill the earth and subdue it'" (Gen 1:27-28a). So, there is something about both the masculinity of men and the femininity of women that is God-like. We get a fuller picture of God and His glory by following the Scripture and likening Him in these and other ways to both sexes!

We must make certain that, while we carefully and thoughtfully guard the unique aspects of God's Fatherhood, we do not either rob Him of glory or dishonor women and motherhood by likening only males to God. And God to males. For God, Himself, declared, "Can a mother forget the baby at her breast and have no compassion on the child she has borne? Though she may forget, I will not forget you!" (Isa 49:15). Let us join Paul in following our tender and meek Lord, "But we were gentle among you, like a mother caring for her little children" (1 Thes 2:7 and Matt 11:28-30).

Response

I thank you God for showing me _____

_____.

STRATEGY

Follow Jesus today, who surprised His disciples by the levels of His gentleness and kindness as seen in **Mark 10:13-16** (Read now)

As I follow Jesus today I will remember _____

_____.

OBEDIENCE (I will statement)

The Spirit is convicting or leading me today to do or stop doing: _____

_____.

PETITIONS (Following your reciting of The Lord's Prayer)

I pray for these scheduled meetings today:

I pray also for these pressing needs of myself, my family, my church, my disciples my world:

CONFESSION and REPENTANCE

I confess these, my sins, with every intention to never repeat them, but rather to live as Jesus would live, by Your enabling grace and Spirit …
*Never confess without a faith that looks to the cross of Christ, where the guilt and penalty of all our sins was paid!

WALK (Think about the following hymn)

My God, How Wonderful Thou Art

1) My God, how wonderful Thou art,
Thy majesty, how bright;
How beautiful Thy mercy seat
In depths of burning light!

2) How dread are Thy eternal years,
O everlasting Lord,
By prostrate spirits day and night
Incessantly adored!

3) How wonderful, how beautiful,
The sight of Thee must be;
Thy endless wisdom, boundless power,
And glorious purity!

4) O how I fear Thee, living God,
With deep and tender fear;
And worship Thee with trembling hope,
And penitential tears!

5) Yet, I may love Thee, too, O Lord,
Almighty as Thou art;
For Thou hast stooped to ask of me
The love of my poor heart!

6) No earthly father loves like Thee,
No mother, e'er so mild,
Bears and forbears as Thou hast done,
With me, Thy sinful child.

7) Only to sit and think of God,
Oh, what a joy it is!
To think the thought, to breathe the Name,
Earth has no higher bliss.

8) Father of Jesus, love's Reward!
What rapture it will be
Prostrate before Thy throne to lie,
And gaze, and gaze on Thee!
(Frederick W. Faber, 1814-1863)

Response

Help me, Jesus, to _____

_____.

VICTORY

Memorize *Matthew 11:28-30*

Be prepared for opposition (spiritual warfare) and expect victory in Jesus' name.

Write down the name (s) of those with whom you shared today _____

_____.

_____ Check when the day is completed, never beating yourself up if you did not finish; but, just asking Jesus to help you next day!

Day Eighty-seven

God – The Healing One

ADORATION

 We all want to be well. To be free from painful sicknesses. To be healed from what hurts our minds, hearts and bodies. Because that desire is universal, healing sells. The promise of healing is nearly irresistible to someone who is deeply hurting. That is what makes false peddlers of healing so harmful. A few seem changed; but, so many are left crippled and diseased. And they are crushed by not being helped. Why was someone healed, and I wasn't? I must be the problem. I must be beyond help. God does not love me.

 Healing was one reason why so many thousands followed Jesus. "Many followed him, and he healed all their sick, warning them not to tell who he was" (Matt 12:15-16). He did not seek fame or glory. He did not sell cloths and make money from His healing power. He healed because He, as God, simply loved those around Him. And He desired to help them. "It is not the healthy who need a doctor, but the sick ... I have not come to call the righteous, but sinners" (Matt 9:12-13).

 As the Life giver, God is also the Healer. "I will heal my people and will let them enjoy abundant peace and security" (Jer. 33:6b). He is sovereign over life and death. They are His servants. "See now that I myself am He! There is no god besides me. I put to death and I bring to life. I have wounded, and I will heal, and no one can deliver out of my hand" (Deut 32:39). This truth was so universally known among his OT people, that it became a proverb. "Fear the Lord and shun evil. This will bring health to your body and nourishment to your bones" (Prov 3:7b-8).

 Christ even gave the gift of His healing power to some. "Crowds gathered also from the towns around Jerusalem, bringing their sick and those tormented by evil spirits, and all of them were healed" (Acts 5:16). The gift of healing never failed. There is no evidence that anyone ministered to by a believer with that gift was left unhealed. Today some claim to have the gift who leave many in despair and illness. We should pray for the sick and expect God to graciously heal whom He will because He is a God of love and power. But we should not claim to have a gift of healing if people are left sick following our attempt to help them. Every disciple of Jesus should be ready to pray for healing in the contexts of "people of peace," whose lives have been marked by sincere receptivity to being discipled, but whose way forward is hindered by illness. Their healing has often opened great doors for Kingdom advancement. Many are being thus healed today, praise the Lord! (See Luke 10:1-12, see Trousdale's Miraculous Movements).

God heals. Let us praise Him whatever means He uses. Miraculously or medically. But let us be careful not to trifle with the hearts of the broken and despairing. Those who need our love and listening. Our time, our help and our prayers. Let us leave their physical healing with God, who often uses our sicknesses and afflictions in ways to humble us, break us down and open our hearts. He also uses our pains to take us places to minister to others who need to hear the Gospel. To some well in body but sick in soul. To others who are sick and do not know that Christ died to heal us from all the power of sin. "Surely he took up our infirmities and carried our sorrows...and by his wounds we are healed" (Isa 53:4-5). Faith in the Gospel heals NOW. The full and permanent effects of that healing will be enjoyed when "there will be no more death or crying or pain, for the old order of things has passed away" (Rev 21:4b).

Response

I thank you God for showing me _____

_____.

STRATEGY

Follow Jesus today, whose healing power was often used during His short public ministry as seen in **Mark 1:21-34** (Read now)

As I follow Jesus today I will remember _____

_____.

OBEDIENCE (I will statement)

The Spirit is convicting or leading me today to do or stop doing: _____

_____.

PETITIONS (Following your reciting of <u>The Lord's Prayer</u>)

I pray for these scheduled meetings today:

I pray also for these pressing needs of myself, my family, my church, my disciples my world:

CONFESSION and REPENTANCE

I confess these, my sins, with every intention to never repeat them, but rather to live as Jesus would live, by Your enabling grace and Spirit …

*Never confess without a faith that looks to the cross of Christ, where the guilt and penalty of all our sins was paid!

WALK (Think about the following hymn)

He Touched Me

1) Shackled by a heavy burden,
'Neath a load of guilt and shame,
Then the hand of Jesus touched me,
And now I am no longer the same.

*He touched me, Oh He touched me,
And oh the joy that floods my soul!
Something happened and now I know
He touched me and made me whole!*

2) Since I met this blessed Savior,
Since He's cleansed and made me whole,
Oh, I will never cease to praise Him
I'll shout it while eternity rolls.
(Bill Gaither, 1963)

Response

Help me, Jesus, to _____

_____

VICTORY

Memorize *Acts 10:38*

Be prepared for opposition (spiritual warfare) and expect victory in Jesus' name.

Write down the name (s) of those with whom you shared today and pray for them. _____
_____.

____ Check when the day is completed, never beating yourself up if you did not finish; but, just asking Jesus to help you next day!

Day Eighty-eight

God – The Happy One

ADORATION

  I think we all would agree that heaven is a happy place. But why? Because no sin, suffering or sorrow are there? Heaven's happiness is not mainly due to what is NOT there. It is the happiest of places because it is filled with the presence of an infinitely happy God. Heaven rejoices (Luke 15:10) because it can't help itself. It is where "thousands upon thousands of angels [are] in joyful assembly" (Heb 12:22). There a triune God forever calls on all around Him to be full of His delightful and joyful love.

  "The Lord your God is with you...He will take great delight in you, he will quiet you with his love, he will rejoice over you with singing" (Zeph 3:17). "You will fill me with joy in your presence" (Ps 16:11). "And the ransomed of the Lord will return. They will enter Zion with singing; everlasting joy will overtake them, and sorrow and sighing will flee away" (Isa 35:10; 51:11; 61:7). Instead of an enemy overtaking us, it will be joy! Everlasting joy!

  One of the great aims of our Christian walk now should be to let faith fill us with the firstfruits of that joy. Paul said, "The fruit of the Spirit is love, joy..." (Gal 5:22), and he prayed, "The God of hope fill you with all joy" (Rom 15:13). In fact, unless we "rejoice in the Lord always," (Phil 4:4) we aren't rightly following Christ.

  "Jesus, the author and perfecter of our faith, who, for the joy set before him endured the cross" (Heb 12:2). Jesus came because the horror of His human passion could not parallel the eternal joy that He would thereby usher in. He was filled with deep delight, even during daily sufferings. "At that time Jesus, full of joy through the Holy Spirit..." (Lk 10:21). As His life reached its awful end, on the very last night, He said, "I have told you this so that my joy may be in you and that your joy may be complete" (John 15:11). Surrounded by suffering and death, He still spoke of joy. And the Spirit shares that grace with us, as Paul testified, "in all our troubles my joy knows no bounds" (2 Cor 7:5). So, faith is now seen by our ability to suffer with a smile. "Do not grieve, for the joy of the Lord is your strength" (Neh 8:10).

  Let Paul's haunting question serve as our constant reminder, "What has happened to all your joy?" (Gal 4:15). The gospel frees from all sin and striving, bidding us sing," I will go to the altar of God, to God, my joy and my delight...Why are you downcast O my soul? (Ps 43:4-5). Joy will win over sorrow. "Weeping may remain for a night, but rejoicing comes in the morning" (Ps 30:5). So, dear disciples, "be joyful always" (1 Thes 5:16).

Response

I thank you God for showing me _____

_____.

STRATEGY

Follow Jesus today, who, though "a man of sorrows" also was often filled with joy as seen in **Luke 10:17-24** (Read now)

As I follow Jesus today I will remember _____

_____.

OBEDIENCE (I will statement)

The Spirit is convicting or leading me today to do or stop doing: _____

_____.

PETITIONS (Following your reciting of <u>The Lord's Prayer</u>)

I pray for these scheduled meetings today:

I pray also for these pressing needs of myself, my family, my church, my disciples my world:

CONFESSION and REPENTANCE

I confess these, my sins, with every intention to never repeat them, but rather to live as Jesus would live, by Your enabling grace and Spirit ...

*Never confess without a faith that looks to the cross of Christ, where the guilt and penalty of all our sins was paid!

WALK (Think about the following hymn)

His Eye is on the Sparrow

1) Why should I feel discouraged, why should the shadows come,
Why should my heart be lonely, and long for heaven and home,
When Jesus is my portion? My constant friend is He:
His eye is on the sparrow, and I know He watches me;
His eye is on the sparrow, and I know He watches me.

*I sing because I'm happy,
I sing because I'm free,
For His eye is on the sparrow,
And I know He watches me.*

2) "Let not your heart be troubled," His tender word I hear,
And resting on His goodness, I lose my doubts and fears;
Though by the path He leadeth, but one step I may see;
His eye is on the sparrow, and I know He watches me;
His eye is on the sparrow, and I know He watches me.

3) Whenever I am tempted, whenever clouds arise,
When songs give place to sighing, when hope within me dies,
I draw the closer to Him, from care He sets me free;
His eye is on the sparrow, and I know He watches me;
His eye is on the sparrow, and I know He watches me.
(Civila D Martin, 1866-1948)

Response

Help me, Jesus, to _____

_____.

VICTORY

Memorize *Philippians 4:4*

Be prepared for opposition (spiritual warfare) and expect victory in Jesus' name.

Write down the name (s) of those with whom you shared today _____
_____.

____ Check when the day is completed, never beating yourself up if you did not finish; but, just asking Jesus to help you next day!

Day Eighty-nine

God – The Uplifting One

ADORATION

When one falls, he usually gathers his strength and stands back up, if the fall is not too severe. But once someone falls too far, the force of the drop usually does permanent damage. Life changes forever. Crutches, wheelchair, inserted rods, pins and pain. No more easy days. Because of "the Fall."

When Adam and Eve sinned, they fell from a state of holiness, happiness and life. That dark day is termed, The Fall of Man. No other crash has ever wrought such ruin as Adam's Fall, whether 9/11 or the stock market crash of 1929, or the Great Fire of London in 1666, or the Black Death (Bubonic Plague) that killed upwards to 200 million people between 1347 and 1351. All death and sadness come from Adam's Fall. Do not be deceived, sin never advances or uplifts or profits our lives. It always, ultimately, takes us down and leaves us desperate! Thanks be to God, He did not leave us cast down, broken and hopeless. He came and offered us His strong, saving hand!

"I will exalt you, O Lord, for you lifted me out of the depths" (Ps 30:1). "He lifted me out of the slimy pit, out of the mud and mire; he set my feet on a rock and gave me a place to stand" (Ps 40:2). Our fall into sin weakens us and opens us up to every foe. "O Lord, see how my enemies persecute me! Have mercy and lift me up from the gates of death" (Ps 9:13). "But you are a shield around me, O Lord; you bestow glory on me and lift up my head" (Ps 3 :3). With such a Helper let us ever say, "Why are you downcast, O my soul? Why so disturbed within me? Put your hope in God" (Ps 42:5a).

Our fallenness is very real. Our depraved and sinful condition is undeniable. So, God is happy when we confess the reality of our own mess and ask Him for help. But those who deny their crippled, broken and desperate condition are often left to themselves until they are humbled. Peter learned this and wrote, "God opposes the proud but gives grace to the humble. Humble yourselves, therefore, under God's mighty hand, that he may lift you up in due time" (1 Pet 5:5b-6; James 4:10). In fact, if we deny our sin, He will expose our proud foolishness to help us assume the correct position of humility before Him. "I am against you, declares the Almighty. I will lift you skirts over your face. I will show the nations your nakedness and the kingdoms your shame" (Nahum 3:5). God takes no pleasure in thus shaming us. But it is really kindness for Him to do it, to lead us first, to reality and then, to repentance. "In all their distress he too was distressed, and the anger of his presence saved them. In his love and mercy, he redeemed them; he lifted them up and carried them all the days of old. Yet they rebelled and grieved his Holy Spirit. So, he turned and became their enemy and he himself fought against them" (Isa 63:9-10). Even His correction is outlined by mercy.

God loves to help the needy and delights when we do the same in His Name. "He raises the poor from the dust and lifts the needy from the ash heap; he seats them with princes" (Ps 113:7-8a). "He who is kind to the poor lends to the Lord, and he will reward him for what he has done" Prov 19:17). Jesus often helped the poor and saw it as a great proof of His divine mission (Matt 11:2-6). May we often lift up others and, so, follow the Lord, "But Jesus took him by the hand and lifted him up to his feet, and he stood up" (Mk 9:27).

Response

I thank you God for showing me _____

_____.

STRATEGY

Follow Jesus today, who loved to lift up the poor and crippled as seen in **Mark 9:14-27** (Read now)

As I follow Jesus today I will remember _____

_____.

OBEDIENCE (I will statement)

The Spirit is convicting or leading me today to do or stop doing: _____

_____.

PETITIONS (Following your reciting of The Lord's Prayer)

I pray for these scheduled meetings today:

I pray also for these pressing needs of myself, my family, my church, my disciples my world:

CONFESSION and REPENTANCE

I confess these, my sins, with every intention to never repeat them, but rather to live as Jesus would live, by Your enabling grace and Spirit ...

*Never confess without a faith that looks to the cross of Christ, where the guilt and penalty of all our sins was paid!

WALK (Think about the following hymn)

He Lifted Me

1) In loving-kindness Jesus came
my soul in mercy to reclaim,
and from the depths of sin and shame
through grace He lifted me.

*From sinking sand He lifted me,
with tender hand He lifted me,
from shades of night to plains of light,
O praise His name, He lifted me!*

2) He called me long before I heard,
before my sinful heart was stirred,
but when I took Him at His word,
forgiven, He lifted me.

3) His brow was pierced with many a thorn,
His hands by cruel nails were torn,
when from my guilt and grief, forlorn,
in love He lifted me.

4 Now on a higher plane I dwell,
and with my soul I know 'tis well;
yet how or why, I cannot tell,
He should have lifted me.
(Charles Gabriel, 1856-1932)

Response

Help me, Jesus, to _____

_____.

VICTORY

Memorize *Psalm 37:23-24*

Be prepared for opposition (spiritual warfare) and expect victory in Jesus' name.
Write down the name (s) of those with whom you shared today _____

_____.

____ Check when the day is completed, never beating yourself up if you did not finish; but, just asking Jesus to help you next day!

Day Ninety

God – The Destroyer of Satan

ADORATION

God is infinitely good. Satan is evil, "a murderer from the beginning" (Jn 8:44). He led the angels astray and they were cast out of heaven. "The great dragon was hurled down—that ancient serpent called the devil, or Satan, who leads the whole world astray. He was hurled to the earth, and his angels with him" (Rev 12:9). He led Eve astray and was condemned on earth, "And I will put enmity between you and the woman, and between your offspring and hers; he will crush your head and you will strike his heel" (Gen 3:15). Her offspring would destroy the devil. And that offspring would come through Abraham (Gen 12:1-3), the first Jew. That promise sparked in Satan a relentless effort to destroy the OT children of God and to obliterate Israel from existence. No Israel means no Messiah. No Messiah means no Offspring to crush my head. He failed. Israel endured by God's grace. Jesus was born. "He too shared in their humanity so that by death he might destroy him who holds the power of death—that is, the devil—and free those who all their lives were held in slavery by their fear of death" (Heb 2:14-15). Or as John summarized, "He who does what is sinful is of the devil, because the devil has been sinning from the beginning. The reason the Son of God appeared was to destroy the devil's work" (1 John 3:8). The noose was tightening.

I hope you sense the reality of this spiritual war because it now includes you if you dare follow Jesus. Yes, God will destroy the devil utterly; but first He crippled him. Jesus said, "Now is the time for judgment in this world; now the prince of this world will be driven out" (John 12:31). The devil was displaced. And he is mad. So, he seeks vengeance against all those Jesus saves. Peter felt his grip (Matt 16:23; 26:69ff) and later wrote, "Be self-controlled and alert. Your enemy the devil prowls around like a roaring lion looking for someone to devour. Resist him, standing firm in the faith" (1 Pet 5:8-9a). Paul rejoiced, "The God of peace will soon crush Satan under your feet" (Rom 16:20). Yes, God uses disciples to oppose and destroy Satan's kingdom! But how?

Very carefully and prayerfully. "Watch and pray so that you will not fall into temptation." (Matt 16:41a). "Put on the full armor of God, so that you can take your stand against the devil's schemes... And pray in the Spirit on all occasions, with all kinds of prayers and requests. Be alert and always keep on praying for all the saints" (Eph 6:11-18). He uses us against Satan as we humbly pray, "deliver us from the evil one" (Mart 6:13). One mark of the faith-filled, content Christian is that "You have overcome the evil one" (I Jn 2:13,14). The doubting, angry Christian gives "the devil a foothold" in his life (Eph 4:27). Instead of standing (humbly) in Christ's victory, such a one often falls (proudly) –just like Satan fell in pride (1 Tim 3:6). Nevertheless, God wins! "And the devil … was thrown into the lake of burning Sulphur … (and) will be tormented day and night forever" (Rev 20:10). Follow Jesus and renounce the devil! Bear your cross of suffering NOW and reign with Him forever.

Response

I thank you God for showing me_____

_____.

STRATEGY

Follow Jesus today, seeing how He claimed to already have defeated Satan as seen in **John 12:20-36** (Read now)

As I follow Jesus today I will remember_____

OBEDIENCE (I will statement)

The Spirit is convicting or leading me today to do or stop doing: _____

_____.

PETITIONS (Following your reciting of The Lord's Prayer)

I pray for these scheduled meetings today:

I pray also for these pressing needs of myself, my family, my church, my disciples my world:

CONFESSION and REPENTANCE

I confess these, my sins, with every intention to never repeat them, but rather to live as Jesus would live, by Your enabling grace and Spirit …

*Never confess without a faith that looks to the cross of Christ, where the guilt and penalty of all our sins was paid!

WALK (Think about the following hymn)

A Mighty Fortress

1) A mighty fortress is our God, a bulwark never failing;
Our helper He, amid the flood of mortal ills prevailing:
For still our ancient foe doth seek to work us woe;
His craft and power are great, and, armed with cruel hate,
On earth is not his equal.

2) Did we in our own strength confide, our striving would be losing;
Were not the right Man on our side, the Man of God's own choosing:
Dost ask who that may be? Christ Jesus, it is He;
Lord Sabaoth, His Name, from age to age the same,
And He must win the battle.

3) And though this world, with devils filled, should threaten to undo us,
We will not fear, for God hath willed His truth to triumph through us:
The Prince of Darkness grim, we tremble not for him;
His rage we can endure, for lo, his doom is sure,
One little word shall fell him.

4) That word above all earthly powers, no thanks to them, abideth;
The Spirit and the gifts are ours through Him Who with us sideth:
Let goods and kindred go, this mortal life also;
The body they may kill: God's truth abideth still,
His kingdom is forever.
(Martin Luther, 1483-1546, trans by Frederic Hedge, 1853)

Response

Help me, Jesus, to _____

_____.

VICTORY

Memorize <u>Romans 16:20</u>

Be prepared for opposition (spiritual warfare) and expect victory in Jesus' name.

Write down the name (s) of those with whom you shared today _____
_____.

____ Check when the day is completed, never beating yourself up if you did not finish; but, just asking Jesus to help you next day!

10-Day Period 10

Discipleship and our Going to Make Disciples of Jesus

**Begin by reading Appendix Ten – *Truly Fulfilling Jesus' Great Commission*

The NT is largely a missionary book which was written by disciples to disciples who were committed to making disciples. To read it in any other way is to misread it. It was not written by Christian leaders to Christians trying to make Christians. Or by church leaders to church goers who were trying to grow their local churches. It was not written by theologians to theological students who were trying to advance their theological opinions. It was written by men who were in the process of discipling the world because that is what their Master had commanded them to do.

You cannot make something if you do not understand its components or elements. If you do not know what "disciple" meant to Jesus and all 1st century rabbis, you will never be able to "make disciples" as He commanded. As I have shown, there were 5 marks of a 1st century disciple[37]. And one of them was what I called "total duplication." That is, every disciple expected to master the rabbi's thought and life sufficiently to be commissioned to go and make other disciples. Because disciples reproduce, you must make reproducers. One's discipleship status is not proven until his or her disciple is making disciples. God bless you as you pray, find people of peace whom the Spirit has readied for discipleship, and then go and make them disciples of Jesus Christ!

---

[37] See my Are You a Christian or a Disciple? *Rediscovering and Renewing NT Discipleship* chapters 1-4

Day Ninety-one

God – The Strong One

ADORATION

"Blessed are those whose strength is in you" (Ps 84:5a). Think of what it would be like to be without strength. With no ability to move. Totally paralyzed. Motionless. The thought causes us to cringe in horror or fills us with pity for a paralyzed person we know.

We have already focused on God's omnipotence. But few of us appreciate how dangerously weak we are and just how desperately we need His strength. The Psalmist pronounces a person "blessed" who learns to live like one who is paralyzed, needing assistance for every moment of daily life. Like a child who cannot yet crawl or walk and cries out for help to get from one place to another. That is a characteristic of childlikeness that we often reject. We want to stand on our own two feet and move forward like grown adults. Such is not the way of wisdom. As Solomon had counseled, "Trust in the Lord with all your heart and lean not on your own understanding; in all your ways acknowledge him, and he will make your paths straight" (Prov 3:5-6). And did not Jesus say, "apart from me you can do nothing" (John 15:5b)?

David sang, "I love you, O Lord, my strength" (Ps 18:1). The deeper the danger from which God rescues us, the stronger is our love for Him. But too many of us never admit being weak enough to need God's powerful help. We certainly rarely begin the day with that sense of desperation. But we should! Many Christians recovering from addictions begin their day that way. They pray, "Thank you Lord for waking me up and letting me see the light of another day. Unless you are with me, I am one bad thought away from disaster. Be my strength." Sounds like David, "God is our refuge and strength, an ever-present help in trouble" (Ps 46:1). If we live in a world where trouble is ever-present, and if we have no natural strength to protect ourselves from its destruction, then we need an ever-present God to help us. Do YOU really believe that you have a need to "be strong in the Lord and in his mighty power" so that "you can take your stand against the devil's schemes" (Eph 6:10-11)?

"The Lord is my strength and my song" (Isa 12:2b). Maybe your song is growing weak because you are singing too often of yourself, putting too much stock in your own strength. Let "the joy of the Lord (be) your strength" (Neh 8:10). Rejoice in what you have in Him—in His strength freely given by His Spirit to you. Let everyone know of your own powerlessness and see your strength residing only in Christ. "I can do everything through him who gives me strength" (Phil 4:13). Make this your constant song: "O my Strength, I sing praise to you; you, O God are my fortress, my loving God" (Ps 59:17).

Response

I thank you God for showing me _____

_____.

STRATEGY

Follow Jesus today, remembering the peerless power with which He will return to the earth as seen in **Matthew 24:26-31** (Read now)

As I follow Jesus today I will remember _____

_____.

OBEDIENCE (I will statement)

The Spirit is convicting or leading me today to do or stop doing: _____

_____.

PETITIONS (Following your reciting of The Lord's Prayer)

I pray for these scheduled meetings today:

I pray also for these pressing needs of myself, my family, my church, my disciples my world:

CONFESSION and REPENTANCE

I confess these, my sins, with every intention to never repeat them, but rather to live as Jesus would live, by Your enabling grace and Spirit …

*Never confess without a faith that looks to the cross of Christ, where the guilt and penalty of all our sins was paid!

WALK (Think about the following hymn)

I Need Thee Every Hour

1) I need Thee every hour,
Most gracious Lord;
No tender voice like Thine
Can peace afford.

I need Thee, oh, I need Thee;
Every hour I need Thee;
Oh, bless me now, my Savior!
I come to Thee.

2) I need Thee every hour,
Stay Thou nearby;
Temptations lose their power
When Thou art nigh.

3) I need Thee every hour,
In joy or pain;
Come quickly and abide,
Or life is vain.

4) I need Thee every hour,
Teach me Thy will;
And Thy rich promises
In me fulfill.

5) I need Thee every hour,
Most Holy One;
Oh, make me Thine indeed,
Thou blessed Son.
(Annie S Hawks, 1835-1918)

Response

Help me, Jesus, to _____

_____.

VICTORY

Memorize *Psalm 28:7*

Be prepared for opposition spiritual warfare) and expect victory in Jesus' name.

Write down the name (s) of those with whom you shared today _____
_____.

_____ Check when the day is completed, never beating yourself up if you did not finish; but, just asking Jesus to help you next day!

Day Ninety-two

God – The Compassionate One

ADORATION

Passion is strong emotions or feelings. Compassion is to have strong feelings for someone else. To come alongside of another with passion, with sympathy, when one is hurting. Never think that God is coldly aloof, without emotion in His nature. The Bible makes it abundantly clear, "You, O Lord, are a compassionate and gracious God, slow to anger, abounding in love and faithfulness" (Ps 86:15). "As a father has compassion on his children, so the Lord has compassion on those who fear him; for he knows how we are formed, he remembers that we are dust" (Ps 103:13-14).

Unlike our human fathers, though, God is infinitely sympathetic towards us, completely understanding our pitiful nature and need. "Yet the Lord longs to be gracious to you; he rises to show you compassion" (Isa 30:18a). We often rise to pursue our own agendas, our daily schedules. God's agenda is compassion. His schedule is kindness. Every morning we awaken to the Lord's kind and compassionate heart. "Because of the Lord's great love, we are not consumed, for his compassions never fail. They are new every morning" (Lam 3:22-23).

Since "the Lord is full of compassion and mercy" (James 5:11b), our hearts are filled with joy and praise. We always have His sympathy. "Shout for joy, O heavens; rejoice, O earth; burst into song, O mountains! For the Lord comforts his people and will have compassion on his afflicted ones" (Isa 49:13). He will wipe away every tear from our eyes.

Over and over we read of the compassion of Jesus, the Son of God. "When he saw the crowds, he had compassion on them, because they were harassed and helpless, like sheep without a shepherd" (Matt 9:36). "When Jesus landed and saw, a large crowd, he had compassion on them and healed their sick" (Matt 14:14). He said, "I have compassion for these people; they already have been with me three days and have nothing to eat. I do not want to send them away hungry, or they may collapse on the way" (Matt 15:32). "Jesus had compassion on them and touched their eyes. Immediately they received their sight and followed him" (Matt 20:34). Every degrading human woe filled our Savior with strong sympathy. He hated to see Satan bring His beloved creatures into such conditions. He hurt for the sin that enslaved the children of Adam. And when He came alongside, He healed. He fed. He delivered. He saved. The issue of sin needed a deeper, long-term solution that

He would provide. Misery did not need to wait. This is how Jesus lived and how He guides those who follow Him today to live!

"Praise be to the God and Father of our Lord Jesus Christ, the Father of compassion and the God of all comfort" (2 Cor 1:3). God gives birth to compassion. To all types of real, lasting comfort. And He turns our hearts in compassion to the suffering ones around us. "Therefore, as God's chosen people, holy and deeply loved, clothe yourselves with compassion, kindness ..." (Col 3:12). Since Christ is compassionate, let us follow Him in having passionate concern for the needy, the sorrowing, the hurt, the lost. Since God cannot be defeated, let us remember that compassion wins! All our efforts to help others in need, out of loving sympathy (not cold pity) and in His Name will be blessed!

Response

I thank you God for showing me _____

_____.

STRATEGY

Follow Jesus today, whose compassion was often expressed as seen in **Matt 9:35-38** (Read now)

As I follow Jesus today I will remember _____

_____.

OBEDIENCE (I will statement)

The Spirit is convicting or leading me today to do or stop doing: _____

_____.

PETITIONS (Following your reciting of The Lord's Prayer)

I pray for these scheduled meetings today:

I pray also for these pressing needs of myself, my family, my church, my disciples my world:

CONFESSION and REPENTANCE

I confess these, my sins, with every intention to never repeat them, but rather to live as Jesus would live, by Your enabling grace and Spirit …

*Never confess without a faith that looks to the cross of Christ, where the guilt and penalty of all our sins was paid!

WALK (Think about the following hymn)

Come unto Me, Ye Weary

1) Come unto Me, ye weary, and I will give you rest.
O blessed voice of Jesus, which comes to hearts oppressed!
It tells of benediction, of pardon, grace and peace,
Of joy that hath no ending, of love which cannot cease.

2) Come unto Me, dear children, and I will give you light.
O loving voice of Jesus, which comes to cheer the night!
Our hearts are filled with sadness, and we had lost our way;
But He hath brought us gladness and songs at break of day.

3) Come unto Me, ye fainting, and I will give you life.
O cheering voice of Jesus, which comes to aid our strife!
The foe is stern and eager, the fight is fierce and long;
But Thou hast made us mighty and stronger than the strong.

4) And whosoever cometh I will not cast him out.
O welcome voice of Jesus, which drives away our doubt,
Which calls us, very sinners, unworthy though we be
Of love so free and boundless, to come, dear Lord, to Thee.
(William C Dix, 1837-1898)

Response

Help me, Jesus, to _____

_____.

VICTORY

Memorize *Psalm 51:1*

Be prepared for opposition (spiritual warfare) and expect victory in Jesus' name.

Write down the name (s) of those with whom you shared today and pray for them. _____

_____.

____ Check when the day is completed, never beating yourself up if you did not finish; but, just asking Jesus to help you next day!

Day Ninety-three

God – The Peaceful One

ADORATION

Picture a still lake, an undisturbed forest, a mind at rest, a couple quietly holding hands as they sit on their porch. In all its many forms, peace is beautiful. Like other good things on earth, the gift of peace "is from above" (James 1:17). Peace is not homegrown within the human heart. As Isaiah wrote, "Lord, you establish peace for us; all that we have accomplished you have done for us" (Isa 26:12). Paul agreed, "But the fruit of the Spirit is …" (Gal 5:22). God is the author of peace.

"There is no peace, says the Lord, for the wicked" (Isa 48:22). Our sins make peace with a sinless God impossible. So, God devised and amazing way to save us from the storm of our sin and provide eternal serenity to our souls. God chose to send and punish Jesus, His Beloved Son, instead of punishing us. "He was pierced for our transgressions … The punishment that brought us peace was upon him" (Isa 53:5). And when Christ came, the father was "through him reconciling to himself all things … by making peace through his blood, shed on the cross" (Col 1:19).

Jesus, alone, is "the Prince of Peace" (Isa 9:6). Long before He came, "Gideon built an altar to the Lord … and called it 'The Lord is Peace'" (Judges 6:24). And after Jesus ascended to heaven, Paul wrote, "Therefore, since we have been justified through faith, we have peace with God through our Lord Jesus Christ" (Rom 5:1).

Peace is as obvious as its opposites: turmoil, confusion and despair. God wants us to be at rest, filled with peace. To experience this special gift, go to Jesus who said, "Peace I leave with you; my peace I give unto you. I do not give to you as the world gives. Do not let your heart be troubled and do not be afraid" (John 14:27).

But how can this peace be attained? Paul answers, "Do not be anxious about anything, but in everything by prayer and petition, with thanksgiving, present your requests to God. And the peace of God which transcends all understanding, will guide your hearts and minds in Christ Jesus (Phil 4:6-7). Peace is achievable only by a faith that is active in prayer. Isaiah taught this truth long before the Messiah came, when he said, "You will keep in perfect peace him whose mind is steadfast, because he trusts in you" (Isa 26:3).

Peace and patience are twins. Peace and pressure are opponents. Trust in God, in His timing, in His plan. In His goodness. And realize that most pressures are put on us by ourselves. We push and struggle for that which we crave, rather than peacefully walking with our God. "…The Lord turn his face toward you and give you peace" (Num 6:26).

Response

I thank you God for showing me _____

_____.

STRATEGY

Follow Jesus today, who spoke of giving peace as seen in **John 14:1-2, 25-30** (Read now)

As I follow Jesus today I will remember _____

OBEDIENCE (I will statement)

The Spirit is convicting or leading me today to do or stop doing: _____

_____.

PETITIONS (Following your reciting of The Lord's Prayer)

I pray for these scheduled meetings today:

I pray also for these pressing needs of myself, my family, my church, my disciples my world:

CONFESSION and REPENTANCE

I confess these, my sins, with every intention to never repeat them, but rather to live as Jesus would live, by Your enabling grace and Spirit …

*Never confess without a faith that looks to the cross of Christ, where the guilt and penalty of all our sins was paid!

WALK (Think about the following hymn)

Peace Perfect Peace

1) Peace, perfect peace, in this dark world of sin?
The blood of Jesus whispers peace within.

2) Peace, perfect peace, by thronging duties pressed?
To do the will of Jesus, this is rest.

3) Peace, perfect peace, with sorrows surging round?
On Jesus' bosom naught but calm is found.

4) Peace, perfect peace, with loved ones far away?
In Jesus' keeping we are safe, and they.

5) Peace, perfect peace, our future all unknown?
Jesus we know, and He is on the throne.

6) Peace, perfect peace, death shadowing us and ours?
Jesus has vanquished death and all its powers.

7) It is enough: earth's struggles soon shall cease,
And Jesus call us to Heaven's perfect peace.

(Edward Bickersteth, 1825-1906)

Response

Help me, Jesus, to _____

_____.

VICTORY

Memorize *John 20:21*

Be prepared for opposition (spiritual warfare) and expect victory in Jesus' name.

Write down the name (s) of those with whom you shared today _____

_____.

____ Check when the day is completed, never beating yourself up if you did not finish; but, just asking Jesus to help you next day!

Day Ninety-four

God – The Opposed One

ADORATION

When we consider how good God is, how patient and loving to us sinners, especially in sending His Son to save us, we should be astounded at how often and deeply we oppose Him! We are so infected by sin that, even as Christians, we frequently find ourselves resisting both Him and His ways. Today I will focus on the madness of opposing Him. Yes, it is insanity, as Job declared, "But he stands alone, and who can oppose him? He does whatever he pleases" (Job 23:13). When facing a selfishly driven dilemma, Peter said, "Who was I to think that I could oppose God?" (Acts 11:17b).

"The kings of the earth take their stand and the rulers gather together against the Lord and against his Anointed One. 'Let us break their chains,' they say, 'and throw off their fetters'" (Ps 2:2-3). Here, David portrays the zenith of human power as being focused against God. Though one man rivals another and one king hates his neighbor, there is One they hate more. One against whom they are willing to lay aside their historic differences in order to try to defeat. And so, we read that when Jesus was crucified, on "that day Herod and Pilate became friends—before this they had been enemies" (Luke 23:12). Later, believers remembered, "Indeed Herod and Pontius Pilate met together with the Gentiles and the people of Israel in this city to conspire against your holy servant Jesus, whom you anointed" (Acts 4:27).

God told Samuel, "Listen to all that the people are saying to you; it is not you they have rejected, but they have rejected me as their king" (1 Sam 8:7). During their wanderings in the wilderness, He said to Israel, "You will not eat it for just one day … but for a whole month –until it comes out of your nostrils and you loathe it—because you have rejected the Lord, who is among you, and have wailed before him saying, 'Why did we ever leave Egypt?'" (Num 11:20).

Why would anyone reject or oppose the Lord? Jesus said, "You are ready to kill me because you have no room for my word" (John 8:37b). We are, like old King Herod, so filled with ourselves that there is no room within us for the will of God. Upon hearing Micah's word of prophecy, "He gave orders to kill all the boys in Bethlehem and the vicinity who were two years old and under" (Matt 2:16b). Jesus, from birth, was "destined … to be a sign that will be spoken against so that the thoughts of many hearts will be revealed" (Luke 2:34b).

Dear friend, what ugliness is revealed within our hearts when we remain aloof from Him and His Word! Repent with me of every thought, feeling and action opposing Jesus! Let us join Paul in "demolishing arguments and every pretension that sets itself up against the knowledge of God" taking "captive every thought to make it obedient to Christ" (2 Cor 10:5). God cannot be mocked. "Those who oppose the Lord will be shattered. He ... will judge the ends of the earth" (1 Sam 2:10). Remember, every opponent of God befriends only confusion, sadness and death. God must win.

Response

I thank you God for showing me _____

_____.

STRATEGY

Follow Jesus today, who was often opposed as seen in **Matthew 16:21-28** (Read now)

As I follow Jesus today I will remember _____

OBEDIENCE (I will statement)

The Spirit is convicting or leading me today to do or stop doing: _____

_____.

PETITIONS (Following your reciting of The Lord's Prayer)

I pray for these scheduled meetings today:

I pray also for these pressing needs of myself, my family, my church, my disciples my world:

CONFESSION and REPENTANCE

I confess these, my sins, with every intention to never repeat them, but rather to live as Jesus would live, by Your enabling grace and Spirit …

*Never confess without a faith that looks to the cross of Christ, where the guilt and penalty of all our sins was paid!

WALK (Think about the following hymn)

Judge Eternal, Throned in Splendor

1) Judge Eternal, throned in splendor,
Lord of lords and King of kings,
with your living fire of judgment
purge this land of bitter things;
solace all its wide dominion
with the healing of your wings.

2) Still the weary folk are pining
for the hour that brings release,
and the city's crowded clangor
cries aloud for sin to cease,
and the homesteads and the woodlands
plead in silence for their peace.

3) Crown, O God, your own endeavor;
cleave our darkness with your sword;
feed the faithless and the hungry
with the richness of your word;
cleanse the body of this nation
through the glory of the Lord.
(Henry S Holland, 1847-1918)

Response

Help me, Jesus, to _____

_____.

VICTORY

Memorize *Romans 1:18*

Be prepared for opposition (spiritual warfare) and expect victory in Jesus' name.

Write down the name (s) of those with whom you shared today _____
_____.

_____ Check when the day is completed, never beating yourself up if you did not finish; but, just asking Jesus to help you next day!

Day Ninety-five

God – The Provider

ADORATION

When the Lord commanded Abraham to sacrifice Isaac, Abraham's faith convinced him that "God himself will provide the lamb for the burnt offering" (Gen 22:8). Abraham trusted God's promise of a nation and Savior through Isaac, so he walked forward by faith even without taking a lamb with them. After the Lord spared Isaac, and provided a ram for the sacrifice, "Abraham called the name of that place "The Lord will Provide" (Gen 22:14). We may trust God to provide all He has promised to provide for those who follow Him.

It is good for the believer to wait on the Lord for those provisions that we so desperately need and cannot rightly supply for ourselves. Paul said to the Philippians, "And my God will meet all your needs according to his glorious riches in Christ Jesus" (Phil 4:19). He may not provide all your desires or fulfill all your dreams; but He will meet your needs. "He who did not spare his own Son, but gave him up for us all—how will he not also, along with him, graciously give us all things?" (Rom 8:33).

Every good thing our good God will provide for the trusting disciple. Sometimes He provides "a vine" to sustain us, and then provides "a worm" and "a scorching east wind" (Jonah 4:6-8) to test us. Whenever we face a day of great temptation or testing, He promises, "… when you are tempted, he will provide a way out so that you can stand up under it" (1 Cor 10:13). Often the way out is not obvious or appear supernatural and can be discerned and appreciated only as we pray. So, "let us … approach the throne of grace with confidence, so that we may receive mercy and find grace to help us in our time of need" (Heb 4:16). He will always be gracious to the sincerely seeking soul.

We must remember that the Lord provides our needs so that we might praise Him, and thus show others where the fount of every blessing really is located. "I provide water in the desert and streams in the wasteland, to give drink to my people, my chosen, the people I formed for myself that they may proclaim my praise" (Isa 43:20-21). Every praise is a pointer for others. And we should always point to Christ, the great Provider.

Jesus "provided redemption for his people; he ordained his covenant forever—holy and awesome is his name" (Ps 111:9). Just as He claimed for His own Isaiah's great prophecy, "The Spirit of the Sovereign Lord is on me because the Lord has anointed me … to provide for those who grieve in Zion - to bestow on them a crown of beauty instead of ashes, the oil of gladness instead of mourning, and a garment of praise instead of a spirit of despair ….." (Isa 61:1-3; Luke 4:17-18). Since Christ provides, let us not fret about little things, but seek first His kingdom and righteousness, knowing "all these things will be given you as well" (Matt 6:33).

Response

I thank you God for showing me _____

_____.

STRATEGY

Follow Jesus today, who provided for those around him as seen in **John 19:25-27** (Read now)

As I follow Jesus today I will remember _____

_____.

OBEDIENCE (I will statement)

The Spirit is convicting or leading me today to do or stop doing: _____

_____.

PETITIONS (Following your reciting of The Lord's Prayer)

I pray for these scheduled meetings today:

I pray also for these pressing needs of myself, my family, my church, my disciples my world:

CONFESSION and REPENTANCE

I confess these, my sins, with every intention to never repeat them, but rather to live as Jesus would live, by Your enabling grace and Spirit ...

*Never confess without a faith that looks to the cross of Christ, where the guilt and penalty of all our sins was paid!

WALK (Think about the following hymn)

Though Troubles Assail Us

1) Though troubles assail us and dangers affright,
Though friends should all fail us and foes all unite,
Yet one thing secures us, whatever betide,
The promise assures us, "The Lord will provide."

2) The birds, without garner or storehouse, are fed;
From them let us learn to trust God for our bread.
His saints what is fitting shall ne'er be denied
So long as 'tis written, "The Lord will provide."

3) When Satan assails us to stop up our path,
And courage all fails us, we triumph by faith.
He cannot take from us, though oft he has tried,
This heart cheering promise, "The Lord will provide."

4) He tells us we're weak, our hope is in vain,
The good that we seek we never shall obtain,
But when such suggestions, our graces have tried,
This answers all questions, "The Lord will provide."

5) No strength of our own and no goodness we claim;
Yet, since we have known of the Savior's great Name,
In this our strong tower for safety we hide:
The Lord is our power, "The Lord will provide."

6) When life sinks apace, and death is in view,
The word of His grace shall comfort us through,
Not fearing or doubting, with Christ on our side,
We hope to die shouting, "The Lord will provide."
(John Newton, 1725-1807)

Response

Help me, Jesus, to _____

_____.

VICTORY

Memorize *1 Timothy 6:17-18*

Be prepared for opposition (spiritual warfare) and expect victory in Jesus' name.

Write down the name (s) of those with whom you shared today _____

_____.

____ Check when the day is completed, never beating yourself up if you did not finish; but, just asking Jesus to help you next day!

Day Ninety-six

God – The Overcomer

ADORATION

Worship is given to God, alone, because He is infinite in His entire being. He is perfect love, endless existence, boundless power. Ultimately, God cannot lose. None is His match or rival. But that does not mean that many have not tried to defeat God—and still do!

David captured the way that the world hates His sovereign power and control: "The kings of the earth take their stand and the rulers gather together against the Lord and against his Anointed One (Christ). Let us break their chains, they say, and throw off their fetters" (Ps 2:2-3). But, not only the earth's rulers join with the devil in opposing the rule of God. It is all "who suppress the truth by their wickedness ... and exchange the truth of God for a lie, and worship and serve created things rather than the Creator" (Rom 1:18,25). Think of it—a man opposing God with a determined and obstinate hatred. This is what comes to mind when we exalt God as the Overcomer.

It is one thing for God to send a Flood, destroying all human life except Noah's family. It is similar when Christ will return on "the Day of the Lord" to avenge all wrong and punish all evildoers. At such times He amply makes His power known and reveals the sheer stupidity of creatures opposing their Creator. But the very word "overcome" implies persistent and planned opposition. Often God allows humans to foolishly plot and plan against Him. He might even allow their plans to appear to succeed. But, ultimately, He overcomes their rebellion and subdues them.

The Psalm writers often meditated on this truth in their inspired songs, "Do not fret because of evil men or be envious of those who do wrong; for like the grass they will wither, like green plants they will soon die away ... Refrain from anger ... do not fret – it leads only to evil. For evil men will be cut off, but those who hope in the Lord will inherit the land. A little while, and the wicked will be no more; though you look for them, they will not be found ... The wicked plot against the righteous ... but the Lord laughs at the wicked, for he knows their day is coming" (Ps 37:1-2, 8-13). Those who oppose God will be overcome.

"They will make war with the Lamb, but the Lamb will overcome them because he is Lord of lords and King of kings—and with him will be his called, chosen and faithful followers" (Rev 17:14). Jesus promises, "To him who overcomes I will give the right to sit with me on my throne, just as I overcame and sat down with my Father on his throne" (Rev 3:21). He overcame for us as the Second Adam. The Son of Man. He did what our original father, Adam, (and we) failed to do. He resisted evil and defeated it!

And, having won the victory, He ascended and poured out His Spirit into us, so we can overcome by His power. "You, dear children, are from God and have overcome them, because the one who is in you is greater than the one who is in the world" (1 John 4:4). It is by His Spirit, alone, that we prevail.

Have pity on those still blinded in their sin. Pursue them, knowing your sure destiny and coming victory. He said, "I have told you these things so that in me you may have peace. In this world you will have trouble. But take heart! I have overcome the world" (John 16:13)

Response

I thank you God for showing me _____

_____.

STRATEGY

Follow Jesus today, who, by His resurrection, overcame all His enemies as seen in **Luke 24:1-8** (Read now)

As I follow Jesus today I will remember _____

_____.

OBEDIENCE (I will statement)

The Spirit is convicting or leading me today to do or stop doing: _____

_____.

PETITIONS (Following your reciting of <u>The Lord's Prayer</u>)

I pray for these scheduled meetings today:

I pray also for these pressing needs of myself, my family, my church, my disciples my world:

CONFESSION and REPENTANCE

I confess these, my sins, with every intention to never repeat them, but rather to live as Jesus would live, by Your enabling grace and Spirit …

*Never confess without a faith that looks to the cross of Christ, where the guilt and penalty of all our sins was paid!

WALK (Think about the following hymn)

They That Overcome

1) Overcoming evil day by day,
This our warfare on the Christian way;
Yet unto those that faithful endure,
God has declared that His promise is sure.

They that overcome, thus saith He,
They that overcome, blessed shall be;
They that overcome the world and sin,
Life and a crown in His kingdom shall win.

Tho' we suffer tribulation here,
Tho' our crosses oft may seem severe,
Think of the joy when trials are past,
Strong in the Lord we shall conquer at last.

Overcoming, O my soul, arise,
Overcoming, thou must reach the skies;
Still journey on, and still overcome,
Rest by and by with the Savior at home.
(Fanny J Crosby, 1820-1915)

Response

Help me, Jesus, to _____

_____.

VICTORY

Memorize *Mark 9:24*

Be prepared for opposition (spiritual warfare) and expect victory in Jesus' name.

Write down the name (s) of those with whom you shared today _____
_____.

____ Check when the day is completed, never beating yourself up if you did not finish; but, just asking Jesus to help you next day!

Day Ninety-seven

God – The Preserver

ADORATION

A life preserver keeps one floating when there is too little strength to swim and drowning threatens us. God is often called both the Creator and the Preserver of life within us. We sink without Him! Death occurs when God stops preserving our life and summons our spirits to leave our bodies and return to Him. God uses an infinite variety of means in supporting all life on earth. "O Lord you preserve both man and beast. How priceless is your unfailing love! Both high and low among men find refuge in the shadow of your wings" (Ps 36:6b-7). What men call "instinct" in the animal kingdom is nothing other than the preserving power of the omnipresent Spirit of God over all His creation!

Those who are healthy and strong often doubt their need of God's help. They wrongly and proudly think that their own strength has caused them to endure. But God says, "All men are like grass, and all their glory is like the flowers of the field. The grass withers and the flowers fall because the breath of the Lord blows on them. Surely the people are grass" (Isa 40:6-7). "Love the Lord all his saints! The Lord preserves the faithful, but the proud he pays back in full" (Ps 31:23).

At every moment our prayer should be, "Keep me safe, O God, for in you I take refuge" (Ps 16:1). "Praise our God, O peoples...he has preserved our lives and kept our feet from slipping" (Ps 66:8-9). And at every moment our minds should be, with the psalmist, focused on the truth of His Word, declaring, "I will never forget your precepts, for by them you have preserved my life" (Ps 119:93).

Even when others do things to harm you, God's plan prevails. So, Joseph told his brothers, "And now, do not be distressed for selling me here, because...God sent me ahead of you to preserve for you a remnant on earth and to save your lives by a great deliverance" (Gen 45:5-7). The very thing we think would save us, often fails us. And that which we disregard and despise, God uses to save us by. He uses weakness to strengthen us. (2 Cor 12:7-20). Meekness to advance us (Matt 5:5). Death to lead to life (John 12:23-32).

God's preserving work is hardly appreciated if we don't regard the dangerous foes set against us, desiring our destruction. Satan is like "a roaring lion looking for someone to devour" (1 Pet 5:8). Sin "is crouching at your door; it desires to have you" (Gen. 4). But sin and Satan are neutralized by the power of Christ, as John said, "We know that anyone born of God does not continue to (live in) sin; the One who was born of God keeps him safe, and the evil one cannot harm him" (1 John 5:18). Jude ends his letter adoring our preserving God with these words: "To him who is able to keep you from falling and to present you before his glorious presence without fault and with great joy—to the only God our Savior be glory...." (Jude 24,25a). Our hope is forever in His help. "The one who calls you is faithful and He will do it" (1 Thess 5:24). Amen!

Response

I thank you God for showing me _____

STRATEGY

Follow Jesus today, who preserves His followers as seen in **John 17:13-19** (Read now)

As I follow Jesus today I will remember _____

_____.

OBEDIENCE (I will statement)

The Spirit is convicting or leading me today to do or stop doing: _____

_____.

PETITIONS (Following your reciting of The Lord's Prayer)

I pray for these scheduled meetings today:

I pray also for these pressing needs of myself, my family, my church, my disciples my world:

CONFESSION and REPENTANCE

I confess these, my sins, with every intention to never repeat them, but rather to live as Jesus would live, by Your enabling grace and Spirit ...

*Never confess without a faith that looks to the cross of Christ, where the guilt and penalty of all our sins was paid!

WALK (Think about the following hymn)

Hiding in Thee

O safe to the Rock that is higher than I,
My soul in its conflicts and sorrows would fly;
So sinful, so weary, Thine, Thine, would I be;
Thou blest "Rock of Ages," I'm hiding in Thee.

*Hiding in Thee, hiding in Thee,
Thou blest "Rock of Ages,"
I'm hiding in Thee.*

In the calm of the noontide, in sorrow's lone hour,
In times when temptation casts o'er me its power;
In the tempests of life, on its wide, heaving sea,
Thou blest "Rock of Ages," I'm hiding in Thee.

How oft in the conflict, when pressed by the foe,
I have fled to my refuge and breathed out my woe;
How often, when trials like sea billows roll,
Have I hidden in Thee, O Thou Rock of my soul.
(William O Cushing, 1823-1902)

Response

Help me, Jesus, to _____

_____.

VICTORY

Memorize *Psalm 119:50*

Be prepared for opposition (spiritual warfare) and expect victory in Jesus' name.

Write down the name (s) of those with whom you shared today _____
_____.

____ Check when the day is completed, never beating yourself up if you did not finish; but, just asking Jesus to help you next day!

Day Ninety-eight

God – The Coming One

ADORATION

It is human nature to want to make some preparations when we know a visitor is coming. We do not want them to come and find the house a mess or us dressed in our pajamas. Throughout Scripture this one great promise is repeated over and over—Get ready, God is coming!

Early prophecies predicted this. "I see him but not now; I behold him but not near. A star will come out of Jacob; a scepter will rise out of Israel" (Num 24:17a; Gen 49:10). But most of the statements spoke of that day of visitation being filled with fury and judgment. "Our God comes and will not be silent; a fire devours before him, and around him a tempest rages" (Ps 5:3). "See the Lord is coming with fire...he will bring down his anger and fury... for with fire and sword the Lord will execute judgment upon all men, and many will be those slain by the Lord" (Isa 66:15-16).

When He descended upon Mt Sinai, it was with thunder and lightning, thick clouds and trumpet blasts, billowing smoke and breaking rocks (Ex 19:16-19). It wasn't the type of coming people wanted from their God. "But who can endure the day of his coming? Who can stand when he appears?" (Mic 3:2). Israel knew God's coming as a day of awesome reckoning for sinners. Mankind was on a collision course with God and that's a crash no creature can survive.

The prophets, though, spoke of another coming. When Messiah would come in meekness and majesty to save (Zech 9:9). As a Shepherd gathering the lambs into His arms (Isa 40:11). As a Light for the blind (Isa 61:1) and the Healer of broken hearts (Isa 61:1-2). This is the Christ of Christmas. The great and good Jesus of Nazareth who "did not come to be served but to serve, and to give his life a ransom for many" (Mk 10:45). The Jesus who came "to seek and to save what was lost" (Luke 19:10). His first coming was not to condemn but to save all those who believed on Him (John 3:16-17). To help us miss the coming collision with God.

Jesus and His followers warned us to watch and be ready for His coming. "I am coming soon. Hold on to what you have, so that no one will take your crown" (Rev 3:11). "Behold, I am coming soon! My reward is with me, and I will give to everyone according to what he has done" (Rev 22:12, 7). "Be patient, then, brothers until the Lord's coming. See how the farmer waits for the land to yield its valuable crop. You, too, be patient and stand firm, because the Lord's coming is near. Don't grumble against each other, brothers, or you will be judged. The Judge is standing at the door" (James 5:7-9) "Since everything will be destroyed in this way, what kind of people ought you to be? You ought to live holy and godly lives as you look forward to the day of God and speed its coming" (2 Pet 3:11,12).

      Nothing could be worse than to be unprepared for Christ's return. Only faith in Him, in His work accomplished for our salvation, can prepare us. We can be saved, accepted, cleansed from sin only by a faith that trusts in Christ. A faith that says, "Amen. Come, Lord Jesus" (Rev 22:20). So, let's live in such a way that it is obvious that God is our future.

Response

I thank you God for showing me _____

_____.

STRATEGY

Follow Jesus today, who spoke of His Second Coming as seen in **Acts 1:1-11** (Read now)

As I follow Jesus today I will remember _____

_____.

OBEDIENCE (I will statement)

The Spirit is convicting or leading me today to do or stop doing: _____

_____.

PETITIONS (Following your reciting of The Lord's Prayer)

I pray for these scheduled meetings today:

I pray also for these pressing needs of myself, my family, my church, my disciples my world:

CONFESSION and REPENTANCE

I confess these, my sins, with every intention to never repeat them, but rather to live as Jesus would live, by Your enabling grace and Spirit …

*Never confess without a faith that looks to the cross of Christ, where the guilt and penalty of all our sins was paid!

WALK (Think about the following hymn)

One Day

1) One day when Heaven was filled with His praises,
One day when sin was as black as could be,
Jesus came forth to be born of a virgin,
Dwelt among men, my Example is He!

*Living, He loved me; dying, He saved me;
Buried, He carried my sins far away;
Rising, He justified freely forever;
One day He's coming—O glorious day!*

2) One day they led Him up Calvary's mountain,
One day they nailed Him to die on the tree;
Suffering anguish, despised and rejected:
Bearing our sins, my Redeemer is He!

3) One day they left Him alone in the garden,
One day He rested, from suffering free;
Angels came down o'er His tomb to keep vigil;
Hope of the hopeless, my Savior is He!

4) One day the grave could conceal Him no longer,
One day the stone rolled away from the door;
Then He arose, over death He had conquered;
Now is ascended, my Lord evermore!

5) One day the trumpet will sound for His coming,
One day the skies with His glories will shine;
Wonderful day, my beloved ones bringing;
Glorious Savior, this Jesus is mine!
(J Wilbur Chapman, 1859-1918)

Response

Help me, Jesus, to _____

_____.

VICTORY

Memorize *1 Peter 4:7-8*

Be prepared for opposition (spiritual warfare) and expect victory in Jesus' name.

Write down the name (s) of those with whom you shared today _____

_____.

_____ Check when the day is completed, never beating yourself up if you did not finish; but, just asking Jesus to help you next day!

Day Ninety-nine

The Wrath of God

ADORATION

The Bible is the Word of God. Its main mission, therefore, is to reveal Him to us, His creatures. We are often amazed at what is said of Him. Sometimes confounded, even shocked. That matters very little, for we must accept God as He is! It makes little sense to try to remake Him in a way that suits our tastes. Besides, sin has affected our tastes. He is all that ultimately matters simply because He is God. And He is good.

Around 175 times, the Bible reveals God as having perfect wrath. This is shown throughout both Testaments and, though overlooked today, was a respected part of how all NT and OT believers perceived God. God's wrath is different from ours. His wrath is his perfect, unchanging opposition to all wrong and His determination to punish it fairly when best suits His purpose. His wrath has nothing to do with his losing emotional control of Himself and blowing up like a super-volcano. But because He is all-powerful, when He chooses to show His wrath—It is an awesome and frightening thing. "Who knows the power of your anger? For your wrath is as great as the fear that is due you" (Ps 90:11). "The Lord is at your right hand; he will crush kings on the day of his wrath" (Ps 110:5).

Read Numbers 16 and see the wrath of God displayed. Note what it was that ended the display of His wrath. "Then Moses said to Aaron, take your censer...and hurry to the assembly to make atonement for them. Wrath has come out from the Lord; the plague has started" (Num 16:46). Great sin caused His wrath to be shown. And it continued until His wrath was perfectly satisfied. What appeases God's infinite, eternal and unchangeable wrath? A satisfactory atonement or offering.

During OT times, God's wrath against Israel's sin was pacified by the offering of animal sacrifices, which all pointed forward to the time when God would come and offer Himself as the human sacrifice for us. Jesus was called "the Lamb of God who takes away the sin of the world" (John 1:29). Because God is holy, all sin (unholiness) must be punished. No one can be accepted by a holy God without having his unholiness purged. This is why Jesus came. "He is the propitiation (atoning sacrifice) for our sins" (1 John 2:2). His offering of Himself on the cross satisfied God's perfect justice and appeased His righteous wrath. So, to reject Jesus is to reject the only way to avert experiencing God's wrath! "Whoever rejects the Son will not see life, for God's wrath remains on him" (John 3:36b). Faith in Christ saves us from God's coming wrath. " Since we have now been justified by his blood, how much more shall we be saved from God's wrath through him!" (Rom 5:9).

The predicted Day of the Lord, the day of vengeance and wrath are coming. Then many will call "to the mountains and to the rocks, fall on us and hide us from the face of him who sits on the throne and from the wrath of the Lamb! For the great day of their wrath has come, and who can stand?" (Rev 6:16-17). You must take refuge in "Jesus, who rescues us from the coming wrath" (1 Thess 1:10b). You can be safe only in Him." (Ps 44:4-7). Do we really believe?"

Response

I thank you God for showing me _____

_____.

STRATEGY

Follow Jesus today, who spoke as a witness against false teachers and others who opposed and denied Him as seen in **John 5:24-47** (Read now)

As I follow Jesus today I will remember _____

_____.

OBEDIENCE (I will statement)

The Spirit is convicting or leading me today to do or stop doing: _____

_____.

PETITIONS (Following your reciting of The Lord's Prayer)

I pray for these scheduled meetings today:

I pray also for these pressing needs of myself, my family, my church, my disciples my world:

CONFESSION and REPENTANCE

I confess these, my sins, with every intention to never repeat them, but rather to live as Jesus would live, by Your enabling grace and Spirit …
*Never confess without a faith that looks to the cross of Christ, where the guilt and penalty of all our sins was paid!

WALK (Think about the following hymn)

O Conquering Now and Still to Conquer

1) Conquering now and still to conquer, rideth a King in His might;
Leading the host of all the faithful into the midst of the fight;
See them with courage advancing, clad in their brilliant array,
Shouting the Name of their Leader, hear them exultingly say:

Not to the strong is the battle,
Not to the swift is the race,
Yet to the true and the faithful
Vict'ry is promised through grace.

2) Conquering now and still to conquer, who is this wonderful King?
Whence are the armies which He leadeth, while of His glory they sing?
He is our Lord and Redeemer, Savior and Monarch divine;
They are the stars that forever bright in His kingdom shall shine.

3) Conquering now and still to conquer, Jesus, Thou Ruler of all,
Thrones and their scepters all shall perish, crowns and their splendor shall fall,
Yet shall the armies Thou leadest, faithful and true to the last,
Find in Thy mansions eternal rest, when their warfare is past.
(Fanny J Crosby, 1820-1915)

Response

Help me, Jesus, to _____

_____.

VICTORY

Memorize *Hebrews 12:29*

Be prepared for opposition (spiritual warfare) and expect victory in Jesus' name.

Write down the name (s) of those with whom you shared today _____
_____.

____ Check when the day is completed, never beating yourself up if you did not finish; but, just asking Jesus to help you next day!

Day One Hundred

God – The Triumphant One

ADORATION

Was Jesus' triumphal entry a hoax or a true parade of victory for the King of kings? Though He was praised as the conquering Messiah, He soon left the city only to return to it and die at the very hands of some who earlier had bowed in praise of Him. So who won? Let's remember that God is infinite. He can wait until the best time. His gracious patience in the face of opposition does not dim the certainty of His triumph. Jesus knew He would reign; but, first He had to destroy death by dying.

The way up is down. Jesus showed that, in this life, humility and death lead to glory and life. We do not really win by crushing others. We follow the One of whom it was written, "A bruised reed he will not break...till he leads justice to victory" (Matt 12:20). It is as both the slain Lamb (Rev 5:6) and as "the Lion of the tribe of Judah" that He triumphs" (Rev 5:5a). Lamb and Lion. In crushing the head of the Serpent, His heel had to be bruised (Gen 3:15b). Why did He have to suffer to win?

He tasted death and defeat for us, so that we would never have to. Through Him we can truly be victorious. "Thanks be to God who gives us the victory through our Lord Jesus Christ" (1 Cor 15:57). Victory is His, always, only His, for He is all powerful, undefeatable. It is His gift to bestow on whomever He chooses. And He wants to give it to His children. "He holds victory in store for the upright" (Prov 2:7a). "The God of peace will soon crush Satan under your feet" (Rom 16:20). It is ours to live by such a faith in Christ that even so great a foe as Satan cannot harm us (1 Jn 5:18b). To be so fully in union with God's Son, that Satan is routed by our prayers in Christ's name (Eph 6:18; 1 Pet 5:8-9).

How many victories have you won in your Christian life? Can you testify, "You are my King and my God, who decrees victories for Jacob. Through you we push back our enemies...my sword does not bring me victory; but you give us victory that we can "be strong in the Lord and in his mighty power" (Eph 6:10)? God's power working through me? Yes, but remember the Lord's formula is "Not by might, nor by power, but by my Spirit, says the Lord Almighty" (Zech 4:6b). "The horse is made ready for the day of battle, but victory rests with the Lord" (Prov 21:31). May our faith be true enough to lead us to say with suffering Paul, "God...always leads us in triumphal procession in Christ" (2 Cor 2:14). Following our Savior, we will suffer; but we are reminded every Spring, "Unless a kernel...falls into the ground and dies it remains only a single seed. But if it dies it produces many seeds. The man who loves his life will lose it, while the man who hates his life in this world will keep it for eternal life" (John 12:24-25). Triumph and tragedy are not always enemies. For the Christian, weakness and winning often go hand-in-hand, for God said, "my power is made perfect in weakness." So, we echo, "Therefore, I will boast all the more gladly about my weaknesses... for when I am weak, then I am strong" (2 Cor 12:9b-10).

Response

I thank you God for showing me _____

_____.

STRATEGY

Follow Jesus today, who has triumphed as seen in **Rev 5:1-14** (Read now)

As I follow Jesus today I will remember _____

OBEDIENCE (I will statement)

The Spirit is convicting or leading me today to do or stop doing: _____

_____.

PETITIONS (Following your reciting of The Lord's Prayer)

I pray for these scheduled meetings today:

I pray also for these pressing needs of myself, my family, my church, my disciples my world:

CONFESSION and REPENTANCE

I confess these, my sins, with every intention to never repeat them, but rather to live as Jesus would live, by Your enabling grace and Spirit …
*Never confess without a faith that looks to the cross of Christ, where the guilt and penalty of all our sins was paid!

WALK (Think about the following hymn)

See, the Conqueror Mounts in Triumph

1) See, the Conqueror mounts in triumph; see the King in royal state,
Riding on the clouds, His chariot, to His heavenly palace gate.
Hark! the choirs of angel voices joyful alleluias sing,
And the portals high are lifted to receive their heavenly King.

2) Who is this that comes in glory, with the trump of jubilee?
Lord of battles, God of armies, He has gained the victory.
He Who on the cross did suffer, He Who from the grave arose,
He has vanquished sin and Satan, He by death has spoiled His foes.

3) While He lifts His hands in blessing, He is parted from His friends
While their eager eyes behold Him, He upon the clouds ascends;
He Who walked with God and pleased Him, preaching truth and doom to come,
He, our Enoch, is translated to His everlasting home.

4) Now our heavenly Aaron enters, with His blood, within the veil;
Joshua now is come to Canaan, and the kings before Him quail;
Now He plants the tribes of Israel in their promised resting place;
Now our great Elijah offers double portion of His grace.

5) He has raised our human nature in the clouds to God's right hand;
There we sit in heavenly places, there with Him in glory stand:
Jesus reigns, adored by angels; man with God is on the throne;
Mighty Lord, in Thine ascension we by faith behold our own.

(6) Holy Ghost, illuminator, shed Thy beams upon our eyes,
Help us to look up with Stephen, and to see beyond the skies,
Where the Son of Man in glory standing is at God's right hand,
Beckoning on His martyr army, succoring His faithful band.

7) See Him, who is gone before us, heavenly mansions to prepare,
See Him, who is ever pleading for us with prevailing prayer,
See Him, who with sound of trumpet, and with His angelic train,
Summoning the world to judgment, on the clouds will come again.

8) Raise us up from earth to Heaven, give us wings of faith and love,
Gales of holy aspirations wafting us to realms above;
That, with hearts and minds uplifted, we with Christ our Lord may dwell,
Where He sits enthroned in glory in His heavenly citadel.

9) So, at last, when He appeareth, we from out our graves may spring,
With our youth renewed like eagles, flocking round our heavenly King.
Caught up on the clouds of Heaven, and may meet Him in the air,
Rise to realms where He is reigning, and may reign for ever there.

10) Glory be to God the Father, glory be to God the Son,
Dying, risen, ascending for us, who the heavenly realm has won;
Glory to the Holy Spirit, to one God in persons Three;
Glory both in earth and Heaven, glory, endless glory, be.
(Christopher Wordsworth, 1807-1885)

Response

Help me, Jesus, to _____

_____.

VICTORY

Memorize *2 Corinthians 2:14*

Be prepared for opposition (spiritual warfare) and expect victory in Jesus' name.

Write down the name (s) of those with whom you shared today _____

_____.

____ Check when the day is completed, never beating yourself up if you did not finish; but, just asking Jesus to help you next day!

The Daily Bible Memory Verses

Day 1	Acts 4:12	Day 40	Psalm 19:11
2	1 Peter 1:15	41	1 Peter 4:19
3	John 8:12	42	Psalm 18:2
4	Hebrews 4:15	Day 43	Psalm 22:11
5	Hebrews 4:16	44	Matthew 6:33
6	Acts 1:8	45	John 14:23
7	2 Corinthians 5:10	46	James 1:5
8	2 Thessalonians 1:6-7	47	John 1:14
9	Matthew 3:11	48	Colossians 3:4
Day 10	2 Corinthians 5:17	49	1 Thessalonians 5:16
11	John 6:35	Day 50	Romans 6:18
12	John 4:24	51	1 Corinthians 10:31
13	Philippians 3:7-8	52	2 Corinthians 13:14
14	Hebrews 10:23	53	Malachi 3:6
15	Acts 16:31	54	1 Timothy 1:17
16	2 Corinthians 13:8	55	Daniel 4:25b
17	Lamentations 3:22-23	56	John 3:16
18	Matthew 10:39	57	Zechariah 1:14
19	John 17:3	58	1 John 1:9
Day 20	Ephesians 2:10	59	Romans 3:10
21	Hebrews 13:5	Day 60	John 4:24
22	Psalm 50:15	61	1 John 3:1
23	Proverbs 3:5-6	62	John 6:44-45
24	1 Corinthians 11:1	63	John 14:6
25	Revelation 22:17	64	1 John 2:27
26	Luke 9:57-58	65	2 Corinthians 9:7
27	Revelation 5:13	66	James 1:2-3
28	John 10:11	67	Psalm 139:21
29	John 15:14	68	Romans 8:28
Day 30	Galatians 2:20	69	Matthew 20:28
31	Psalm 2:1-3	Day 70	John 3:17
32	Luke 11:13	71	1 Corinthians 6:19-20
33	1 John 3:23	72	1 Peter 1:6-7
34	Luke 22:20	73	1 Peter 2:21
35	Proverbs 21:15	74	Acts 1:8
36	John 1:17	75	Matthew 11:28
37	Romans 3:20	76	1 Corinthians 13:4
38	Psalm 34:7	77	Colossians 1:13-14
39	John 4:34	78	Psalm 16:11

The Daily Bible Verses, continued

79	Psalm 37:4	Day 90	Romans 16:20
Day 80	1 John 5:4b	91	Psalm 28:7
81	2 Timothy 1:7	92	Psalm 51:1
82	John 15:7	93	John 20:21
83	John 17:20-21	94	Romans 1:18
84	Psalm 34:15	95	1 Timothy 6:17-18
85	Isaiah 41:10	96	Mark 9:24
86	Matthew 11:28-30	97	Psalm 119:50
87	Acts 10:38`	98	1 Peter 4:7-8
88	Philippians 4:4	99	Hebrews 12:29
89	Psalm 37:23-24	Day 100	2 Corinthians 2:14

The Book of Psalms was compiled over centuries. In its final form, it is composed of 5 sections, each of which closes with an appropriate conclusion. Here are the 5 sections (Psalms 1-41; 42-72; 73-89; 90-106; and 107-150).

The doorway to the Psalms was carefully and powerfully portrayed in Psalms 1 and 2. Their Hebrew construction reveals that they were intended to serve as both an introduction to the Psalter and a description of the person most likely to embrace the spirit of the Psalms, with Psalm 1 leading the way. May its way of life portray your way of life as a disciple of Jesus.

Psalm One

(1) Blessed is the man who walks not in the counsel of the wicked,
nor stands in the way of sinners,
nor sits in the seat of scoffers;
(2) but his delight is in the law of the Lord,
and on his law, he meditates day and night

(3) He is like a tree planted by streams of water
that yields its fruit in its season,
And its leaf does not wither.
In all that he does, he prospers.
(4) The wicked are not so,
but are like chaff that the winds drive away.

(5) Therefore, the wicked will not stand in the judgment,
nor sinners in the congregation of the righteous;
(6) for the Lord knows the way of the righteous,
but the way of the wicked will perish. (ESV)

Appendix One
Are YOU a Christian or a Disciple?

Are you a Christian or a disciple? No, it is not a trick question. The two nouns are different words. Both biblical.[38] Both good. But both coming from very different origins. The Bible amply explains these words and gives us the background we need for rightly understanding and using them today. Please try to remember this: All true disciples are Christians. But not all Christians are true disciples. My goal is to help you see why this is a big deal. And the mess that has resulted from our confusing these words.

Here's a 21st century parable. Let's say Jesus wants to make an apple pie for the Father. So, He tells you to go to the market and get Him some nice tart Granny Smith apples. When you arrive, you become mesmerized by all the beautiful fruit you see. They are ripe and cheap. You begin to reason… if He likes one fruit, He will like these other types as well. If He can use Granny Smiths, think of the fruit salad he could make from all of these. So, you go wild and begin to buy bananas, oranges, kiwi, grapes, pomegranates, mangos and pineapple. Oh yes, you also get some nice Granny Smith apples in case He still wants them when He sees all the other options. And then you return.

What would you think Jesus will say? Well done? Good job? I should have thought of that? This is what I think. Jesus would look at you and say, how can I make an apple pie from these other fruits? My Father loves apple pies and I live to please Him. Yes, I know that an apple is a fruit. But not all fruits are apples. Yes, all fruits are good. But I asked you to go and buy apples—one specific kind of fruit—because only apples will produce the pie that My Father desires. You can do whatever you want with the other fruit. They are of no value to My plan. Give me those Granny Smith apples.

Jesus has given the Church a Great Commission. He has clearly told us what we are to do: "Go and make disciples." But, instead we focus on making Christians. What's the big deal, you might ask? Simply this—like the difference between apples and fruit--*all true disciples are Christians*. But *not all Christians are disciples*. He has a very specific goal in mind. The goal that the Father gave Him to accomplish. The goal to make disciples. We have a much more general goal. To make Christians. Jesus has commanded us to follow Him and make apple pies. We have gone out and chosen rather to make fruit salad.[39]

---

[38] Christianos or Christian(s) is used 3 times in the NT. Matheteis or disciple(s) is used over 250 times.
[39] If you need more time to think and work through the difference between being a church-going Christian and a Christ-following disciple, get my *Are You a Christian or a Disciple?*

Appendix Two

A Faith that does not Save[40]

Evangelicals emphasize faith. We often seize on those many texts that link faith with true salvation. One reason for doing this is to help others see that trusting in their good works to save them will not work. They must believe in Christ. But, here again, many Evangelicals do not realize that not all faith in Christ leads to salvation. The Bible teaches that there are different types of faith. And Jesus clearly spoke of some with faith or belief who were not going to enter His kingdom. Since we affirm that salvation is by faith, it is hard for some Evangelicals to conceive of someone with faith in Christ as not being saved. Listen to Jesus explain some of His Parable of the Sower,

"Those on the rocky ground are the ones who receive the word with joy when they hear it, but they have no root. They **believe for a while**, but in the time of testing they fall away. The seed that fell among thorns stands for those who hear, but as they go on their way they are choked by life's worries, riches and pleasures, and they do not mature. But the seed on good soil stands for those with a noble and good heart, who hear the word, retain it, and by persevering produce a crop." (Luke 8:13-15).

Now, you need to draw a conclusion. Do you think those who receive the seed (the Word) on rocky and thorny soil are saved? Few interpret the text that way. Those on rocky soil "believe for a while." So, there is a faith or a capacity to believe that is temporary in nature rather than permanent. That type of faith, if remaining at that stage, does not lead to salvation.

Jesus also distinguished some of those who "believed" from those who were His disciples. John wrote, "Even as he spoke, many put their faith in him. To the Jews who had believed him, Jesus said, 'If you hold to my teaching, you are really my disciples. And you will know the truth, and the truth will set you free." (John 8:31-32).

As their discussion goes on, Jesus says to the same people, "Why is my language not clear to you? Because you are unable to hear what I say. You belong to your father, the devil; and you want to carry out your father's desire." (John 8:43-44)

James rebukes those with a fruitless "faith" saying, "You believe that there is one God? The demons believe that--and shudder" (James 2:19). So,

---

Rediscovering and Renewing New Testament Discipleship. This 100 Days with Jesus is meant for those who are ready to be His disciples and understand the cost such a relationship will demand. Do NOT rush. This can save and transform your life, making it incredibly fruitful.

[40] Appendix two is largely excerpts from *Are You a Christian or a Disciple?* chapter 7

demons have a type of faith, we might call it "a faith in the existence of God" or an historical faith. But I know of none who teach that demons will be saved.

Demonic professions of faith

Those who insist that all expressions of faith lead to salvation have trouble when they are forced to examine the statements that come out of the mouths of the demonized. The biblical facts reveal that demons use people and:

*Call Jesus, "the Holy one of God" (Mk 1:23).
*Run and fall on their faces before Jesus (Mk 5:6).
*Call Jesus, "Son of the Most High God" (Mk 5:7).
*Believe that they will be destroyed by Jesus "at the appointed time" (Matt 8:29).
*Warn sinners with words like, "These men are servants of the Most High God, who are telling you the way to be saved." (Acts 16:17).

So, going forward in a church service or running forward and bowing down before Jesus will not necessarily lead to salvation. Calling Jesus "Lord", "God", "Messiah" or any other name will not by itself save you. Understanding biblical truth and doctrines do not guarantee salvation. And even taking part in evangelistic outreaches (like Judas Iscariot did - Mark 6 & and Matt 10), will not necessarily lead to your salvation. The sobering words of Jesus warn us all, "Not everyone who says to me, 'Lord, Lord' will enter the kingdom of heaven, but only he who does the will of my Father in heaven. Many will say to me on that day, 'Lord, Lord, did we not prophesy in your name, and in your name drive out demons and perform many miracles? Then I will tell them plainly, 'I never knew you. Away from me you evildoers!'" (Matt 7:21-23).

Jesus is not saying in this text that a person is *justified* by works. But He is saying that true faith is proven by its link with repenting of evil and turning away from it to follow Him. He is saying that salvation, in its widest sense, demands discipleship.

Is your Faith Active?

Evangelicals have to be more careful how they use the word "faith." We should not be too quick in assuring converts of their being born again at the moment of their first profession of faith. Let them prove themselves. Why? Because it is safe, wise and biblical to do so. As Paul said at the close of his last letter to the Corinthians, "Examine yourselves to see whether you are in the faith; test yourselves." (2 Cor 13:5).

We have simply got to learn that if our lives on Monday-Saturday do not back up what we sing on Sunday, those words may not be words of faith—but expressions of exaggeration or delusion. Idleman amplified this problem by writing,

> "When I was studying about the word "belief" I came across a secular article written by a psychiatrist…. When the psychiatrist was speaking about his patients with beliefs that had no basis he didn't call them "beliefs." Do you know what he called them? He called them "delusions." …A belief, no matter how sincere, if not reflected isn't a belief; it's a delusion."[41]

Richard Stearns, president of World Vision, put it this way, "It's not what you believe that counts; it's what you believe enough to do."[42] No one has ever said it better than Jesus when He marveled, *"Why do you call me, 'Lord, Lord,' and do not do what I say?" (Luke 6:46)*.

The amazing content of Hebrews 11 demands that we define and depict faith as something that always is active. By faith Noah built an ark. By faith Abraham left his homeland. By faith Rahab hid the spies. By faith Moses chose to suffer. Hebrews 11 demands that we declare this--true faith produces some action of godliness. True faith is never without some corresponding works. Faith works! And Hebrews 11 leads into precisely what saving faith looks like in all NT era believers—true discipleship! "Therefore, since we are surrounded by so great a cloud of witnesses (those mentioned in Heb 11!), let us also (like they did) lay aside every weight, and sin which clings so closely and let us run with patience the race that is set before us, looking to Jesus…." Discipleship is living while looking to Jesus! So, what is your faith producing? What are the witnesses doing while looking at your life? Are they cheering or booing?

We can with great ease throw around words like salvation, grace and faith—and still be lost. Our premise is that the true disciple is called by Jesus to forsake the world and follow Him from conversion onward. Salvation is based on a faith that lives and works through love. It is a sure, objective reality. Not a sinless reality, for it is based on the Gospel which gives us a sinless Savior by whose righteousness we are perfected. And by whose sufferings on the cross our sins are fully and completely atoned for. A faith that rightly grasps the gospel follows Christ. A grace that leads to heaven is a

---

[41] From Kyle Isleman's *Not a Fan*, 32-33
[42] From Richard Stearns' *The Hole in our Gospel*, 87

costly grace. And the salvation that Jesus came to deliver does not usually begin and end with a secret prayer.

Sixty-five years ago, the renowned leader A.W Tozer saw the problems we are addressing and said,

> "We pursue God because, and only because, He has first put an urge within us that spurs us to the pursuit.... The impulse to pursue God originates with God, but the outworking of that impulse is our following hard after Him....
>
> The whole transaction of religious conversion has been made mechanical and spiritless. Faith may now be exercised without a jar to the moral life and without embarrassment to the (natural) ego. Christ may be "received" without creating any special love for Him in the soul of the receiver. The man is "saved" but he is not hungry nor thirsty after God."[43]

The personal passion and fearless focus of faith that empowered Christ's first followers seem to be absent from many Christians today. Let us all beware of a biblical familiarity that masquerades as a true discipleship. Saying and singing the great words of salvation do not make them so in our lives. For that salvation to be rooted, we need Jesus, our Savior, to be with us and ever going before us. He is there for you who need and want Him.

---

[43] From AW Tozer's *The Pursuit of God*, 10

Appendix Three

Is Total Submission Too Radical for YOU?[44]

As we now begin to apply the five marks of a 1st century disciple of Jesus, we need to start with the one element that was understood to be the foundation of all rabbi-disciple relationships. We need to recognize that, as difficult as the other terms of discipleship are, this seems to be the most difficult for 21st century Christians living in the Western world. This aspect of discipleship is at the core of everything else. When the official relationship was established, **every disciple would totally submit to the rabbi he followed.**

If it ever came to the point where the disciple could not agree and live by the rule of the rabbi, there was one option—leave. Many questions were asked, and debate was encouraged. But the goal of a disciple was not to reform the group or change the rabbi's mind. It was to learn and apply the wisdom of the sage. The will of the rabbi was final. Today we have a Christianity without the living Christ as its authority figure. In His place we have set up a calm and benign Christ who does not demand too much. A quiet coup has occurred, and Jesus has been chased away. Rebellion against one's rabbi was unthinkable in the time of Jesus. Disciples obeyed. Today it is different. And that difference has been disastrous.

I think many of us have struggled at this very point. We talk about having "a personal relationship" with Jesus, but it falls far short of a discipleship relationship. Is that reality acceptable? Should we who call Christ the center of our lives be able to determine in what ways our faith may affect our lives? Does living 2000 years later allow us that luxury? I don't think so. We are not left with the liberty to choose what kind of relationship we are going to have with Christ. That is His right alone. He determined that the defining nature of our relationship would be framed along the lines of a rabbi-disciple relationship. And doing so, He determined that our faith in Him should control every single aspect of our lives. So, Christianity was never meant to grow from a soil other than true, biblical discipleship. Today's loose way of following Jesus simply is not working well. It is neither radically transforming the Christian nor is it being seriously noticed by the world. The salt has lost its savor! And Jesus told us what happens to useless salt. Notice that the context of this hard saying is the strongest teaching on discipleship Jesus ever gave!

---

[44] Appendix 3 is largely excerpts from *Are You a Christian or a Disciple?* chapter 11

"If anyone comes to me and does not hate father and mother, wife and children, brothers and sisters—yes, even their own life—such a person cannot be my disciple. And whoever does not carry their cross and follow me cannot be my disciple.... In the same way, those of you who do not give up everything you have cannot be my disciples. "Salt is good, but if it loses its saltiness, how can it be made salty again? It is fit neither for the soil nor for the manure pile; it is thrown out. "Whoever has ears to hear, let them hear." (Lk 14:26-35).

I hope by now you have ears to hear.

Our largely comfortable and indulgent Christianity is not different enough from the world. The world needs to see and feel the stark reality of a new way. Our neighbors need to encounter what *"a new creation in Christ"* looks and acts like. Not the warmed-over worldliness that so many Christians exhibit and are quite comfortable with. The Spirit's new creation does not flow through Christians who stay in control of their lives. Our relationship needs to reflect total submission to Jesus. By total, I do not mean perfect. But I do mean every part of us. A disciple was not partly his own and partly his rabbi's. As David Bivin writes,

"The term 'rabbi' is derived from the Hebrew word *rav*, which in biblical Hebrew ... was sometimes used to refer to high government officials or army officers (e.g., Jer.39:3,13). In Jesus' day *rav* was used to refer to the master of a slave or of a disciple. Therefore, *rabbi* literally meant 'my master' and was a term of respect used by slaves in addressing their owners and by disciples in addressing their teachers."[45]

Jesus reflected this truth when he linked the relationship of slave and master with that of disciple and rabbi. He declared, *"A disciple is not above his teacher, nor a servant above his master"* (Matt. 10:24-ESV). Most scholars I have read refer to this verse as the most basic principle of 1st century discipleship. How free was a bond slave to pursue his own will? It would be unthinkable for him to look at his master and tell him he was taking the rest of the day off. The parallels between disciple and slave were fully known and heartily accepted by all those who answered His call and entered an official disciple-rabbi relationship with Jesus. How many follow Jesus today reflecting this total submission?

The first followers of Jesus knew they were to leave their independence when they followed the Master. It was neither a hobby nor a

---

[45] David Bivin, *New Light*... 10

part-time pursuit. Mark makes it clear at the beginning of his Gospel, how Jesus called His first disciples.

"Passing alongside the Sea of Galilee, he saw Simon and Andrew the brother of Simon casting a net into the sea, for they were fishermen. And Jesus said to them, 'Follow me, and I will make you become fishers of men.' And immediately they left their nets and followed him. And going on a little farther, he saw James the son of Zebedee and John his brother, who were in their boat mending their nets. And immediately he called them, and they left their father Zebedee in the boat with the hired servants and followed him" (Mark 1:16-20).

It is truly remarkable what we do **not** see happening here. There is not a long pause between the call and the response. The men do not then discuss the plausibility of leaving their jobs. They had already done that. They had counted the cost. Jesus calls and there is but one response: immediate and total submission to the call. They have entered a relationship of obedience to Him. They became His disciples.

Submitting all 4 aspects of our being to Jesus

Humans who are well have the capabilities to think, to feel, to speak and to act. We are to submit our whole selves entirely to Jesus as Lord. So, believers often are warned concerning these four defining areas of **intellect**, **emotion**, **speech** and **action**. Our thoughts, feelings, words and deeds belong to Jesus as our Lord and Master... as Paul succinctly said, *"You are not your own"* (1 Cor 6:19b).

Appendix Four

Jesus and Obedience[46]

Obedience is an indispensable topic that many Christians today want to dispense with. The reason we must obey is that it is God who has issued the commands, not some mere human. Jesus the eternal Son of God says, "Follow me." Our options, then, are not many. They are not, "I can wait." Or, "I will watch at a safe distance." Or, "what does that really mean for me today?" When Jesus calls, His disciples follow. They obey. Not perfectly, but sincerely. And when we choose to sin, the options are not many, either. We repent, denying ourselves, taking up our crosses and following Him again. Sure, this emphasis runs the risk of being misunderstood. As appearing to be "holier than thou." Or of letting obedience become an end, where legalistic robots roam around with neither smiles nor grace. Sure, there is a chance of works displacing grace. But I agree with Bonhoeffer's assessment here: *"The word of cheap grace has been the ruin of more Christians than any commandment of works."* I fear for the Christianity that has no more "MUSTS" in it. That has exalted God's grace so highly that we, in fact, are left without anything that must be done. A Christianity without imperatives is not the Faith of the Apostles of Christ. But it is, sadly all too often, the Church today. Let that truth sink in as we take some time and look at some significant ways many Bible-believing churches turn away from obeying Christ's commands.

How good works became bad

I regretfully must admit that following my conversion the phrase "good works" was NOT spoken of positively by the Christians I knew. How could that be? Because the one thing I was taught about good works was that they could NOT save you. Good works were what liberals substituted for saving faith. Good works were leading many to hell. So, a very biblical phrase was largely discarded because some had abused it. Of course, my mentors would not have stopped teaching the importance of being good or serving others. But they would stay clear of calling these "good works." I am afraid that their throwing away of a good, biblical phrase had a long-term negative impact upon me and many others. ...Among other things, the biblical call of obedience was undermined. Gladly, today, there has been an increasing rejection by Evangelicals of this dualism. But there are millions still who view good works with suspicion.

---

[46] Appendix 4 is largely excerpts from *Are You a Christian or a Disciple?* Chapter 9

A different missionary mandate and way of praying

The pride of many Evangelicals is the Great Commission. Yet, in His Great Commission Jesus said, "teach them to obey everything I have commanded" (Matt 28:20). The prayer of many Evangelicals is, "Your kingdom come." But, the very next petition of The Lord's Prayer following that petition is, "Your will be done on earth as it is done in heaven." And how do angels in heaven do the will of God? Is it by hearing His command and altering it or by obeying it explicitly? We know the answer. The word "angels" means messengers. They are given a message to deliver or a mission to perform and they do it. When we do His will on earth like the angels do it above, we live like disciples. We obey explicitly....

Obedience or "application"

I hope that we all agree that the Word of God should be applied to every culture into which it goes with care and sensitivity. As a missiologist, I have been carefully trained to understand and appreciate this truth. The truths of Christ can and should be at home in every culture. Since this is not a book focusing on cross-cultural ministry, I want to focus on the American scene one more time. Just to show again that we are not quite as close to following Jesus as we might think.

I want to consider how many of us normally hear the Word of God when it is preached to us. Jesus said, "Therefore consider carefully how you listen. Whoever has will be given more; whoever does not have, even what he thinks he has will be taken from him" (Lk 8:18). We kind of pride ourselves in our preaching. And an important part of our preaching is our application of the texts. But let me ask an important question: What is the difference between applying a text and obeying a command in a text? We know that some texts give commands only for its original hearers. But are there no commands that are supra-cultural, applying to all disciples everywhere? I think there are many such commands of Jesus. Many today rightly go to great lengths developing precise steps for a text's proper applications. But few books encourage simple obedience. It is easier to write on how to apply a text than it is on how to obey it. We need to be careful not to remove clear, relevant commands by our applications. Jesus concluded His longest and most detailed teaching with these words: "Everyone then who hears these words of mine and does them will be like a wise man who built his house on the rock. And the rain fell, and the floods came, and the winds blew and beat on that house, but it did not fall, because it had been founded on the rock. And everyone who hears these words of mine and does not do them will be like a foolish man who built his house on the sand. And the rain fell, and the floods came, and the winds blew and beat against that house, and it fell, and great was the fall of it." (Matt 7:24-27 - NIV).

Commenting on these verses, Bonhoeffer again reminds us,

"Humanly speaking, we could understand and interpret the Sermon on the Mount in a thousand different ways. Jesus knows only one possibility: simple surrender and obedience, not interpreting it or applying it, but doing and obeying it. That is the only way to hear his word. The only proper response to this word which Jesus brings with him from eternity is simply to do it. Jesus has spoken: his is the word, ours the obedience."[47]

I understand that my scorecard on Evangelicalism has not been very flattering. But these accommodations have avalanched into a deadly culture of disobedience. I have lived in it and around it for decades. Aren't you concerned, too, by the deadly trend towards disobedience that the preceding areas reveal?

It appears to me that wherever in the New Testament literal obedience to Christ is demanded, many Christians find a loophole. It looks almost like we are allergic to obedience. We literally seem to grow sick when we must give up something to do what Jesus says....

We treat obedience like a cancer that threatens the life of the Church, when in fact it is part of our healthy immune system! It is only as we embrace obedience to Christ and keep Him central that we can diagnose the diseases that threaten the vital organs of the Church, the Body of Christ.... Bonhoeffer spoke to this point with proper passion.

"All along the line we are trying to evade the obligation of single-minded, literal obedience. How is such absurdity possible? What has happened that the word of Jesus can thus be degraded by this trifling, and thus left open to the mockery of the world? When orders are issued in other spheres of life there is no doubt whatever of their meaning. If a father sends his child to bed, the boy knows at once what he must do. But suppose he has picked up a smattering of pseudo-theology. In that case he would argue like this: "Father tells me to go to bed, but he really means that I am tired, and he does not want me to be tired. I can overcome my tiredness just as well if I go out and play. Therefore, though father tells me to go to bed, he really means: "Go out and play." If a child tried such arguments on his father or a citizen on his government, they would both meet with a kind of language they could not fail to understand—in short, they would be punished. Are we to treat the commandment of Jesus differently from other orders and exchange single-

---

[47] Bonhoeffer, *The Cost of Discipleship*, 219.

minded obedience for downright disobedience? How could that be possible?"[48]

So what hope do we have? Where does this leave us? What can we do? First, you must not despair! Whenever Jesus is involved, the solution to our problems is closer than we think. The Gospel-embracing disciple will never take his/her eyes off Jesus for long. Emphasizing obedience does not doom us to becoming proud, self-righteous and smug hypocrites—if we always lift Jesus. If we refuse to take credit for the good we might do, and clearly give Him the glory for it. If we humbly admit our many sins against Him and one another. And if we carefully by faith keep Him between us and even our every obedience, so that we do not make them our idols!

Secondly, take heart and do not be discouraged. Remember … disciples of Jesus are obeying Him with amazing simplicity all over the world. This will most surely humble us as it spurs us on to change. Our western ways have not prepared us well to follow Jesus. He is just too simple, too truthful and too poor for our liking. We can't follow Him and live lavish, comfortable, self-absorbed lives. We all need the help of God to admit the many ways we have turned a deaf ear to Christ's commands. The good news is, if we really want His help, He is willing to give it!

---

[48] Bonhoeffer, 59

Appendix Five

Following Jesus by a Memorized Mastery of His Word[49]

In looking back to the 1st century, I do not want us to get lost in analyzing another day and time. Bogged down with minute details that could create unnecessary distance between us and them. Rather, I want us to see how our following of Jesus can parallel theirs. How the Spirit today can bear similar fruit in us, our churches and our culture. Our goal is to produce, with Jesus, what He called "fruit that remains."

We cannot, though, deny some very basic differences between the 1st and 21st centuries. It is good to appreciate how different that time was from ours! How unique it was with its combination of Roman, Greek and Jewish influences.[50] Paul portrayed the epoch as being *"the fullness of time"* (Gal. 4:4). It was the perfectly prepared time in human history for the Messiah to come. The progress and perfection of disciple making was certainly one of the many ways in which history had been specially prepared by God for Jesus. The teachings of Messiah would have been treasured and shared in the highly developed system of training that was 1st century discipleship. It is estimated that hundreds of rabbis filled 1st century Palestine making disciples. As David Bivin notes,

> "The rabbis were sincerely interested in leading more and more people to 'take upon themselves the yoke of Torah,' a rabbinic expression for accepting God's reign over one's life, to live according to his will. To accomplish this, they trained advanced students as disciples, and they taught the masses. To 'make many disciples' was one of the three earliest sayings recorded in the Mishnah, and perhaps the highest calling of a rabbi. Often, he could select and train large numbers of disciples, but he was perfectly willing to teach as few as two or three students. It is recorded that the Apostle Paul's teacher Gamaliel had one thousand disciples who studied with him"[51]

---

[49] Appendix 5 is largely excerpts from *Are You a Christian or a Disciple?* chapter 12
[50] [50] See JG Machen's *Introduction to the New Testament and its Literature* chap 2 – The Roman Background of Christianity, chap 3 – The Greek background of Christianity, and chaps 4&5 – The Jewish Background of Christianity (both in Palestine and the Diaspora), pp 20-43 or Michael Green's "Evangelism in the Early Church," chap 1 - Pathways for Evangelism, 13-28.
[51] Bivin, 10.

More powerful than the internet

In our age of massive amounts of information technology at a touch, few would consider that epoch as being better suited for learning and spreading the Faith than ours. But it was. And one of the reasons is that they did **not** rely primarily on printed resources. They listened carefully and memorized the rabbi's teachings word-for-word. Picture the disciples following Jesus and sharing what they heard with one another. They hung on His every word. The Pharisees of the 1st century transmitted their teaching orally. This "Oral Torah" was not written down until after 200AD in the Mishnah. The accuracy of oral memorization by discipleship groups was surprising.

"The transmission of oral literature by rabbis and their disciples approached 100% accuracy, far greater accuracy than could have been achieved through written transmission…. It is hard for us to appreciate the trustworthiness and accuracy of oral transmission within rabbinic circles of the first century. The disciple of a sage was not permitted to alter even one word of a tradition he had received from his teacher when quoting him to others."[52]

Does it really matter that few believers today actually memorize the Word of God verbatim? I think so. Because it is hard to overstate the role that our thinking plays in our lives.

Gospel texts demanding memorization

Jesus expected His disciples to master His words. And He taught them that His words would become a most valuable and powerful force in their lives. How deeply do we value His Word? How seriously have we taken to heart the following texts which either demand or imply the mental mastery of His teaching? How many Bible College students or seminarians memorize more of God's Word than their lecturers' notes, which are soon forgotten after the exam is taken? Though many more could be given, I will limit myself to just a handful of texts showing Jesus' teaching on mastering His Word.[53]

We are the followers of Jesus. He knew and quoted the Word of God. What did it mean when He told the disciples to "abide in my word"? Abide means to remain and reside. Is the word of Christ your residence? Your address? Where your mind naturally hangs out? Are you a committed disciple or merely a church-goer?

We will likely not choose to memorize what we do not have to. Since so many Christians have entered the Faith on their own terms, they do not

---

[52] Bivin, p 34 and comments on m. Eudicot 1:3.
[53] See Matt 4:3-4; 10:27; 24:35; Mk 4:24; 8:38; Lk 2:19; John 8:31; 12:48; 15:7, 20

feel it their duty to do much of anything! It will certainly surprise many of us to see the upcoming demands made on our brothers and sisters who lived in the 1st century Church.

If we who are adults do not so love the Word of Christ that we want to master it, how can we teach our children to? We certainly should not force them. Love must lead the way. They will likely love and want to do what we love and do.

When I was dating my wife-to-be, it did not take me long to memorize her phone number and address. No one had to force me to do that. I even memorized her clothing size, so I could buy her something nice if I saw it. I remembered that she liked dark chocolate instead of milk chocolate. I still remember and cherish what she says because I love her. Let's admit it—we do not memorize God's Word because we do not love God with our whole being! If we loved Him we would love what He has said, simply because His Word flows from Him.

Put your mind to it

The apostles and early missionary church planters saw themselves as passing on the teachings of Christ. Paul said, *"Be imitators of me, as I am of Christ" (1 Cor 11:1)*. Peter wrote, *"For to this you have been called, because Christ also suffered for you, leaving you an example, so that you might follow in his steps" (1 Pet 2:21)*. The followers of Jesus made it clear in their teachings that they expected His disciples to carefully memorize His teaching and theirs, which was always focused on Christ. I hope you take this seriously and consider the following texts as calling us to a life of memorized mastery of the Words of Christ, too[54]

Those believers did not have the Bible in printed form. It was not to them a Book to refer to. Its words were memorized or mastered so that its life changing truths could master them. And change the world.

Notice how the texts from Revelation focused on the words "keep" or "kept"? To keep is to treasure. We are not keeping what we routinely forget. What good is it to have multiple books of biblical resources if we do not treasure the words of Christ in our hearts? We can regularly use our Bible concordances, studiously discovering every place that a biblical word is used throughout the Bible, without regularly remembering a single verse of what we studied!

Many of us believe that every word of the Bible is the inspired Word of God. And we defend the full inerrancy of Scripture. But what is the sense of standing for a strict doctrine of biblical inerrancy if we do not fight off the

---

[54] Acts 20:35; Phil 3:15-17; Col 3:16; 1 Tim 6:3-4; 2 Tim 1:13; 2 Pet 1:12-15; Jude 1:17; Rev 1:3; 2:26; 12:17; 22:7

apathy that allows our minds to be filled with worldly darkness instead of biblical light?

Appendix Six

Following Jesus' Teaching concerning the Old Testament Law[55]

When a sage or rabbi developed a following, he wanted a close-knit group who would all unite in believing and following the Old Testament Law similarly. They did think and live like a very disciplined team.

"The idea of a fellowship among a core of disciples came from the schools of the Pharisees. The disciples of the Pharisees organized themselves into small fellowships called *chaverim*. A *chaver* (which means 'friend') was a fellow who lived according to the same legal standards as the rest of the fellowship."[56]

While the followers of Jesus did not have the same degree of rigid ceremonial standards that the Pharisaic and Essenic groups promoted, they were highly disciplined. Their focus was not on rigid outward rules of cleansing but on the inward spiritual/moral disciplines of the heart and mind. Jesus wanted His followers, even more than other rabbis, to live like a close-knit family. Even though they came from very different and antagonistic backgrounds, Jesus' disciples were expected to be responsive, kind and forgiving. To look for opportunities to serve one another with the same zeal that most pagan leaders pursued in establishing their own position of power. To be meek and gentle towards one another rather than aggressive.

"The *chaverim* of the Twelve was, for all practical purposes, a family. Just as the disciples of Hillel were called the House of Hillel, so too the disciples of Yeshua (Jesus)were a household of which He was the head. They were brothers. They ate together, lived together, traveled together, worked together, prayed together and learned together. They were the new family of the master. They were *Beit Yeshua* (the House of Yeshua)."[57]

The unity of His followers was very important to Jesus. His followers must believe and live as one. Today, we need a transformation just to be able to seek to relate to other believers as true brothers and sisters. Our churches will not step towards missional unity if we remain comfortable with our present status of animosity and competition within the Kingdom.

Just before we look at what Jesus believed concerning the Old Testament Scriptures, it is good to understand how binding His views would have been to his official disciples.

---

[55] Appendix 6 is largely excerpts from *Are You a Christian or a Disciple* chapter 13
[56] D Thomas Lancaster, King of the Jews, 54.
[57] Lancaster,55.

"If a rabbi ultimately agreed to a would-be-disciple's request, and allowed him to become a disciple, the disciple-to-be agreed to totally submit to the rabbi's authority in all areas of interpreting the Scriptures for his life. This was a cultural given for all observant Jewish young men - something each truly wanted to do. As a result, each disciple came to a rabbinic relationship with a desire and a willingness to do just that - surrender to the authority of God's Word as interpreted by his Rabbi's view of Scripture."[58]

One obvious truth that the gospel writers wanted to convey is that Jesus did the choosing and the calling. The disciples obeyed the call of Jesus because it was to them the call of Messiah, full of power and authority.

Christ's school of discipleship in a snapshot

The most important section in the Gospels for discovering what Jesus believed about the Old Testament is the Sermon on the Mount. We could call this an introduction to Jesus' School of Discipleship. Many authors have shown how His style in this section paralleled the way other rabbis would interact to debate. Let's focus on the whole context, looking at the opening and closing statements. The text begins, *"Seeing the crowds, he went up on the mountain, and when he sat down, his disciples came to him. And he opened his mouth and taught them, saying: Blessed are...." (Matt 5:1-3)*. Jesus receives His disciples while the people are watching and listening. And then He blesses them. He pronounces on them, in these Beatitudes, the blessings which all of Israel have longed to have fulfilled upon themselves and the earth.

. At the end of the address, Matthew notes, *"And when Jesus finished these sayings, the crowds were astonished at his teaching, for he was teaching them as one who had authority, and not as their scribes" (Matt 7:28-29)*. The crowds left astonished. Jesus had spoken of many being deceived. He had demanded His followers not only call Him, "Lord, Lord" but to do what He said. The way of wisdom was evidenced only by those who grasped and followed His teachings. All other options were equated with the way of foolishness, sinking sand and destruction. Jews who had been raised on the Proverbs could not fail to understand. Jesus was demanding an all-in relationship by his disciples. Please listen to Bonhoeffer,

"We have listened to the Sermon on the Mount and perhaps have understood it. But who has heard it aright? Jesus gives the answer at the end. He does not allow his hearers to go away and make of his sayings what they will, picking and choosing from them whatever they find helpful, and testing them to see if they work. Humanly speaking, we could understand and interpret the Sermon on the Mount in a thousand different ways. Jesus knows only one

---

[58] Doug Greenwold, Preserving Bible Times -*Reflection # 307* - worldwide internet .

possibility: simple surrender and obedience, not interpreting it or applying it, but doing and obeying it. That is the only way to hear his word."[59]

The Beatitudes – Those whom God blesses will be blessed

This is not like any sermon you have ever heard. Most of which call for your attention and some small response, if any at all. Not so with this teaching. Jesus demands everything. And if He did this for His 1st century disciples, what evidence do you have to support that His standards have changed for you and me today? If you want the blessings that Jesus is about to pronounce, you must agree to the way of life that Jesus is about to proscribe. Jesus begins with a blessing. There is much hard teaching to come. But Jesus wants the crowds and the disciples to know where this is all heading. What the end goals are. Nine blessings await the disciples of Jesus. The blessings were likely expected. It was the personal price that must be paid that probably took many people by surprise. Even His disciples. Little do we know just how necessary suffering is for anyone to follow Jesus. We need to be transformed by the Spirit of God so that the cross God gives us to bear is not despised but embraced with all joy. Do we really want these blessings at this price?

Disciples as "salt" and "light"

The disciples of Jesus are special. Their existence is here declared by Jesus as indispensable to the life of the world. This is what Jesus said next in the Sermon on the Mount. *"You are the salt of the earth.... You are the light of the world" (Matt 5:13-16)*. He is explaining what His gracious call and power has made them. Disciples are also the light of the world.

The verifiable testimony of thousands of Muslims coming to faith in Christ today is that the love of Christ flowing through His disciples, faced them with a power greater than which they had ever experienced. Jerry Trousdale interviewed several former imams who had become disciples of Jesus. All of them had been in prison for following Jesus. He asked them why they remain in that dangerous region, putting their lives at risk when they could easily move to a safer area. Here are their answers, in their own words. Listen to what the love of Christ sounds and looks like in the 21st century:

"We could leave the Muslim community and live comfortably amidst other Christians, but we would not be fulfilling the Great Commission if we did that... There are over 2 billion Muslims who need to hear the gospel.... We have a unique love for these people because we all came from them. It is

---
[59] Bonhoeffer, 218-219.

we who can understand them, and we know that Muslim people have a great unsatisfied hunger for salvation.... Every day their prayers open with, 'Show us the right path,' from the first chapter of the Qur'an. We are the answer to that prayer! We want to be there to show them the right path.... In prison, we get a double blessing. 1st, we get to stand and tell others that we are followers of Isa (Jesus), and we get to tell them the truth of God's Word. 2nd, we see many leaders of violent Muslim groups in prison, and we get to share the gospel with them. Then they get released and become committed leaders for Isa, sharing the gospel with people we couldn't reach otherwise. So now many Muslim leaders are saying, 'Keep them out of prison, because they just multiply there!'"[60]

Transformation comes into us and through us to others when we let God's love fill us and flow through us by the Spirit. It is an incredible power. A power, that Paul said, "never fails"!

Christ and the Law

Next, Jesus answers a very serious accusation. He said, *"Do not think that I have come to abolish the Law and the prophets; I have not come to abolish them but to fulfill them." (Matt 5:17)* This whole context concludes with Jesus' remarkable assertion, *"For I tell you, unless your righteousness exceeds that of the scribes and Pharisees, you will never enter the kingdom of heaven" (Matt 5:20)*. That statement is the defining statement for understanding the entire text.

Jesus came and perfectly kept the Law so that those whom He calls might have a righteousness that exceeds that of the most religiously observant Jews of that day. The righteousness of the Pharisees was not good enough. The issue is not with the Law. It is with us. We cannot keep it. So, we need a perfect Son of Man to come and keep it for us, so that its blessing may come on us. Jesus does not attack the Law. He instead, lifts it higher than anyone else had ever done. And so, placing it beyond anyone's ability to keep, presents himself as the only one ever to fulfill its demands.

Jesus claimed to do what no scribe or Pharisee could do. And with that claim He presented the gospel. So, it became life for those who believed in Him. But it was viewed as death to His opponents. He now would expose their misinterpretations and reveal the real intent of the Law by His interpretations. Who but God could thus speak so authoritatively? Rabbinical leaders for ages had offered their measured opinions on the Law. Jesus was here speaking like none of them. He was clear, unambiguously direct and bold. He quoted no earlier rabbi as His source. Indeed, *"he was teaching them as one who had authority, and not as the scribes" (Matt 7:29)*. We as disciples follow

---
[60] Trousdale, 143-144.

the One and Only who fulfilled and fully taught God's holy Law. Our focus and life are in Him, alone.

Have you enrolled in the School of God?

It is past time to enroll in the school of God. But the doors are not closed! When you pass through them, what will Christ first teach you? The same thing He taught the Thessalonians. *"Now concerning brotherly love, you have no need for anyone to write to you, for you yourselves have been taught by God to love one another, for that indeed is what you are doing to all the brothers throughout Macedonia" (1 Thes 4:9-10).* The one church plant of Paul called *"a model to all believers" (1 Thes 1:7),* was his model because they were taught by God how to love.[61] When you are schooled by God, you are taught how to love one another. The God of love became flesh and showed His disciples what love looked like in every setting of life. The disciples of Jesus were primarily discipled in a life of love.

Jesus is the fulfillment of the Law, bringing the blessings of its perfect obedience into our lives, replacing the curse we deserve by our innumerable transgressions of it. How does this happen? By faith alone. That is Good News! We can know the power of His resurrection over death. How? By a faith that works through love. A faith that is willing to follow Christ even in sharing "his sufferings." The path of biblical discipleship does not pretend to be an easy path. But it is joyful because every step of the way Jesus is with us, bidding us, "Follow me." His presence transforms every inch of the hard way into a life-giving way. As were the first disciples of Jesus, you should be thrilled with the "school" or the "House of Jesus." It is as different from the world as light is from darkness. Do not shrink back from the great moral and spiritual demands Jesus makes of His disciples. They are demands of love for us and the world. Demands which His Spirit empowers us to embrace. As we live a life of self-denying love, some of those who love only themselves will be led to repent and join as we follow Jesus, together.

---

[61] See my book, *The Amazing Love of Paul's Model Church*

Appendix Seven

Following Jesus' Way of Life[62]

In this (appendix), I will encourage you all to follow Jesus by a living faith. One great benefit of ours is that we can see just what walking with God looked like through the lives of His early disciples. First century disciples tried to imitate the way that their rabbis lived as closely as they could.

"In Judaism, in the days of the apostles, the job of a disciple was well understood. A disciple's job was to become like his… teacher. So, it is written for us in the gospel of Luke, *'Every [disciple], after he has been fully trained, will be like his teacher" (6:40)*. At its simplest, discipleship is the art of imitation. It is the art of walking after a teacher. When the disciple was fully trained, he became the teacher and passed on the teaching to disciples of his own, who in turn, when fully trained, became teachers and raised up disciples of their own."[63]

A visual often helps fasten a concept to our mind. One of the earliest sages quoted in the Mishnah, Yose ben Yoezer, who lived over 100 years before Jesus, said, "Let your home be a meeting-house for the sages, and cover yourself with the dust of their feet, and drink in their words thirstily." Commenting on this quote, David Bivin wrote,

> "For the long-term disciple, learning from a rabbi meant considerable traveling as well. One literally had to follow a rabbi to learn from him, so if your rabbi traveled, you did too. To this day the unpaved roads of Israel are covered with a fine dust and as a result when people walk along these roads they invariably raise a considerable cloud of dust. Any group of disciples following a rabbi would be covered with dust at the end of the journey, and if one wanted to travel with a rabbi, one literally had to cover oneself with the dust of his feet!"[64]

The more you admired your rabbi, hanging on every word and watching every step, the closer you would walk to him. The closer you walked, the more dust you would wear. We slow down when driving behind another car on a dirt road because we do not want to "eat their dust." How many today follow a Jesus who is walking just ahead of them? Clearing the way before us. Setting everything up so that it all works together for the good

---

[62] Excerpts from *Are You a Christian or a Disciple?* chapter 14
[63] D T Lancaster, *King of the Jews*, 51
[64] M. Avot 1:4 – quoted in David Bivin, *New Light*, 12-15.

of the called-out ones who love Him. I guess if we say we are following Jesus, there ought to be some close similarity between His words, His walk and ours. How like the Jesus-way is your way of life?[i] How much of His dust are you wearing?

What Jesus most often spoke about

In His Great Commission, Jesus linked obeying everything He has commanded with being His disciple. And He said that His followers should pursue this guideline *"to the end of the age."* That would seem quite clearly to include you and me today. Are you ready to look at what Jesus taught and how He lived so you can align your life with his? Are you ready to imitate Jesus as a disciple should?

I have chosen to focus on what one scholar called "the prominent lines" or some of the often-repeated topics about which Jesus demanded the obedience of His disciples. There were six areas which Jesus very often addressed. While we can't spend much time on each, I hope to help you appreciate what it looked like to follow Jesus as a disciple then. Only if this is done will you be able to similarly follow Him today. The six topics Jesus repeatedly brought before His disciples involved: *possessions, honor, force, attachment to others, faith and suffering.* I hope that you, like the first disciples, will not overlook or neglect the less frequently mentioned commands Jesus gave. By His definition true disciples obey everything He has commanded us. But we will mention just six prominent areas.

(1) Jesus on possessions

Remember how the first disciples would have heard the words of Jesus. How they would have hung on every word, mastering them with the intent of doing and teaching them. As hard and strange as these words of Jesus sound to us, do your best to hear them as one listening to the miracle-working, God-attested Messiah in whose being lay all the hopes of Israel and the world! Karl Barth noted, "For us Westerners, at any rate, the most striking of these main lines is that which Jesus…obviously commanded many people, as the concrete form of their obedient discipleship, to renounce their general attachment to the authority, validity, and confidence of possessions, not merely inwardly but outwardly…."[65]

---

[65] Karl Barth, *The Call to Discipleship*, 48ff. The reader may be surprised that I choose Karl Barth, the Swiss theologian whom most Evangelicals do not often quote. Although Barth's view of biblical inspiration differs from mine, his brilliance and grasp of theology and the New Testament are obvious. Few 20th century authors better comprehended the content of the

Disciples hear and follow their rabbi's teaching. It is we, alone, as followers of Jesus, who have an immortal Rabbi. Heaven and earth will pass away. His word never fails. Let's not play around in the quicksand of materialism. Our treasures are elsewhere. And if we have been blessed with much more than what we need, let us do with it what the early disciples were taught to do. What a response of amazement would be produced in today's onlookers if this one area in our lives was transformed by Christ! There are some churches in the USA which are repenting and taking these commands seriously. For one thrilling example, read Pastor David Platt's book, Radical.

(2) Jesus on honor

The demand of Jesus to honor and serve one another was one big reason why there were not many *"wise by human standards, not many were influential; not many were of noble birth" (1 Cor 1:26).* The higher ranks of Roman culture were not going to let slaves, uneducated and uncouth women and children assume a level or even exalted position above themselves. That was simply madness to them.

What Jesus taught and modeled concerning honor, the disciples learned, followed and taught to others. So, the early Church leaders all taught a new perception of honor that was astonishing, admirable and very challenging to the core values of cultures of their day. A quick perusal of texts from throughout the New Testament shows that the standards of Jesus were advanced long after He had ascended into the glory of heaven.[66]

Every believer is to extend to all other believers the dignity of being treated as fellow citizens in Christ's Kingdom. There is no place for special favoritism as we are equally pardoned and accepted through Christ. We are fully adopted children of God. We are called, thereby, to treat one another as fellow members of God's family. And to bestow on every other member in the Body of Christ more importance and dignity than we see ourselves deserving. It takes the love of God filling us by the Spirit to call and treat fellow disciples as our beloved brothers and sisters. Many live in this glorious truth and no longer want the walls of denominationalism or theological nuances to divide us. Why not reject the honor your clique bestows on you when you join them in attacking other believers? Embrace His transforming love today.

---

words of Jesus, so his suggested list of five areas where Jesus repeatedly demanded obedience remains very helpful for us who love Jesus and want to obey his Word. Barth also bravely resisted the rise of Hitler and Nazism in Germany—a stand which cost him his job at the university and sent him home to Switzerland.

[66] See Rom 12:10, 13-16; 14:13-19; 1 Cor 12:20-26; Gal 1:10; 5:13; Phil 2:3-9; James 4:10; 1 Pet 3:7,8; 5:5-7; 1 John 2:15-17

(3) Jesus on the use of power or force

We all want our side to win and our way to be followed. We reluctantly seek others input and rarely yield willingly to their control. I am constantly baffled by the resistance of Christians to work together for the Kingdom. I doubt that biblical or theological differences are really the issue here, though they matter. We think we are right and will rarely yield. Because down deep, we do not want to change. We are often caught in the web of our pride, our fear and our mistrust of others. We want power over others. What we cannot gain by reasoned argument, we will take by force where possible. Such is the sad history of the world. And it has been so because the world, in all its eras, has been plagued by people like you and me.

Transformation in our lives and contexts are possible. But in a world controlled by the Sovereign Savior, we only get to where we need to go by following Him. We win by losing. We only live by dying. The way up is down. Safety and strength is in our complete and total surrender. Don't misunderstand me, I am not advocating an unbiblical pacifism. But the way of biblical discipleship is a joyful bearing of a cross. Maybe many crosses. We will serve rather than dominate. We will pray and bless when opposed for His sake. For letting go of "power moves" in favor of moves of meekness.

(4) Jesus on attachment to others

The preceding focus showed that following Jesus and seeing His Kingdom advanced demand that we relinquish illegitimate uses of power against our opponents. Our next often-mentioned line of Jesus' teaching deals with our loved ones. They can also pose a problem. So, He teaches that disciples must not lean too much on the good, natural relationships we have with family and friends. Jesus is Lord over everyone and will not yield that right others. May He help us learn how to resist one of the most natural of all idolatries—the exaltation of family and friends over Him. All we truly need is Him and those who follow Him.

(5) Jesus on religious traditions and spirituality

Jesus grew up as an observant or Orthodox Jew. He lived among a very religious people. While He clearly exalted God's Law (Matt 5:17-19), keeping it the way God intended, He criticized some of the strictest keepers of the Law – the Pharisees. In His day, they emphasized outward observance. Jesus noted the importance of that, too, but emphasized what was in the heart. Motivation mattered to Jesus. Our hearts must be powered by faith and love.

Sometimes following Jesus will demand a vast restructuring because His new wine cannot flourish in old wineskins (Matt 9:14-17). We can promote traditions that actually "nullify the word of God for the sake of (our) tradition" (Matt 15:5). Paul aptly summarized this conflict saying, "For in Christ Jesus neither circumcision nor uncircumcision has any value. The only thing that counts is faith expressing itself through love" (Gal. 5:6).

(6) A closing word on suffering

We have seen five of the most frequent themes that run throughout the teachings of Christ. And I hope, as we commit ourselves to treasuring and obeying these teachings, we anticipate for ourselves the kind of transformation that drastically altered the lives of the 1st century disciples.

"There is another equally prominent line of concrete direction we have not yet touched upon.... In many of the New Testament records the call to discipleship closes with the demand that the disciple should take up his cross. This final order crowns, as it were, the whole call, just as the cross of Jesus crowns the life of the Son of Man."[67]

Are you ready to follow Jesus? To receive the crowning mark of a true disciple. Are you ready to step out, be counted and suffer? Hopefully, by now you will not hesitate. That whatever the cost Jesus demands of you as you follow Him down the road of this life, you will joyfully accept. Frankly, it is only if you concretely follow Jesus along the lines outlined above that you can understand and appreciate what it means to walk with Him. What sense can we make of the lives of the apostles, the early missionaries and church planters apart from their simply being His disciples? As they wrote to the new generations of disciples being raised up by the Spirit under their ministries, they constantly brought them back to the reality of His call. Of their first commitment and their first love. They did not condition their growth upon their learning new truths. They simply reminded them that they were to live as closely to Jesus as possible. Closer even than disciples who once wore the dust that He raised. They were to live as those who were "in Jesus."

Dear friend, if you started your walk with Christ as a disciple—just keep going down that same path with thankfulness. It will take you where you want to go. If you have gotten off the path, return. And if you did not start this way—then start now.

---

[67] Barth, 67ff

Appendix Eight

Truly Witnessing like NT Disciples[68]

Western Evangelicals historically have thought they knew the best and most biblical ways to evangelize. We have wanted to be known for it. One of the issues of this book, though, is to challenge what we Evangelicals have identified as evangelism. The problem that many if not most Evangelicals have embraced is a Christianity without true discipleship. This has happened because, though we emphasize the Great Commission and its command to make disciples, disciples simply are not being made. Instead of looking hard at our goal, we have changed it. Our goal has in fact become making Christians. To be sure, Evangelicals know how to make Christians. But the problem is that once they are made, many of them bear little likeness to the disciples who were first called Christians at Antioch.

Two ways to reach the world

William McDonald concluded, "The New Testament seems to present two principle methods of reaching the world with the gospel. The first is by public proclamation; the second is by private discipling." He then adds, "The second is the method which the Lord Jesus used in the training of the twelve…The apostle Paul not only practiced this method himself but urged Timothy as well in 2 Tim 2:2."[69]

When this truth struck me, my eyes were opened. I could see why my forced, pressurized approach to evangelism produced so few positive results. Hearers normally felt abused. The evangelists felt uneasy, programmatic and result-driven, rather than responsive, prayerful and peaceful. And, to be frank, I was rarely excited with "going out fishing" this way. I was also nervous but could not show it. Because I was the leader, the trainer. The pro. The truths conveyed through the various forms of Christ's sending His disciples were transformational. When I became willing to change my approach, I was liberated.

My way to reach the world

I left how I was taught to do evangelism or missions and reach the lost by my early pastors, teachers and models. I thank God for them all, but

---

[68] Appendix 8 is largely excerpted from chap 6 (Jesus and Evangelism) from Are You a Christian…?
[69] William McDonald, *True Discipleship*, 74

I have now learned a much more fruitful way. My way was pretty much as follows:

> -Try to manipulate every conversation so the plan of salvation was woven into as many of them as I could. I was always seeking the loophole to turn the conversation from what it was towards the gospel message.
>
> -Once we were there, I tried to pressure the person with as many arguments as I could to "turn or burn." The goal was to get them to believe and repent before we parted ways. Who knows, it may be their last chance—so I went into the conversations as I was trained—like a fireman into a burning house. Hell was and still is very real to me.
>
> -The goal was simple--Get them to pray some form of the sinner's prayer and ask Jesus into their hearts. THAT was the expression of faith and repentance I was looking for.
>
> -If they prayed, and it appears they were at least somewhat sincere, I assured them that they were saved and no one or nothing could remove their possession of eternal life. Like your first birth, you are "born again" only once.
>
> -Then I moved on to the next lost soul to do the same.

After decades of doing this and hundreds of sinners praying, I saw two undeniable things. First, not many whom I led to Christ this way stuck. They did not become lifelong followers of Jesus. Second, I could never get more than 10% of any church plant or established church I pastored to implement this approach as their normal and natural strategy for outreach. However hard I prayed and trained and tried. It just didn't work well. I and many others have found a better, more loving, more discerning and less rude way. A peaceful, less stressful way to reach the lost. The way of *discipleship evangelism*.

Jesus' way to reach the world

When Jesus evangelized, it was the purest expression of the gospel that the world has ever experienced. But it was very different from simply declaring "the plan of salvation" as we have learned it. It was much bigger than and yielded many more powerful results than what our evangelism often produces. Let's look at one classic example:

> *"And as he was setting out on his journey, a man ran up and knelt before him and asked him, "Good Teacher, what must I do to inherit eternal life?" And Jesus said to him, "Why do you call me good? No one is good except God alone. You know the commandments: 'Do not murder, do not commit adultery, do not steal, do not bear false witness, do not defraud, Honor your father and mother.'" And he said to him, "Teacher, all these I have kept from my youth." And Jesus, looking at him, loved him, and said to him, "You lack one thing: go, sell all that you have and give to the poor, and you will have treasure in heaven; and come, follow me." Disheartened by the saying, he went away sorrowful, for he had great possessions." (Mark 10:17-22)*

Few have better captured the difference between how Jesus evangelized and how most of us have been taught, than John MacArthur did when reflecting on this very text:

"What kind of evangelism is this? Jesus would have failed personal evangelism class in almost every Bible College or seminary I know! He gave a message of works, and at this point did not even mention faith or the facts of redemption. Nor did He challenge the man to believe. He failed to get closure. He failed to draw the net. He failed to sign the young man up. After all, when a person comes along saying he wants eternal life, you can't let him get away, right? Wrong. Our ideas of evangelism cannot indict Jesus; rather, He must judge contemporary methods of evangelism. Modern evangelism is preoccupied with decisions, statistics, aisle-walking, gimmicks, prefabricated presentations, pitches, emotional manipulation, and even intimidation. Its message is a cacophony of easy-believism and simplistic appeals.

Unbelievers are told that if they invite Jesus into their hearts, accept Him as personal Savior, or believe the facts of the gospel, that's all there is to it. The aftermath is appalling failure, as seen in the lives of multitudes who have professed faith in Christ with no consequent impact on their behavior. Who knows how many people are deluded into believing they are saved when they are not?"[70]

So, what do you think about that? Could it be that our way is fundamentally different from the way Jesus evangelized? Did you notice what Mark recorded just before Jesus' outlandish demand that the rich young ruler gives up everything? In case you didn't, Mark wrote, *"And Jesus, looking at him loved him and said...."* How can love lead someone to say and do what Jesus said and did to this young seeker?

---

[70] John MacArthur, *The Gospel According to Jesus*, 79

Our way of evangelizing has often been to make the good news as clear and irresistible as we can, leaving out what may sound like bad or difficult news. Jesus did not do that. Kyle Idleman expressed his surprise in discovering how Jesus evangelized the crowds as follows:

"Finally, a thought crosses my mind: I wonder what Jesus taught whenever he had the big crowds. What I discovered would change me forever. Not just as a preacher, but as a follower of Christ. I found that when Jesus had a large crowd, he would most often preach a message that was likely to cause them to leave."[71]

Why did Jesus often make the way harder rather than easier?

I think it is in answering this question that we may come to understand how different our evangelism may be from that taught by Jesus and followed by the early disciples. One reason Christ's evangelism was so different than ours is that when the Lord was on earth, He searched hearts by probing and loving questions. He reached down into the sewer that is our own selfishness and stirred the mess around. No wonder that what often resulted wasn't a neat and pretty "confession of faith," but rather a sad departure. When Jesus had touched the seeker's deeply-cherished idol, He looked at the "seeker," and issued the exact form that repentance must take for the idol of his heart to be discarded. He did not mince any words. This is how He often evangelized. See Luke 9:57-62 as three examples.

How many conversions today are based upon the well-thought-through cost it will likely demand to continue to identify with Jesus? The places one might not be able to continue to go and those where Jesus might lead him that are new and challenging? How many invitations to be saved today carry with them the once-and-for-all nature of 1st century discipleship? Or the implicit warning that trouble lies ahead when the loved ones of our own family may think we have gone crazy and bring every pressure they can to rejoin their slow walk to death?

To all these seekers, "who came forward" and offered themselves to Jesus, the Lord had something else to say. And it wasn't, "Just repeat this prayer after Me." What He said to them and everyone else was virtually, "I am God. You must follow Me. And the way I will lead you down is not an easy road, but one of great difficulty. A road where there will be a cross for you to bear every day. But at the end of which, salvation in its fullest will come breaking into your life and you will enter into unparalleled joy." In some form, the demanding cost of discipleship met the converts of Jesus and His disciples. In our evangelism, most often, these words are left unsaid. The difference? Jesus obviously knew they were necessary and we do not think

---

[71] Kyle Idleman, not a fan, 11

they are. His goal was to make disciples for the here and now. Ours is to get people into heaven later.

The call of Christ

Evangelicals say they believe that in the process of "getting saved," the deep, heart-work done in the sinner is by the Spirit of God. God saves, we do not save. Why then do we try to make it so easy? Why do we speak so little of repentance when Jesus and His disciples spoke so much about it? Why do we dumb down the gospel to its simplest core and offer baby aspirin when the sinner needs a heart transplant? The reason we say one thing and do another is because we do not really believe that God saves when, where and how it pleases Him. And it always pleases Him to be worshiped and served for who He is! The one living and true God.

Unfortunately, the form that our gospel often takes does not involve bowing down before a King. Rather we have in our mind a Savior who stands outside the door (without a handle) and knocks patiently to come in. Once He comes in, He is just happy to be inside and will take any place we give Him. Instead of submitting our lawless lives to His Holy Rules, and doing whatever He tells us to do, our gospel very often leaves the sinner without a clue. An evangelist who has not been discipled cannot easily make disciples when he evangelizes. Yet this is exactly what Jesus and the apostles did when they evangelized. They made disciples.

We must stop sharing a gospel that works against discipleship! And begin to preach the gospel in such a way that *"the power of God unto salvation"* is seen immediately. How do we do this?

We must begin to believe again that *"all power has been given to Jesus … on earth,"* and share the gospel that reveals His supernatural power. The gospel of the cross is the same as the gospel of the kingdom. Our evangelism must unite them as one. The good news that Jesus died for my sins is the good news that Jesus reigns—and His reign has conquered and subdued me to Himself.

Can't you see this power revealed in the Gospels through the call of Christ as given in Mark 1:16-20 and Luke 19:1-6? Jesus is God and when God speaks with the intention of being heard, He is heard. There is a general and a selective call. Many are outwardly called but few are chosen. Only those who are called or chosen, like Lydia, respond like Lydia of whom it is written, *"The Lord opened her heart to respond to Paul's message" (Acts 16:14).* Zacchaeus was called and responded because God graciously opened his heart. When some of Jesus' disciples heard this teaching, they turned back. *"Stop grumbling among yourselves… No one can come to me unless the Father who sent me draws him…." (John 6:43-44).*

Perhaps the greatest example in the Gospels of the power of the call of Jesus in making a disciple is the simple story of the call of Matthew (Levi – Mark 2:13-17). Can you imagine the setting? Jesus walks past a rebellious Jew collecting taxes for Rome, looks at him and calls him to follow. Immediately he gets up, leaves everything, and follows. Why are we not given more details? Why does Mark not fill in the blanks here, for Matthew must have had some process involved in making such a monumental decision? The reason is simply this—Mark wants his readers to be amazed at the power of the call of Jesus. As Bonhoeffer so well put it when reflecting on Matthew's call,

> "(In) Mark 2:14 - The call (to Levi) goes forth, and is at once followed by the response of obedience...How could the call immediately evoke obedience? ...For the simple reason that the cause behind the immediate following of the call is Jesus Christ himself. It is Jesus who calls, and because it is Jesus, Levi follows at once. This encounter is a testimony to the absolute, direct, and unaccountable authority of Jesus."[72]

What we want to see in our evangelism is the "absolute, direct, and unaccountable" power of the call of Christ going out through us to lost sinners. That will rarely be seen unless we turn from decisional evangelism and embrace discipleship evangelism. Someone can get out of their pew or raise their hand apart from the power of God. Emotions can move us to do certain things. But to leave everything and to follow Jesus as your God—now that is evidence of an amazing power in your life.

I can hardly wait to tell you where you can read the stories of present-day disciples who are going out to make disciples just as Jesus taught His disciples to go. They are preaching the gospel and making disciples by the thousands. And what do they do when their word is rejected? They are obeying their Lord, wiping the dust off their feet as a witness against them and going until they encounter a person of peace prepared by the Spirit to obey the gospel. We need to re-learn how to share the gospel, so we can see Christ call His own through us.

So, ask yourself, what would happen if our evangelism returned to the method Jesus used? Is it too much to think that we would have similar results—and see even greater things? Well, my friends, throughout the world that is happening! There are some today whose initial conversion includes a faith response that powerfully follows Jesus, forming groups of disciples who become over time disciple making movements (DMMs). We are praying for DMMs to happen more widely here in the West. In and through evangelical

---

[72] Dietrich Bonhoeffer, *The Cost of Discipleship*, 61-62

churches and everywhere the Spirit finds hearts ready to submit completely to Jesus.

When decisional evangelism is laid aside for discipleship evangelism, there will be amazing fruit that remains. Having already counted the cost, converts hear His call and commit their lives to following the living Lord into the fields that are truly white already to harvest. Join us and evangelize in the way and with the goals first taught by Jesus to his first disciples!

Appendix Nine

Why Most Christians Prayers are NOT Answered

The Prayer Promise by Jesus	The Context of Discipleship
1. Matthew 7:7-11	1. Matthew 5:1
2. Matthew 18:19	2. Matthew 18:1
3. Matthew 21:22	3. Matthew 21:20
4. Mark 11:24	4. Mark 11:14
5. Luke 11:9-13	5. Luke 11:1
6. John 14:13	6. John 13:5, 22, 35
7. John 14:14	7. John 13:5, 22, 35
8. John 15:7	8.. John 15:8
9. John 15:16	9. John 15:8
10. John 16:23	10. John 16:17
11. John 16:24	11. John 16:17
12 John 16:27	12. John 16:17, 29

The above promises of the power of prayer by Jesus were all spoken specifically to His disciples. That is what each context of the prayer promises reveal. The promises were NOT given to all who read the Bible. Or to all who go to church. Or to all who are raised in a Christian home. Or to all Christian leaders. Or to all Christians praying at a church's prayer meeting! The promises are given to the disciples of Jesus. Alone.

One of the reasons I wrote the book, Are *You a Christian or a Disciple?* was to convince Christian readers that many of them are NOT committed disciples of Jesus. And, as such, they are outside the group to which Jesus often gave specific teaching, authority and promises. No matter how much they might read the Bible and pray, that does not make them disciples of Jesus.

To get a good idea of how amazingly God is answering the prayers of simple disciples TODAY, read Jerry Trousdale's book, Miraculous Movements: *How Hundreds of Thousands of Muslims are Falling in Love with Jesus.*

Appendix Ten

Truly Fulfilling Jesus' Great Commission[73]

Christ's form of discipleship follows the trend of Scripture in demanding a commitment to spiritual reproduction[74]. Disciples eventually multiply, as we can see in the book of Acts. No one takes a vacation, but prayerfully finds receptive "people of peace" who soon become reproducing disciples. The movement grows exponentially because it involves multiplication (with each disciple reproducing), not simply addition (with one active soul winner doing most of the work).

The accounts of Disciple Making Movements (DMMs) all over the globe are many and indisputable. They are there for you to read and be amazed by.[75] I am not asking you to take a leap without looking. To do something foolish or unbiblical. Jesus wants us to carefully count the cost. And to build all we do on Him alone, which means constantly assessing and evaluating everything by the truth of Scripture. I just don't want you to be crippled by fear any longer, even if those around you are. It's time to follow Him for yourself. Who knows but your little step of obedient faith may be the first step leading to a great DMM in your area. Satisfy yourself by doing your own diligent research and pray for God's saving grace to descend upon your own life and area in similar ways!

The basics of how Jesus made disciples

This is not chiefly a book on HOW to make disciples. There are many good books, new and old on that theme. The Lord is choosing not to bless just ONE model but many different ones. And there will be many, many more as facilitators in each culture adapt the training of Jesus to each

---

[73] Appendix 9 is largely excerpted from chap 15 (Following Jesus in Making Disciples) from *Are You a Christian…?*
[74] See my Fruitful or Unfruitful: Why it really Matters, for a survey of OT and NT texts demanding faith's sharing and reproduction from believer to non-believer.
[75] For instance, Jerry Trousdale's, Miraculous Movements; David Garrison's, A Wind in the House of Islam, David Watson's, Contagious Disciple Making, Steve Smith's, T4T: A Discipleship Re-Revolution and Kurt Urbanuk's, Cuba's Great Awakening.

specific context. There are certain constants in the most effective models that I have examined. Some of them would be as follows:

- They call for love in its fullest agape sense to drive disciple making.
- The love of Christ gives birth to a love for prayer and a reliance on it for everything involved in disciple making.
- They are Word and obedience based. Though stressing faith, it is ever a faith that works through love (Gal 5:6). These movements really "teach them to obey everything Christ commands"!
- They start slowly, forming intimate relationships of true fellowship—and they grow fast—in His time. Multiplication does arise because if the group keeps following Jesus, it will never remain inwardly focused.
- They expect suffering and sometimes see God using miracles to accelerate the growth and multiplication of the group.

One big warning: *DON'T JUST COPY THE METHOD FROM ONE CONTEXT AND THINK IT WILL WORK AS EFFECTIVELY IN YOURS*. This is all about following Jesus. He wants that to be personal and intimate. Be guided by what the word **disciple** meant in the 1st century and to how Jesus trained His followers.

We tend to take the models and USE them, hoping they will PRODUCE for us, too. And if they do not produce what we want, we get discouraged and throw them away. I am afraid that many of us have dragged our consumerism right into our Christianity. Unless we repent, we will never truly follow in life transforming power the sacrificing, giving, loving Christ. Biblical discipleship is more than merely a model to use. It is a transforming call from Christ that changes the person we are, giving us an intimate relationship with Him through the Spirit. And sending us out to make disciples in His name.

While thinking briefly on method or form, I do want to mention one rather obvious method of Christ's training of His disciples. In other words, this is clearly how He made them fishers of men. After calling disciples to follow Him, these are the steps Jesus used in making them disciples. And, Scripture bears out that the way He discipled, they would go out and use in discipling others. If you follow the progression of the Gospels, you will notice His training took a four-step pattern of:

1. ***Watch me do it***
    2. ***We will do it together***
        3. ***I will watch and guide you doing it***
            4. ***You are ready-Go, do it yourself***[76]

Whether it is a mom teaching her son how to make his bed or a construction expert training a new worker, this has always been the most simple and effective way to train. It takes presence and patience to be a truly effective trainer. Why do many young adults flounder in so many areas of life? One big reason--they were never trained when growing up. So, it is with every area of our life. We need helpful mentors. Without them we often fail, resorting to trial and error methods and their haphazard results which often lead us to give up before we learn how to succeed.

As you begin or continue to follow Christ for yourself, you must get ready to disciple others. When He sent the Twelve out, He said, *"Freely you have received. Freely give." (Matt.10:8)*. Biblical discipleship is never about you alone. You must "go and do likewise."

4 Truths to remember when making disciples

(1) It is useless to try to make serious gospel progress with one in whom the Lord is not yet working. It is God who "opens their eyes…" So, you should carefully follow Christ's commands when you "go." Do not cast

---

[76] These were not four totally distinct stages as Jesus was showing and teaching them all along the way. But the texts show His inclusion of them in the work and His sending them out for "trial missions" before He would send them lastly on the Great Commission just before His ascension. And even with that, He promised to be with them, though not physically – Matt 28:20. They were to follow Him by faith throughout the world as they had followed Him by sight with growing faith during their discipleship training. See John 21:18-22.

Watch me (Matt 4:23-25; 8:14-17, 28-34)
    We work together (Matt 9:9-11, 14-17, 19, 35-38; 11:28-30; Mk 6:35-44; 8:4-10
        I will watch you (Matt 10:1-11:1; Mk 6:7-13; Lk 10:1-24; Mk 8:38-41; Mk 10:13-16)
            Go do it yourself (Matt 28:16-20; Mk 16:15-20; Lk 24:36-49; John 20:19-23; Acts 1:8)

your pearls before pigs. He said it, not I. PRAY for God to send you to a "person of peace." Familiarize yourself with Luke 10 and follow it. I do. I go almost daily to study in public places and pray, "Peace to this place" every time I enter. The results have been amazing.

When the Lord of the harvest connects you with a person ready to be discipled, remember next (2) It takes **the love of God** to make disciples. The one you are mentoring will stretch you and test you, just as the Twelve did our Lord. You need a greater love than your own. We need the love that is patient, kind and never fails. Spending the time needed to get the disciple grounded in Christ and His Word will take love. Your flaws and weak faith will be exposed. Jesus will be thus exalted. Don't go without His love filling you. Otherwise when you meet them, you will see them—not Jesus—Who stands between you and them calling you to love and disciple them in His name.

(3) Remember that it takes **the whole gospel** to make disciples. Jesus died for our sins. That we know. By faith in His shed blood for us, we are forgiven. But Jesus also lived for us, too. Faith in Him puts His perfect obedience on our account before a holy God, making His righteousness ours! That means we can be honest with those we disciple, not pretending to be spiritual supermen and superwomen. This guards us from the cancers of pride, self-righteousness and of judging others wrongly. Believers need to have the gospel repeated to them many times a day! The gospel reminds us that we are now the adopted, empowered children of God—not orphans left on our own. You are the salt and light of the earth!

(4) Lastly, to walk with others truly, we need to readily **confess or share our sins and struggles** with those whom we are discipling.[77] This is not confession for justification. It is for bonding and help. Mutual confession of sin creates true fellowship, showing we are both imperfect humans in need

---

[77] I suggest you read 1 John 1 carefully in this light. Notice its emphasis on fellowship (vv. 3, 6,7) with God and one another. It is the mutual confession of our sins, rather than denying them, that specially bonds us together with God and each other. There is no individualistic "I" in 1 John 1. It is always "we" and "you" plural. So, 1 John 1:9 is NOT talking about justification before the Father – "If we confess our sins, he is faithful and just and will forgive us our sins and purify us from all unrighteousness" (1:9). That follows the wonderful promise of 1:7 – "But if we walk in the light, as he is in the light, we (as believers) have fellowship with one another, and the blood of Jesus, his Son, purifies us from all sin." And the warning of verse 8 – "If we claim to be without sin, we deceive ourselves and the truth is not in us." In this light see also Matt 18:15-20; John 20:22-23.

of Jesus. This takes wisdom as we cannot share everything with everyone. Confession lifts Jesus as the King, Head and Leader of His Church. We have but one great Hero—and it is not Paul, Cephas, Apollos, Augustine, Francis of Assisi, Luther, Calvin, Wesley, Mother Teresa or Martin Luther King, Jr. It is Jesus. We all have sinned and fall short of His glory. But as we imperfectly go and make disciples, Jesus reminds us of His transforming presence and power. It is He we ultimately follow, not some well-intentioned discipler. Mutual confession keeps us humble, truthful and Christ-focused. It helps to keep us where the Spirit can use us. Never forget, "God resists the proud!"

Why not YOU here and now?

Many of those whom God is using to make disciples around the globe through very brief training and impressive obedience reveal that they rely on at least 10 important discipleship truths. These would include:

1. Jesus is God and is in control—even on earth.
2. God is opposed by Satan and his demons, who must be forsaken and resisted through Christ.
3. To follow Jesus means the disciple has left a former way of life and submits entirely to Him, even being ready to die for Him. This is symbolized through the obedient step of baptism—showing union with Christ in death and life.
4. The Spirit of God must prepare a person's heart before the Word can be accepted and followed
5. Jesus has said, "Go" – and this should be obeyed
6. Jesus taught disciples to pray FIRST - It is foolish to go before you pray and know where you are to go. And to keep on praying as Satan constantly opposes a disciple's life and mission.
7. The Lord will lead you to the ones He has prepared
8. The Gospel saves and transforms the worst of humans
9. The Word of God demands obedience of its hearers
10. The Spirit of God is the best Teacher

Every disciple should be making disciples. The forms now being used everywhere are not complicated. They are simple as Christ's was in the 1st century. The best disciplers of others today will be those who are the best disciples of Jesus, themselves. Those who live by faith looking to His guidance for their every step through life.

Obey His command as a major goal of your life

In the last book that he wrote, just prior to his death in 2011, John Stott decided he should share his heart on the theme of discipleship. In his very helpful book, Radical Discipleship, he wrote,

> "Nearly all our failures stem from the ease with which we forget our comprehensive identity as disciples. Our Heavenly Father is constantly saying to us what King George V kept saying to the Prince of Wales, "My dear child, you must always remember who you are, for if you remember your identity you would behave accordingly."[78]

Did you get that summary? "Nearly all our failures stem from the ease with which we forget our comprehensive identity as disciples." I totally agree. What you have read in this book is a pivotal, foundational, indispensable issue in your life, as well as in the lives of your family and church. As John Stott asked, "Is it your identity?" Which brings us back to the first question: Are you a Christian or a disciple?

As I close, nothing will be of greater help to you than prayerfully returning to and re-reading the Gospels. Ask the Shepherd to teach you. He will. And as He guides you by His Spirit, step out and do as He leads. Because when it is all said and done, what Jesus clearly promised His first disciples, is His promise to you: *"Now that you know these things, you will be blessed if you do them" (John 13:17)*. Don't go it alone. Disciples need disciples! Now, "GO and make disciples."

---

[78] John Stott in *Radical Discipleship*, p 99.

CPSIA information can be obtained
at www.ICGtesting.com
Printed in the USA
BVHW040023191120
593542BV00003B/14